The Jerusalem Alternative

The Jerusalem Alternative is a collection of the best presentations from the first Jerusalem Summit held in October 2003 in Israel's capital.

The Jerusalem Summit is an international forum of outstanding thinkers and public leaders committed to building peace on the basis of common moral values, determined to resist the new totalitarianism of radical Islam, and believing in Israel's central spiritual and strategic role.

The inaugural Jerusalem Summit gathered over 100 prominent figures from the United States, Europe, Russia, India, and Israel.

Among the participants were Hon. Richard Perle, Senator Sam Brownback (R-KS), Prof. Daniel Pipes, Ambassador Alan Keyes, David Aikman, Frank Gaffney, and Cal Thomas, as well as key Israeli Cabinet ministers Benjamin Netanyahu, Ehud Olmert, Avigdor Liberman, Benny Elon, and Uzi Landau.

The first Summit focused on developing a moral and efficient alternative to the failed Oslo process and mapping out ways to bring democracy and freedom to the Middle East.

The Jerusalem Alternative

Balfour Books

Moral Clarity for Ending the Arab-Israeli Conflict

First printing: January 2005

ISBN: 0-89221-592-5
Library of Congress Number: 2004106977

Editor: Dmitry Radyshevsky
Assistant editor: Jenny Grigg

Cover by Janell Robertson, Green Forest, Arkansas

Printed in the United States of America

Please visit our website for other great titles:
www.balfourbooks.net

For information regarding author interviews,
please contact the publicity department at (870) 438-5288.

Acknowledgments

The editors wish to express their deep appreciation to Mr. Michael Cherney, whose generous support made possible the First Jerusalem Summit, as well as the transcripts of its best presentations gathered in this volume.

Contents

PART I
BASIC PRINCIPLE: DEMOCRACY FIRST
Diplomacy against Peace: When Negotiations Embolden Evil

PART II
THE DEATH PROCESS
Land of a Tiny Democracy for Words of Huge Tyrannies

PART III
ANTI-ZIONISM: MORAL CANCER
OF INTERNATIONAL POLITICS

PART IV
PUSHING FOR ARMAGEDDON:
RAMIFICATIONS OF A PALESTINIAN STATE

PART V
THE RIGHT COURSE OF ACTION

Foreword

Senator Sam Brownback (R-KS)

The common purpose that has brought all of the participants to the Jerusalem Summit is support for Israel. However, this Summit stands unique in its purpose of asserting a common set of values that transcends time, place, or culture.

The paradigm shift this summit has produced will reshape the way alliances and strategic choices are viewed. Instead of fair-weather allies and decisions made without a moral compass, we will stand for and by countries that embrace these values.

The decision to support Israel may seem like a given to many participants of the summit, but it can only be made if viewed through this prism. The challenge of this summit is to make this shift in thinking a reality.

The gathering of so many people from so many faiths makes it clear — our united stand for Israel is just.

To hold the summit in Jerusalem sends a powerful message to the region and to the world regarding our values and the vital role Jerusalem plays as the capital of Israel and center of Jewish identity.

This point is essential. Jerusalem has been the capital of the Jewish people for three thousand years. Jerusalem has never been the capital for any other state other than for the Jewish people.

The United States must have a more explicit position regarding the status of Jerusalem. Our embassy cannot remain in Tel Aviv while we claim to support and defend Israel's right to exist.

I am honored to be part of the Jerusalem Summit and wish it a great success.

Introduction

Uniting in the True Center

Dmitry Radyshevsky
Executive Director of the Jerusalem Summit

On the crossroads of history, Jerusalem has produced new ideas which changed the world and advanced it toward the great ideals of truth and peace. Now is the time of a worldwide crisis when new ideas are especially needed for developing an alternative to the twin dangers of modernity: religious totalitarianism of the East, as represented by radical Islam, and moral relativism of the West, as represented by atheistic globalization.

New ideas, even the most efficient and needed, are accepted with great difficulties.

Jerusalem Summit strives to gather in the capital of Israel the best minds and souls from around the world to present the most innovative socio-political ideas, so that the combined wisdom of participants will propel the best of these ideas to the global status.

The most burning problem of today is terrorism. The radical Islam is the third onslaught of totalitarian evil on mankind in the last 100 years. The first two were fascism and communism. The free world managed to defeat them by uniting, working out a joint strategy, and mastering resolve to fight and prevail. Now, too, is the time to unite and lay out a coherent moral and political strategy in this crucial fight.

The present international bodies designated to protect international law and provide moral leadership are totally inefficient. They have abused the democratic principle of simple majority and have sunk into corruption, cynicism, and immorality. The world needs to unite on the new basis and in the new center.

We believe that the center of such an alliance has to be in Jerusalem. Not for nothing these forces of evil chose Israel as the focus of their attack: here lies the front line of that new battle. If Jerusalem falls, so will fall the entire free world.

The new basis for international unity is reclaiming moral values of our civilization, values which first shone to the world from Zion. It is highly symbolic that the Jerusalem Summit was inaugurated on Sukkot, the Jewish holiday prophesied in the Bible to become the festival of all nations (Zech. 14:16).

The goal of the Jerusalem Summit is to develop practical ways to advance that prophetic vision: the principles for a new international alliance based on morality, and ways to make Jerusalem its coordinating and inspirational center.

The immediate goal of the first Summit was to discuss and offer an alternative to the so-called Oslo process. The stand on the war waged by the Arab world on Israel lies at the heart of international politics. We have to counter the deeply immoral, false, and delusional paradigm engraved in the international politics that peace in the Middle East can be bought only by territorial concessions of a tiny democracy to the huge tyrannies. We discussed viable and moral alternatives to that process and ways to introduce these alternatives into the discourse of international politics.

We hope that with the help of the Almighty, the Jerusalem Summit will pave the way for productive and inspiring progress toward uniting all the people of good will around Israel's capital, Jerusalem, and toward building peace on truth.

PART I

BASIC PRINCIPLE: DEMOCRACY FIRST

Diplomacy against Peace: When Negotiations Embolden Evil

Introduction to Part I

In the foreseeable future, Palestinians are capable of creating only a terrorist state: they didn't give up on the phased plan and brought up a generation of shahids. Such a state will destabilize the region. It will pose multiple security threats to U.S. national interests. It will lead to the destruction of Israel, and to further enslavement, poverty, and catastrophe for the Palestinian people. Israel should reject negotiations till Palestinians meet the conditions of President Bush's landmark June 24, 2002, speech, in which he called for the democratization of Palestinian society.

DANIEL PIPES is director of the Middle East Forum, a member of the presidentially appointed board of the U.S. Institute of Peace, and a prize-winning columnist for the *New York Sun* and the *Jerusalem Post*. His website, <www.danielpipes.org>, is the single most accessed source of specialized information on the Middle East and Islam. Dr. Pipes has published in such magazines as the *Atlantic Monthly, Commentary, Foreign Affairs, Harper's, National Review, New Republic*, and the *Weekly Standard*. Many newspapers carry his articles, including the *Los Angeles Times, New York Times, Wall Street Journal, Washington Post*, another 90 dailies, plus hundreds of websites. Dr. Pipes serves on the Special Task Force on Terrorism and Technology at the Department of Defense. He sits on five editorial boards, has testified before many congressional committees, and worked on four presidential campaigns. Dr. Pipes founded the Middle East Forum, which publishes two journals, the *Middle East Quarterly* and the *Middle East Intelligence Bulletin*, as well as sponsors Campus Watch, a project to review, critique, and improve Middle East studies.

Dr. Daniel Pipes is a member of presidium of the Jerusalem Summit.

Rethinking the
Arab-Israeli Conflict

by Daniel Pipes

Recent years will be remembered as a low point in the long conflict between Palestinians and Israelis, when diplomacy came to a standstill, emotions boiled over, blood ran in the streets, and the prospects of all-out war drew closer. Anti-Zionist and anti-Semitic furies, seemingly put to rest, suddenly revived with stunning vehemence. The existence of Israel appeared imperiled as it had not been for decades.

This picture is accurate as far as it goes, but it omits one other salient feature of the current landscape. The year also witnessed a host of new plans, initiatives, and schemes for fixing the situation. None of these ideas came from the Palestinian side — hardly surprising, given that Yassir Arafat seems to see violence against Israelis as the solution to all his problems. Instead, they issued from various parties in Israel and the United States, with an echo or two from Europe and the Arab states.

These plans, of which the best known is the Bush administration's "Roadmap," run the gamut from tough-seeming to appeasing. But they have two qualities in common. All of them give up on the Oslo-era assumption of Palestinian-Israeli comity as the basis for negotiation. But at the same time, all of them proceed from a fundamentally flawed understanding of the conflict and therefore, if actually implemented, would be likely to increase tensions. None of them can lead to a resolution of the conflict; that requires an entirely different approach.

Suggestions for resolving the conflict fall into three main categories. The first consists of proposals for Israel to retain a significant portion of the territories won in the 1967 war while effectuating a unilateral separation from the Palestinians living there. The toughest idea under this heading calls for an involuntary "transfer": expelling the Palestinians, if necessary against their will, from the West Bank and perhaps from Gaza as well. Once a fringe view, this proposal, thanks to protracted Palestinian violence, has begun to win support in Israel. A February 2002 poll showed 35 percent of respondents wanting to "transfer the residents of the territories to Arab states." A March 2002 poll, asking more specifically about "annexing the territories and carrying out transfer," found 31 percent in favor.

In a milder version of the same idea, some Israelis have called for encouraging a voluntary transfer. Under this plan, Palestinians who chose to leave Israeli-controlled areas could sell their land to the government of Israel, which in turn would help them get established in their new homes. An October 2001 poll reported 66 percent of Israelis supporting this scheme.

Some Israelis would like to redirect Palestinian aspirations toward Jordan, a country that already has a Palestinian majority. Benny Elon, head of the Moledet party, is today the most prominent exponent of this idea, which, under the name of "Jordan is Palestine," has in the past been associated with such figures as Vladimir Jabotinsky, Yitzhak Shamir, and Ariel Sharon. Another idea along these lines, espoused by the Labor party politician Ephraim Sneh, involves a territorial swap: the Palestinian Authority would get some Arab-majority areas inside Israel's 1967 borders in return for giving up its claims to some Jewish-majority areas on the West Bank. Perhaps the simplest proposal for separation is the one that does not require moving people. It is to build a physical wall between the two populations. Prime Minister Ariel Sharon favors a version of this plan, and has made it become a reality.

The second grouping of proposals concentrates on ways of working around the present impasse toward some sort of mutual accommodation.

Here, the key distinction is between those who emphasize a change in Palestinian leadership and those who emphasize mechanisms for improving the existing climate of mistrust. The former, focused on getting Yasir Arafat out, divide again between some (like Benjamin ben Eliezer of Labor) who favor a policy of waiting until a new Palestinian leadership emerges on its own and others (like Benjamin Netanyahu of Likud) who urge Israel to actively remove Arafat and replace him with a more pragmatic and flexible leadership that Netanyahu says is "waiting in the wings."

As for those who stress new mechanisms, they would offer benefits to the Palestinians on condition that the latter make certain changes in their internal arrangements. One such condition is good governance. Originally proposed by Natan Sharansky, Israel's deputy prime minister, this idea was picked up by George W. Bush, who devoted a major policy speech on the subject in June 2002. Proclaiming that it is "untenable for Palestinians to live in squalor and occupation," the president outlined a vision whereby, as a means toward acquiring a state that would live in peace alongside Israel, the Palestinians would develop "entirely new political and economic institutions based on democracy, market economics, and action against terrorism." He specifically mentioned transparent financial institutions, independent auditing, and an independent judiciary.

The "Roadmap," first adopted in September, might be thought of as the State Department's belated answer to the president's June 2002 proposal. The product of consultations by the "quartet" (the United States, Russia, the European Union, and the United Nations), it bears a name (the "concrete, three-phase implementation Roadmap") that suggests its incremental quality. The first phase, proposed for early this year, would have the Palestinians hold "free, fair, and credible elections" and Israel withdraw to its positions of September 28, 2000, "as the security situation improves." The second phase, to kick in later in the year, will "focus on the option of creating a Palestinian state with provisional borders based upon a new constitution." The final phase (2004–05) will see Israeli-Palestinian negotiations "aimed at a permanent-status solution." Once these are achieved, Israel would pull back from territories it won in 1967 "to secure and recognized borders."

The American government regards the dates in the Roadmap as guidelines, whereas the other three parties prefer to consider them hard and fast. Others find the whole Roadmap process too slow. Thus, the Israel Policy Forum, an American advocacy group, has developed a detailed four-step "on ramp" in anticipation of the Roadmap's inception. No less impatiently, Prime Minister Tony Blair announced a series of meetings in London to include the quartet, the Palestinians, and officials from Egypt, Saudi

Arabia, and Jordan. (To make an agreement easier to reach, Blair conveniently left out the Israelis.)

The Roadmap is vague about conditions to be imposed on the Palestinians — and specifically about what, if any, penalties they would pay for noncompliance. But there are some — and they make up the third grouping in the constellation of new ideas — who chafe at conditions altogether, preferring to proceed in the hope that an ample supply of carrots will lead to the desired result. Henry Hyde, chairman of the House International Relations Committee, has proposed a "Marshall Plan" for the Middle East that promises the Palestinians (and others) a comprehensive economic development program. The core of this idea, which has the support of Tom Lantos, the committee's ranking Democrat, is, in Hyde's words, that "people who had hope of a better life in economic terms would not resort to violence."

Martin Indyk, a former U.S. ambassador to Israel and more recently an advisor to John Kerry, favors a more muscular and faster device. He calls for international troops to establish a "trusteeship" over the West Bank and Gaza and thereby lay the basis for "credible, representative, accountable, and transparent institutions." Thomas Friedman, the *New York Times* columnist, has proposed a scheme whereby "a joint American-Palestinian security force" would replace Israeli control over the territories, followed by American troops who would stay on "indefinitely."

Finally, there is the most popular idea of all: no transfer, no wall, no change in leadership, no conditions, no Roadmap, and no foreign troops. Rather, Israel should immediately withdraw all its forces from the territories, dismantle all the Jewish towns and outposts there, and close down whatever remains of its machinery of control. The goal is to inspire a reciprocal mood of accommodation by the Palestinians or, failing that, a de-facto separation that would benefit both sides. "Leave the settlements, return to ourselves" is how the left-wing Israeli organization Peace Now promotes this notion. This was the basis of the "Geneva Accords" that received so much attention in December 2003. Variants of the same idea have been put forward by such figures as Amram Mitzna (the recent Labor candidate for prime minister), by Saudi Crown Prince Abdallah, by virtually every European government, and by the overwhelming majority of leftists, academics, journalists, and diplomats around the world, not to speak of religious and business leaders.

Each of these plans has major deficiencies. The forceful removal of Palestinian Arabs from Israeli-controlled territories would indeed reduce Israeli casualties, but the political price, both abroad and within Israel, would be incalculable, rendering this option more fantastical than real.

The voluntary departure of Palestinians is even more unrealistic. Jordan-is-Palestine is a non-starter for many reasons, of which the single most important is that neither Jordanians nor Palestinians show the slightest readiness to go along with it. Since there is no inclination among Palestinians to accept Jordan as a substitute for Palestine, much less Amman for Jerusalem, the only conceivable outcome of such a policy, were it somehow implemented, would be to add Jordan as a base for the Palestinian conquest of Israel.

As for fences and buffer zones, they offer some protection, but are far from invulnerable. Terrorists can go over a fence in gliders, around it in boats, or under it in tunnels; they can fire mortars or rockets over a wall, pass through checkpoints using false identification papers, and recruit Israeli Arabs or Western sympathizers on the wall's other side. Once a wall goes up, moreover, Israel effectively surrenders much of its influence over what happens beyond it, within the Palestinian Authority, including the latter's ability to import weapons and foreign troops. Nor, finally, does hunkering down behind a fence send the Palestinians the intended message, convincing them to give up on violence; on the contrary, it reinforces an impression of Israel as a cowering and essentially passive society, thus spurring further violence. In sum: a fence has utility as a tactical tool to save lives, but none as a basis for ending the conflict.

What about changes in Palestinian leadership? Every piece of evidence suggests, and every opinion poll confirms, that the assault on Israel initially was wildly popular among Palestinians, though less so now. Indeed, there is ample reason to believe that the "street" was more aggressively anti-Zionist than the leadership. Although Arafat promotes the ambition of destroying Israel, he is not the source of that ambition, and his removal would not eliminate it. More particularly, the ben Eliezer plan — waiting for a change of leadership — rests on the far-from-obvious supposition that the next leaders will be better than the existing ones, while the Netanyahu plan suffers from the kiss-of-death syndrome that applies to any Palestinian leadership selected by Israel.

Which brings us to the various proposals for conferring benefits on the Palestinians in hopes of moderating their hostility. The reasoning here is backward. Although good governance, for example, is certainly welcome in principle, it is less than desirable so long as the Palestinians continue to seek Israel's destruction. It brings to mind the notion of ending the cold war by encouraging "entirely new political and economic institutions" in the Soviet Union even as that system's core ideology remained fully intact. Why should anyone want to enhance an aggressor's competence and economic reach?

The same criticism, and more, applies to Congressman Hyde's update of the Marshall Plan. To the extent the original Marshall Plan worked, it filled a need for capital, which is hardly the Palestinian economy's main challenge; the PA's terminally corrupt leadership would pocket much of the aid, and the Palestinian war against Israel has very little to do with poverty or any other economic issue. Fundamentally, though, the Hyde proposal suffers from the same conceptual mistake as good governance: it promises to reward the Palestinians even as they make war on Israel. Is it too banal to note that the original Marshall Plan was instituted three years after the crushing defeat of Nazi Germany in war?

Then there is the Roadmap, which asks the Palestinians to undertake a temporary reduction in violence, in return for which they will gain a state; as such, the Roadmap imposes even fewer demands on the Palestinians than the failed Oslo process that it has been designed to replace, and makes even less pretense of expecting the Palestinians to comply with its conditions. The "on ramp" and other such plans share precisely the same errors, some to an even greater extent. And the various proposals to use foreign soldiers and intermediaries in what is now a war zone are plainly unworkable. Can anyone seriously imagine Americans, Canadians, and Europeans accepting fatalities just to keep Palestinians from attacking Israelis? It is preposterous, no matter how bravely they might talk in advance.

Finally, we have the immensely popular plan obliging a unilateral Israeli pullback from the West Bank and Gaza in return for precisely nothing, which is by far the worst option of all. If proof were needed, a precedent does exist: namely, the entire past decade, when, under Oslo, Israel took uncounted "steps for peace" and was rewarded by its Palestinian "partner" with a much more aggressive enmity. The outstanding instance, however, remains the unilateral Israeli pullback from Lebanon in May 2000, undertaken in the firm conviction that it would purchase quiet on Israel's northern border. Not only has that not happened, but, given Hizbullah's massive arsenal and overconfidence, the violence there is likely to get much more intense, possibly leading to all-out war. In the meantime, Israel's withdrawal from Lebanon played a major role in spurring the outbreak of Palestinian violence in September 2000. One can only shudder at the carnage that would follow upon Israel's headlong flight from the majority-Palestinian territories.

In truth, all these plans lead in the wrong direction, rendering resolution further off than before. Real progress requires a different and more honest way of looking at the conflict as a whole. Let us begin by recalling certain basic points.

Although a neutral term like "Arab-Israeli conflict" makes it sound as if both sides were equally to blame for this decades-long war, and must therefore be brought to compromise by splitting the differences between them, this is, as Norman Podhoretz has rightly insisted, "a deceptive label." A more accurate term is the "Arab war against Israel."

Israeli control of the West Bank and Gaza cannot be the core of the problem. The Arab war against Israel predated Israel's taking those territories in 1967; in fact, it was underway even before Israel formally came into existence as a state.

Rather, the root cause of the conflict remains today what it has always been: the Arab rejection of any sovereign Jewish presence between the Jordan River and the Mediterranean Sea.

The conflict continues into its sixth decade because Arabs expect they can defeat and then destroy the state of Israel.

Israel cannot end this conflict unilaterally, by actions of its own. It can only take steps that will make it more rather than less likely that the Arabs will give up on those expectations.

At the heart of the problem, in other words, stands Arab rejection. However cunningly conceived, plans that attempt to outflank, leap over, or otherwise finesse this stubborn fact are doomed to failure. Instead of ignoring it, would-be peacemakers would do better to start by recognizing that the conflict will diminish only when the Arabs finally surrender their dream of obliterating the Jewish state, and then to concentrate on finding ways to get the Arabs to undergo what I call a "change of heart." How might that be achieved?

A glance at some of the conflicts of the 20th century provides a clue. Those that ended did so because one side wholly abandoned its war aims. Closure was achieved when, and because, there was no longer a fight. This is what happened in World War II and the cold war, and also in the wars between China and India, between North Vietnam and the United States, between Great Britain and Argentina, between Afghanistan and the Soviet Union, and most recently between the United States and Afghanistan. Conflict ended neither via negotiations nor by means of a wall but by one side accepting defeat.

Such a surrender can occur as a consequence of a military trouncing, or it can occur through an accumulation of economic and political pressure. However achieved, the result must be unequivocal. Should the losing side retain its war goals, then new rounds of fighting remain possible, and even likely. After World War I, for example, defeat left the Germans still looking for another chance to dominate Europe. In like fashion, the wars between North and South Korea, Pakistan and India, Iraq and Iran, and

Iraq and Kuwait have not ended, for the losing side has interpreted every defeat as only partial and temporary.

This historical pattern has several implications. First and foremost, it means that Israel's enemies must be convinced that they have lost. Actually, not all its enemies, just the Palestinians. Although weak by any objective measure as compared with the Arab states, Palestinians are the ones for whom this war is being fought. Should they, having suffered a necessary defeat, give up on the attempt to destroy Israel, others will find it difficult to remain as extremists.

What will help bring about this Palestinian change of heart is Israeli deterrence: maintaining a powerful military and threatening credibly to use force when aggressed upon. This is not just a matter of tough tactics, which every Israeli government of the left or right pursues. It is a matter of a long-term strategic outlook. The trouble with deterrence from the Israeli point of view is that, rather than offering a chance to initiate, it is by nature a reactive approach: boring, unpleasant, expensive, seemingly passive, indirect, and thoroughly unsatisfying, quite out of step with the impatient spirit of the Israeli populace. But it works, as Israel's own experience in the period 1948–93 shows.

A bedrock condition of such a strategy — and one no less frustrating in the short term — is that Palestinian acceptance of Israel is a binary proposition: yes or no, without any in-between. This suggests, in turn, the futility of negotiations — at least until the Palestinians do accept the Jewish state. Such matters as borders, water, armaments, the status of Jerusalem, Jewish communities in the West Bank and Gaza, so-called Palestinian refugees — in brief, the central issues of the Oslo period — cannot productively be discussed as long as one party still aims to murder the other. In principle, something along the lines of the Oslo agreement could turn out to be workable — but only after the Palestinians definitively and unequivocally, and over an extended period of time, demonstrate that they have made their peace with the existence of the state of Israel as an irreversible fact.

If, moreover, we have learned anything over the past decade, it is that interim Israeli concessions are counterproductive and must be discouraged. As the Oslo experience proved, they inflame, rather than tamp down, Arab aggression. By offering repeated concessions even as the Palestinians failed to live up to a single one of their obligations, Israel signaled weakness. That is how, beginning in 1993, the effect of Oslo was to take a bad situation — there was some violence in the late 1980s and early 90s, but a mood of caution still prevailed on the Palestinian side — and make it far worse. Only when Palestinians are convinced there is no other way will an end to the conflict become conceivable, along with the mutual concessions that will seal it.

U.S. diplomacy has long proceeded on the theory that one must start with agreements between Israel and unelected Arab leaders; after such a leader has affixed his signature to a piece of paper, it is thought, feelings of amity will in due course develop among his subjects. That has not happened. Quite the contrary: whenever leaders like Anwar Sadat or King Hussein — and this even applies somewhat to Arafat — have signed agreements, their populations have become more, not less, hostile to Israel. It is as if the government is understood to be passing on the anti-Zionist burden to other institutions: the media, the educational system, religious leaders, the unions, trade associations. A piece of paper cannot of itself produce a change of heart, but can only symbolize it; treaties must follow, not precede, deep shifts for the better on the Arab side.

By the same token, it is a mistake to discuss "final-status" issues — i.e., how things will look when the conflict is over. There has been, indeed, much speculation about a future Palestinian state: its borders, the nature of its sovereignty, and so forth. All such talk encourages Palestinians to think they can win the benefits of a state without accepting Israel. This is not to say that policy planners in some sub-basement should not be thinking through the contours of a final-status agreement; but it is not for those in responsible positions of power to broach the topic.

Beyond these general considerations, there are specific steps that could be taken by the government of the United States. For one thing, the time has come for the president to recognize Jerusalem as Israel's capital. By now, Congress makes an almost yearly habit of trying to force the move of the U.S. embassy to Jerusalem, but the initiative invariably fails because the embassy issue is understood by the White House as purely a matter of symbolism, and the price to be paid in Arab and Muslim anger for a purely symbolic move is always regarded as too high. But the issue is not just symbolic. U.S. recognition of Jerusalem as Israel's capital, especially if properly presented, would go far to indicate to the Palestinians that the existential issue is closed: Israel is there, it is permanent, and the sooner they come to terms with this fact, the better.

For another thing, much more pressure could and should be placed on the Palestinian side to put an end to violence. The U.S. government tends to see this violence as an aberration, a temporary anomaly in Palestinian behavior. Rather, violence stands at the very heart of the Palestinian attitude toward Israel, and stopping it therefore needs to be the priority of U.S. policy — including, in the first instance, by refusing to reward it financially or diplomatically. If the hope in Washington has been that, by gaining ever more of their goals, Palestinians would curb violence on their own, that approach has clearly failed; the time has come to focus directly on the violence itself.

Washington has also been largely indifferent to the massive campaign of lurid anti-Semitism and fanatical anti-Zionism conducted by the institutions of the Palestinian Authority, some of which are subsidized by American taxpayers. In particular, it has paid little heed to the hideous incitement of children to engage in "martyrdom" operations. This is an error that needs urgently to be reversed.

Finally, there are the so-called Palestinian refugees. Alone among all the masses of dislocated peoples in the years following World War II, Palestinians are frozen in the status of refugee — in some cases, unto the fourth generation. (The vast majority of those claiming refugee status were born after the events of 1948–49 that engendered the problem in the first place.) The reason for this anomaly is plain: the rejectionist impulse is sustained through the fantasy of a mass "return," and the ever-proliferating numbers of alleged refugees amount to an ever-sharpening dagger at Israel's throat. In this cruel charade, the U.S. government has been complicit for over a half-century, contributing a substantial percentage of the funds used to maintain the Palestinians' refugee status and to discourage their integration into the Arab states. The time has come to insist that they be assimilated.

There is no short cut, and there is no alternative. The only way to make progress in the Palestinian-Israeli conflict is by inducing the Palestinians to surrender their murderous intentions vis-à-vis Israel. Not only would the rewards of such a surrender be very great but, ironically, they would be yet greater for the Palestinians than for Israel.

Although Israel today suffers from blood in the streets and an economy doing poorly, and although it is the only Western country that is constantly forced to defend its very existence through military force, it remains, for all its problems, a functioning society, with a boisterous political life and a vibrant culture. In contrast, the Palestinians are in desperate straits. The areas nominally ruled by the Palestinian Authority are anarchic, with curfews, road blocks, and violence defining the immediate parameters, and dictatorship, corruption, and backwardness being among the larger consequences. In the words of one sympathetic observer, Palestinians have been "ravaged by widespread poverty, declining health status, eroding education, physical and environmental destruction, and the absence of hope."

The Palestinians, in other words, are suffering even more from the consequences of their own violence than is Israel. So long as they persist in their ugly dream of destruction, they will be haunted by failure and frustration. Conversely, only when they accept the permanence of Israel will they be released to fulfill their considerable potential by building a prosperous economy, an open political system, and an attractive culture.

Much as the Israelis have to gain from a victory over the Palestinians, the Palestinians have more to gain from defeat. From the point of view of American policy, helping them to achieve a change of heart is thus an unobjectionable goal, beneficial to both parties. And while ultimately it is up to the Palestinians to liberate themselves from the demons of their own irredentism, others, especially Israelis and Americans, can indeed help — by holding firm against the seductive appeal of Roadmaps that lead exactly in the wrong direction.

DAVID AIKMAN, senior fellow with the Trinity Forum, is a journalist, author, and specialist on Russia, China, East Asia, and the Middle East.

Civilization's Fight — Before and After September 11, 2001

By David Aikman

> This is not, however, just America's fight. And what is at stake is not just America's freedom. This is civilization's fight. This is the fight of all who believe in progress and pluralism, tolerance and freedom.
> — President George W. Bush, September 20, 2001

Speaking to a joint session of the U.S. Congress in an address broadcast all over the world, President George W. Bush on September 20, 2001, defined his own response to the terrorist atrocities inflicted upon New York and Washington just nine days earlier. Many Americans considered it one of the greatest presidential addresses in many decades. It was thoughtful, careful, resolute, and rousing, warning Americans that the struggle against their global terrorist adversaries would be lengthy, that there would be "new and sudden challenges," and that "great harm" had indeed been done to the nation.

But, the president insisted, "In our grief and anger we have found our mission and our moment. Freedom and fear are at war. The advance of human freedom — the great achievement of our time, and the great hope of every time — now depends on us."

Bush's words resonated everywhere. One of the most striking consequences of the September 11 attacks was the spontaneous surge of patriotic sentiment across the United States. In many parts of the country, it became impossible after a few days to buy a U.S. flag of any description. From radio antennae of sedans and poles rising from pickup trucks, the stars and stripes flapped in the wind along freeways across the country. Millions of dollars were offered spontaneously to the families of the estimated 5,000 victims of the September 11 terrorism by thousands of individuals and communities.

There were other, unanticipated, effects also. In a *Time* magazine article September 24, 2001, essayist Roger Rosenblatt thought that one unexpected benefit of the tragedy was that the "age of irony" had come to an end. "For some 30 years — roughly as long as the Twin Towers were upright," Rosenblatt wrote, "the good folks in charge of America's intellectual life have insisted that nothing was to be believed in or taken seriously. Nothing was real." His comment: "Are you looking for something to take seriously? Begin with evil." Several commentators reflected on the tragedy as demonstrating the folly of post-modernist relativism. In *U.S. News and World Report*, writer John Leo excoriated both multiculturalism and "the therapeutic culture," which he characterized this way: "There is no evil, no right and wrong, only misunderstandings that can fade if we withhold judgment and reach out emotionally to others. Everything can be mediated and talked out. . . ."

These assaults upon postmodernism and multiculturalism prompted one academic name long associated with both streams of thought, Professor Stanley Fish, currently dean of the college of liberal arts and sciences at the University of Illinois at Chicago, to respond in a *New York Times* opinion piece. Relativism, he asserted, was indeed alive and well, "if by relativism," he said, "one means the practice of putting yourself in your adversary's shoes." Anyway, he asserted, relativism was just "another name for serious thought."

Well, there has certainly been a lot of serious thought in both the United States and the world as a whole since September 11, 2001. One question that many Americans have asked themselves is how to account for the passionate anti-American venom demonstrated both by the meticulously well-organized hijackers and the mobs that have filled streets in many parts of the world since then, cheering on the perpetrators of the September atrocities. President Bush in his September 20 address put it this way: "Americans are asking, why do they hate us?" Then he answered his own question this way: "They hate what they see right here in this chamber — a democratically elected government. Their leaders are self-appointed. They hate our freedoms — our freedom of religion, our freedom of speech, our freedom to vote and assemble and disagree with each other."

All of this was true, but it was far from a full explanation of why 19 Arabs, nearly all of them of Saudi Arabian nationality, plotted and planned for years to take over U.S. civilian airliners and deliberately crash them into New York's World Trade Center and the Pentagon in Washington, killing themselves and as many people as possible. Who was Osama Bin-Laden, and what was his organization, al Qaeda? How could there be prospective terrorists based in as many as 60 countries, including the United States (where the FBI estimated there might still be as many as 1,000 "sleepers" waiting to be mobilized for some future outrage) willing to try something similar at the first opportunity, as U.S. government officials said was the case? Were the teachings of Islam "good and peaceful," as President Bush said they were in his speech to the U.S. Congress, and had the terrorists simply been out to "hijack Islam itself," as he told Americans?

In the United States, the debate over the origins of the ideology behind suicide hijackings caused some observers to blame religion, any religion, in general. In the *New Republic*, Andrew Sullivan, a self-proclaimed Roman Catholic and an ardent supporter of gay rights, made the case that any set of firm, monotheistic religious beliefs, including those of his own Roman Catholic tradition, needed to be carefully corralled by secular state power to prevent its inflicting harm upon the human race. After the prominent Baptist leader Rev. Jerry Falwell declared on TV that the World Trade Center attacks were God's judgment upon the United States because of gay rights activism, ACLU efforts to restrict public religious expression in the United States, and other acts of wickedness, some commentators declared that this merely proved that any set of clearly defined, ardently held beliefs, including Christian ones, constituted generic "fundamentalism." There was no difference in principle, some felt, between Rev. Jerry Falwell and Osama Bin-Laden. (The fact that Falwell subsequently apologized for his public intemperance and has never been known to advocate mass murder upon civilians was not commented upon by those who had made this case.)

Among students, scholars, and practitioners of Islam, however, the debate on the origins of Osama Bin-Laden's ideology became more focused.

Some scholars argued that there was a spirit of militancy and intolerance at the very heart of Islam itself, expressed in the sacred words of the Koran, Islam's holy scripture. Others claimed that Bin-Laden had essentially "hijacked" Islam, trying to assert as mainstream a tradition that had always held only a minority place in the historical development of the religion.

A third interpretation was that Bin-Laden's ideology was essentially the heir to the totalitarian ideologies of the 20th century, notably communism, nazism and fascism, and was a savage political thought system best described as "Islamofascism," a theocratic, triumphalist coda bent upon global theocratic domination. What almost all scholars agreed was that politicized, ideologically dictatorial Islam should best be termed "Islamism," a word that accurately suggests the transformation of a religious world view into a totalitarian ideology.

In this briefing, we will try to put the ideology of al Qaeda (literally "the base"), the loose-knit but tightly disciplined international network of pro-Bin-Laden Islamist terrorist groups into the context of Islam as a whole. Of course, how the United States responds to the attack in its efforts to track down and destroy al Qaeda is likely to take months, perhaps years, to be unveiled. The atrocity and tragedy of September 11 is a challenge both to the United States and to the whole of the civilized world. As with all crises, however, it could turn into one of the great national and diplomatic opportunities for the United States as this nation seeks to lead the world against one of the most savage outbursts of barbarism in decades.

The Setting of Historical Islam

The core facts about the history of Islam are simple. It was founded by Mohammed, an Arabian born to a distinguished family in Mecca around A.D. 570, but orphaned in his early years and brought up subsequently by first his grandfather, and then an uncle. Engaging in the caravan trade as a trader, Mohammed, around 595, married a wealthy widow, Khadija, to whom alone he remained married until her death. Subsequently, he was to have nine other wives.

In the year A.D. 610, during a personal retreat to a cave not far from Mecca, Mohammed began to receive the first of what Muslims believe were divine revelations, mediated to him in person by the angel Gabriel. Early on, the revelations were accompanied by sweating, rolling on the ground, and groaning, causing Mohammed to be deeply worried about the source of the revelations. His wife, Khadija, reassured him that what he was hearing came from God. Muslims believe that the first instructions to Mohammed, through Gabriel, were "Recite!" Gradually, the visits of the angel Gabriel led to a whole series of revelations, which together constitute the Koran. Some of them were received while Mohammed was in Mecca, where he experienced great opposition. Others were received after he moved to Medina in 622 (the date of the *hijrah*, or beginning of the Islamic formal calendar).

Muslims believe that the Koran is a holy book entirely dictated by God. They are thus deeply hostile to any kind of textual analysis or criticism analogous to what various critics and skeptics of the Bible for some 250 years have leveled at the sacred book of Christians and Jews. They also believe that Mohammed could not read or write, and thus could not have derived the Koran from knowledge of any other book. But what they do not deny is that the emergence of the Koran as the revelation of God came about in a setting in which Mohammed heard about the beliefs of Jews and Christians who lived in Arabia in his own day, argued with them, actually fought with the Jews, and finally rejected both communities.

Muslims believe that some of the Jewish biblical figures — for example, Abraham, Moses, and King David — were prophets, and that Jesus was a prophet of his own era, but that neither Christians nor Jews really understood what God was revealing to them. Mohammed, Muslims believe, is the "seal of the prophets," the last human being to whom God — Allah — has revealed his message for the human race. Islam means "submission" (i.e., to God's will as expressed in the Koran); a Muslim is someone who has submitted to God's will. In the Islamic cosmology, Abraham himself was actually a Muslim, since Islam was not only God's original message, but the only one.

The rejection by the Jews of Mohammed's message while Mohammed was still based in Medina led to his changing the direction of prayer, the *qibla*, from Jerusalem, the original direction, to Mecca. The Jewish Sabbath day of rest was also changed into the Muslim Friday. Mohammed's struggle with the Jews was also not merely a theological one. Because they resisted both his temporal and spiritual authority in Medina and later Mecca, he eventually expelled all of them from Mecca, massacring hundreds of Jewish men in a final struggle with them.

According to Islam, Jews and Christians are "people of the book," spiritually a step up from rank polytheism, which was the dominant religion of the Arab world until Mohammed imposed Islam upon all the Arabian tribes of the Peninsula, but clearly of inferior status to Muslims. In the Koran, there are verses where Muslims are asked to be gentle with Christians and Jews: "Bear patiently with what they [the unbelievers] say and leave their company without recrimination" (Sura 73:10), or "Be courteous when you argue with people of the book, except with those among them that do evil. Say: 'We believe in that which has been revealed to us and which was revealed to you. Our God and your God is one. To Him we submit' " (Sura 29:46).

But there are other verses that are entirely different. The reason for the change is that after Mohammed's triumphal entry into Mecca in 630, he no longer needed to placate either Christians or Jews for political reasons. In Sura 2:193 we read, "Fight against them until idolatry is no more and God's religion reigns supreme," and in 9:29, "Fight against such of those to whom the Scriptures were given as believe in neither God nor the last day, who do not forbid what God and His apostle have forbidden, and do not embrace the true faith, until they pay tribute out of hand and are utterly subdued." The Koran goes on: "The Jews say Ezra is the son of God, while the Christians say the Messiah is the son of God. Such are their assertions, by which they imitated the infidels of old. God confound them! How perverse they are!" (Sura 9:130).

It is impossible to read the Koran without concluding that Mohammed himself had a deep and abiding dislike for Jews, and contempt for Christians, who Muslims believe have actually mistranslated or misinterpreted the original message of the gospels. In fact, Sura 5:58 admonishes Muslims: "Believers, do not seek the friendship of the infidels and those who were given the book [the Bible] before you, who have made of your religion a jest and a diversion." Two verses later, the Koran says that Allah has transformed these unbelievers (i.e., Jews and Christians) "into apes and swine, and those who serve the devil."

Mohammed died in 632, but his successors led Arab armies to victories over the Byzantines and other foes in Syria, Egypt, and Iraq, and created within less than a decade of Mohammed's death a vast new Arab empire. As leaders of the *umma*, a concept unique to Islam of a community that is *both* spiritual *and* temporal, they were called "caliphs," from the Arabic word *khalifa*, who considered themselves "servants" of the prophet.

The Shi'ite strand of Islam, comprising about 15 percent of all the world's estimated 1.2 billion Muslims (there are an estimated 1.9 billion Christians), grew out of a dispute over the legitimacy of Ali, the fourth caliph and Mohammed's son-in-law. Not surprisingly for a religion that expanded in part through military conquest, three of the four caliphs were themselves assassinated, and the caliphate quickly became a hereditary post taken over by whatever dynasty or ruling ethnic group dominated the Muslim world. The last caliph, a Turk, was deposed in 1924 when the newly secularized republic of Turkey, no longer the Ottoman Empire, abolished the position entirely. What is striking about the ideology of al Qaeda and associated Islamist groups is that many of them wish to re-establish the caliphate on a global scale, in effect imposing Muslim world government upon the entire human race.

The vast Arab empire that grew out of the early Islamic conquests quickly spread in the seventh century A.D. across North Africa, into Central Asia, to the borders of China, and into northern India within decades of Mohammed's death. Muslim armies had overrun Spain by the first few decades of the eighth century, and would have brought Islam right into the heart of Western Europe had they not been stopped by Charles Martel at the Battle of Tours in 732.

The pattern of Muslim conquest had by then become plain. The victorious Arab armies forced pagans and various polytheists to convert to Islam, but they permitted the Christian communities they conquered to continue in their more ancient faith as long as they paid a poll tax to the Muslim rulers and abided by certain strict regulations. The status of conquered Jews and Christians was specifically designated as *dhimma*, inferior to Muslims. *Dhimmis* in much of the Arab world in medieval times were forbidden to ride horses, bear arms, build new houses of worship, or repair old ones. They were required to wear special clothes, a practice that the Taliban rulers of Afghanistan tried in the year 2001 to re-impose on Hindus living in Afghanistan until international outrage prevented them from carrying this out.

Apologists for Islam, whether from within or outside the faith, have often pointed out, correctly, that Jews at certain stages of Arab Muslim history were treated much better under Islam than they were in the Christian world of their day. The greatest figure of medieval Judaism, Maimonides (1135–1204) was court physician to Salah ed-Din (Saladdin), the Kurdish warrior who led Arab armies to victory over the Crusaders in 1187. Jews, after their expulsion from Spain in 1492, took refuge in the Muslim Ottoman Empire and its newly conquered capital Istanbul. Still, even Maimonides, at the height of his own attainment in the court of Saladdin, lamented over the situation of the Jews in general caught in the *dhimmi* status. "God has cast us into the midst of this people, the nation of Ishmael, who persecute us severely, and who devise ways to harm and humiliate us," he complained.

It is significant also that one of the most admired intellectuals in all of Arab literature, the historian ibn Khaldun (1332–1406) was unequivocal in the destiny he thought was deserved by Jews and Christians. "It is for them to choose between conversion to Islam, payment of poll tax, or death," he wrote in his classic philosophy of history, *The Muqaddimah*. Ibn Khaldun was also unequivocal in his estimate of the value of *jihad*, or war as a religious duty. He wrote, "In the Muslim community, the holy war is a religious duty, because of the universalism of the Muslim mission and the obligation to convert everybody to Islam either by persuasion or force."

Interpretations of Jihad

The word *jihad* literally means "struggle," and it can include the "struggle" against sin as well as the concept of struggle on behalf of Islam, including means not limited to warfare. Mohammed himself spoke of the "greater jihad" (meaning struggle against personal sin) and the "lesser jihad," meaning warfare against foes of Islam. But it is simply erroneous to suggest that jihad means merely "a struggle to improve the quality of life in society, struggle in the battlefield for self-defense," as argued by the Council on American-Islamic Relations, an American Islamic group strongly antagonistic to any criticism of Islam or Islamic practices around the world. The most prominent Western scholar of Islam, Bernard Lewis, has asserted that "the overwhelming majority of classical theologians, jurists and traditionalists . . . understood the obligation of jihad in a military sense."

In fact, Islamic jurists early on in Muslim history developed the concept of the world as divided into Muslim and non-Muslim zones. The Muslim zone, *Dar al-Islam,* (abode of Islam) was implied to be in perpetual war with the non-Muslim world, *Dar al-Harb* (abode of war). This did not mean that Muslims should force non-Muslims to convert at the point of a sword, but simply that they should obtain political primacy through conquest and then create conditions in which Muslim rulers could enforce through *sharia*, or Islamic law, the ethical and social principles of the Muslim *umma*. In fact, it is true that Sura 2:256 declares, "There shall be no compulsion in religion," a Koranic injunction frequently cited to demonstrate Islam's alleged pacific nature. Obviously, though, if you are a non-Muslim living in a Muslim-ruled state there is no freedom of religious practice in any way comparable to what exists in all Western nations and in much of the rest of the world today.

Throughout most of Islamic history, jihad meant armed resistance by Muslims when the Muslim umma came under attack. But at different times, some groups within Islam have elevated jihad in its meaning of wars of conquest to impose Islam upon adversaries to be central to Islamic thought. This was the case of Kharijites in the 7th century, the Assassins in the 11th century, and in the writings of the legal philosopher ibn Taymiya (1268–1328).

All Muslims believe in the "five pillars of faith" of Islam: the profession of faith ("There is no God but God and Mohammed is his prophet"), prayer five times a day, charitable giving, fasting during Ramadan, and the pilgrimage to Mecca. But the Kharijites made jihad the sixth "pillar of Islam." It is significant that presently one of the most notorious of the London-based Islamic militants, Sheikh Omar bin Bakri Muhammad, who has raised money for the Palestinian terrorist organizations Hamas and Islamic Jihad, shares this view. "Jihad," he has written, is "one of the main Pillars of Islam after *Tawhid* [profession of monotheistic faith] and *Da'wa* [proselytizing]. In fact, Jihad is . . . Da'wa by the Islamic state as its foreign policy." Sheikh Bakri presents himself as the spokesman for Bin-Laden's International Islamic Front for Jihad Against Jews and Christians.

The concept of the Dar al-Islam (abode of Islam) is an even broader concept than the umma, denoting any part of the world which is actually under the governance of Muslims. The Dar al-Harb (abode of war) has always meant those other parts of the world not yet acquired by Islam through conquest or conversion, and thus potentially the locus of continuing struggle.

Over the centuries, particularly when Islamic communities have become softened by wealth, success, or compromise with surrounding cultures, many Islamic thinkers have sought to return Islam to a hypothetical golden age when the Muslim law, *sharia*, was rigorously implemented upon the umma and when every Muslim sought with all his energy to take the message of Islam to the farthest corners of the world. Invariably, Muslim scholars of this point of view have elevated jihad to a priority status in correct Islamic conduct.

Ibn Taymiya sought to return Islam to what he considered its pristine state of purity at the time of Mohammed. A ruler who failed to implement the sharia rigorously, in ibn Taymiya's view, forfeited his right to rule. In fact, ibn Taymiya characterized any Muslim who failed to live up to his definition of the righteous Muslim as, de facto, an unbeliever. One of the worst categories of human beings, in ibn Taymiya's universe, was a Muslim who converted himself into the category of unbeliever through his failures in Muslim conduct. In effect, bad Muslim behavior was tantamount to reverse conversion, in ibn Taymiya's formulation. In particular, he regarded jihad, meaning warfare to extend the Dar al-Islam, as central to the obligations of all Muslims, and especially of their rulers.

Ibn Taymiya's writings exerted a profound influence on another Islamic sectarian firebrand, Muhammad ibn Abd al-Wahhab (1703–1792) whose sect of puritannical Islam, *Wahhabism*, rose to power in Saudi Arabia 200 years ago and has dominated it ever since. Through huge financial support by Saudi Arabian government agencies and private individuals, Wahhabism has been nurtured in Muslim communities from Central Asia to North Africa, from Indonesia to the United States.

The Taliban are Wahhabists, and many of their leaders were trained at *madrasas*, (religious schools) in Pakistan funded by Saudi money. In fact, essentially all of the Islamists linked to al Qaeda are Wahhabists. In the first of his declarations of war against the United States, the August 1996 document issued by Osama Bin-Laden after the bombings of U.S. embassies in East Africa, Bin-Laden himself quotes ibn Taymiya at great length. "To fight in defense of religion and belief," he cites ibn Taymiya, "is a collective duty; there is no other [greater] duty after believing than fighting the enemy who is corrupting the life and the religion. There are no preconditions for this duty and the enemy should be fought with the best of one's abilities."

In effect, harking back to ibn Taymiya, Bin-Laden believes that Muslim rulers who fail to resist and fight against unbelievers have abandoned the right to be called Muslim (i.e., the current ruling family of Saudi Arabia). Bin-Laden has targeted the United States at the outset because he believes it is propping up a corrupt, and indeed "infidel," Muslim regime in the Arabian peninsula. In fact this belief, that the United States has suppressed democratic movements in the Arab and Islamic world primarily for its own selfish motives of maintaining an uninterrupted supply of oil, is widely shared in the Arab world. Where Bin-Laden goes far beyond most Muslims, however, is in believing that the United States, the West, and indeed the entire civilized world as we understand it (i.e., not subject to Islamic theocracy and rule by terror), must be overthrown.

The Rise of Islamism

The Muslim Arabs captured Jerusalem in A.D. 638 from the Byzantines. But the Arab claim to the rulership of the Muslim umma was ended by the rise of the Ottoman Turks, who first conquered the Byzantine Empire in 1453 and then extended Turkish rule throughout the Arab world with their taking of Jerusalem in 1517 (the same year in which Martin Luther nailed his 95 Theses to the door of Schlosskirche in Wittenberg) and their move south into the Arabian peninsula. The Turks threatened the heart of Europe in both the 16th and 17th centuries, only finally being pushed back from the gates of Vienna in 1683. By then, though, the tide of global power and learning had swept back decisively in favor of the Christian West.

The Protestant Reformation, the rise of Western science, the exploratory, commercial and migratory thrust of European powers throughout the world, the revolution in social organization accomplished in Western societies, rendered all competing civilizational groups, from the Islamic world to Moghul India to Ching Dynasty China irrevocably vulnerable to the great Western advance. The French Revolution and the Industrial Revolution further accelerated these social and political changes. Even though Napoleon's defeat in 1815 led largely to a status quo diplomatic settlement in Europe called the Concert of Europe (1815–1854) that included the Ottoman Empire, this once formidable world power sank beneath the weight of its cumbersome institutions, its absence of the means of self-correction, and the yearnings of its subject populations for cultural and political self-expression. Throughout most of the 19th century the Ottoman Empire was known as "the Sick Man of Europe."

The Sublime Porte, as the Ottoman regime was universally dubbed, did attempt reforms during this time, but the social and political core of the empire seemed to most observers to be the victim of a terminal illness. When the Ottoman Empire rashly joined Germany and the Central Powers in 1914, it provoked the Arab world over which it ruled into a revolt that changed forever the political geography of the Middle East. Arab leaders and intellectuals now came to terms with concepts like national independence, statehood, cultural modernity, and international competition.

Of course, the implementation of those concepts was in most instances shaped by the rival ambitions of the Western powers after World War I broke out, a point alluded to specifically in the video released by Osama Bin-Laden on October 7 just after President Bush's announcement of the U.S. military campaign against al Qaeda. Bin-Laden complained about the "more than 80 years of humiliation and disgrace" suffered by the Arab world. He was obviously referring to the carving up of Muslim Arab states by the British and the French in the wake of the defeat of the Turks after World War I. That slicing up of the Dar al-Islam not only helped the Jewish state of Israel come into existence — a point of ongoing rage to devout Muslims in the Arab world — but it set in place the authoritarian Arab monarchies that either survive today (as in Saudi Arabia and Jordan) or metamorphosed into secular nationalist republics deeply antipathetic to revivalist Islam (Saddam Hussein's Iraq and Bashar Assad's Syria).

But it was in 1928 that an Egyptian schoolteacher, Hassan al-Banna, was to found an Islamic revival organization that helped eventually set much of the Islamic world on fire and was the direct ancestor of all modern Islamism. The organization he founded, the Muslim Brotherhood, was intended to achieve the complete re-Islamization of the state and the purification of the Muslim faith. Seeing himself in the line of purifying reform exemplified by the Saudi sectarian ibn al-Wahhab, al-Banna sought to spread as broadly as possible "belief in the unity and perfection of the Muslim system, the identification of the state with religion, the execution of the Muslim law, the return to the Koran and the Hadith [sayings attributed to Mohammed] and to no other sources, to refrain from scholastic theology, the opposition to mystic innovations, and the imitation of the early righteous ancestors." The *Ikhwan*, as the group became universally known, from the Arabic for "brothers," spread throughout the Arab and then the Islamic world by means of underground cells. Often they resorted to terrorist acts against foreigners or prominent political figures. In 1954, they tried to assassinate Nasser himself, and six of the conspirators were hanged.

Islamism During and After the Cold War

As long as the Soviet Union was locked in a cold war struggle for global primacy with the United States, and offered a secular alternative to Western democratic capitalism, secular pan-Arabism was attractive to many Arabs. But it was the catastrophic defeat of Syria, Egypt, and Jordan by Israel in the Six-Day War in 1967 that disillusioned much of the Arab world that regarded socialist secularism as a vehicle for achieving Arab national greatness. From the late 1960s onward, Islamist thinking gained more and more followers among Arabs and then in the Shi'ite Muslim nation of Iran. Anger with both Western capitalist "imperialism" and Soviet-style atheistic socialism helped propel Iran dramatically out of the Western orbit when the Ayatollah Khomeini took power in 1979. Khomeini's "Death to America" slogan and his humiliation of the United States by taking 50 American diplomats hostage for 444 days was a turning point for many Arab Islamists. They now came to believe that they could, by similar tactics, re-Islamize their own societies.

The decisive moment for Osama Bin-Laden, of course, was not what happened in Iran, but events in Afghanistan. Born in 1957 to a prosperous Saudi business family, Bin-Laden, like many Saudi young men, had for a time enjoyed the fleshpots of Beirut as a playboy. But his father rediscovered his own Islamic faith during a business project to re-construct the Grand Mosque in Mecca, and his newfound piety deeply affected the son. The younger Bin-Laden grew a beard, invariably the sign of Muslim piety, became much more deeply observant in the practice of his faith, and cast around for an Islamic cause into which to throw himself. He found it when the Soviet army invaded Afghanistan in December of 1979.

Almost immediately, Bin-Laden set about organizing support for Afghan freedom fighters, and training and recruiting thousands of Arabs who wanted to participate in the new jihad against the Soviets. Bin-Laden became the chief recruiter for a virtual foreign legion of "Afghan" Arabs from countries as diverse as Egypt, Algeria, Saudi Arabia, and Morocco who wanted to join the jihad. It helped him, of course, that the U.S. government itself was using first Saudi Arabia, and then Pakistan, as a conduit for finances and weaponry to build up the *mujahedeen* ("holy warriors"). At the time, most Americans saw the fight against the Soviets as a vital part of the Cold War. They applauded this novel effort to weaken Moscow by bleeding its armies to death in an unwinnable war in the mountains of Central Asia.

It was one of Afghanistan's neighbors who first drew the attention of Washington to the dangers of this policy. "You are creating a new Frankenstein," then Pakistani Prime Minister Benazir Bhutto is said to have told then U.S. President George Bush in the late 1980s. What she meant was that this new, international fraternity of combat-hardened Arabs and other Muslims, exultant at their successes against one superpower and deeply indoctrinated into Islamist jihad, would eventually turn against the superpower that had encouraged them into existence in the first place. The fact that the United States essentially abandoned Afghanistan once it had helped force the Soviets to retreat is clearly a factor that embittered Bin-Laden and his fellow "Afghan" Arabs, by now numbering several thousand.

But what turned Bin-Laden savagely from his anti-Soviet posture to a raging anti-Americanism was the invitation extended by the Saudi government to U.S. troops to be based on Saudi soil during the build-up to the Gulf War in 1990. Even though the Americans were in his country to protect it against the entirely secular forces of Iraq's Saddam Hussein, Bin-Laden saw their presence not merely as another of the ongoing "infidel" slights to Islam, but proof that the United States would do everything possible to prop up the Saudi royal family. The Saud family banished Bin-Laden in 1991 and stripped him of his Saudi citizenship. He settled for a few years in Sudan. In his eyes, meanwhile, the ruling dynasty of Saudi Arabia had already fulfilled ibn Taymiya's definition of Muslim leaders who had become infidels by abandoning the principles of their faith.

But there is obviously far more to the passionate anti-American venom of Bin-Laden than theological resentment at the House of al-Saud. In many respects, Bin-Laden's hatred of the West is a hatred of modernity, of the success and achievements of globalization that to a striking degree have bypassed the Arab world and much of the Islamic world as a whole. A columnist for the Egyptian magazine *Al-Ahram Al-Arabi* wrote gleefully after the terrorist destruction of the World Trade Center towers, "The world has discovered that the strength of the oppressed is great when the situation becomes unbearable. . . . The city of globalization, with its economic, political, and military symbols, has collapsed, and the theory of globalization will be buried with the establishment of the false coalition [of world powers allied against al Qaeda]."

That hatred, of course, is also partly based on envy, and indeed incomprehension, of a phenomenon — modern international capitalist culture — that obviously is the antithesis of the ethos of traditional Islam. Much of the Islamist hatred of the West derives from a sensibility deeply offended by Western vulgarity: pornography on the Internet, crass popular music, casual sexuality, the endless search for novelty and distraction by spoiled young people; in effect, the mass popular culture of large cities not just in the Western world but in those countries of the world increasingly integrated with globalization.

Then, of course, there is Israel. This non-Islamic presence, of Jews no less — those original critics and mockers of Mohammed — this outpost of Western thought and democracy in the heart of the Dar al-Islam, has been an offense to many Muslims, perhaps to most Arab Muslims, since the day of its independence in 1948. Muslims almost universally believe that Israel could not have continued to survive, much less defeat its adversaries, without American support and encouragement.

For all Islamists, Israel's very existence, not to mention the absence of a Palestinian state, is a living repudiation of Islam's self-image as a religion perpetually moving forward and the Dar al-Islam as being a place where the despised dhimmis can be kept in their place. As if a Jewish state in itself were not enough of an affront to Islamists, Israel's control of access to Islam's third holiest site, the al-Aqsa Mosque in Jerusalem, is profoundly resented by most Arabs.

For Bin-Laden, the Palestinian issue was not initially front and center; it was subordinate to his declaration of war upon America for having its troops in Saudi Arabia. But after September 11, when Bin-Laden realized that he needed a broader platform of support from Muslims than the hitherto rather narrowly focused objections to Americans on Saudi soil, Palestine emerged as prominent among his grievances. In the October 7 video, he said, "As to America, I say to it and its people a few words: I swear to God that America will not live in peace before peace reigns in Palestine, and before all the army of infidels depart the land of Mohammad, peace be upon him."

In effect, Bin-Laden now wants to use the Palestinian issue as his most prominent banner to rally Muslims all around the world to his cause. It will almost certainly be one of the greatest challenges to U.S. diplomacy during the war against al Qaeda to maintain its alliance with Israel and its absolute commitment to Israel's survival in the face of a probable growing chorus of voices demanding pressure upon Israel to concede a state to the Palestinians in short order.

America is certainly hated in much of the Arab world because of its support for Israel. But it is also hated simply because it is America. There is a diffusely felt resentment on the part of much of the world toward the world's only military superpower, the political and economic colossus that somehow always manages to ensure that international conflicts are resolved in ways helpful to American interests. Many in the world, and not just the Arab world, believe that Americans demonstrate a screechy and even hypocritical moralism, denouncing human rights abuses in other nations but not always owning up to their own social, political, and economic shortcomings. It does not seem to matter to Bin-Laden and to millions of Muslims around the world that the U.S. military interventions in the Balkans, in 1995 and 1999, were initiated to rescue Muslim communities from ethnic cleansing by non-Muslims. Nor does it make a difference that the United States is one of the most consciously self-critical societies in the world, willing and at times even eager to listen to harsh attacks upon its character and its policies. Nor does it appear to matter that the United States has usually tried hard to bring its own NATO allies and the United Nations into the decision-making process of its foreign policy in recent years.

Bin-Laden and his cohorts are also unimpressed by former Secretary of State Madeleine Albright's comment, while still ambassador to the U.N. during the first Clinton administration, that she favored an "assertive multilateralism." What they probably remembered her saying were words that she uttered as Secretary of State in February 1998 during one of the many U.S.-Iraqi crises of the past decade. Albright said, "If we have to use force, it is because we are America. We are the indispensable nation. We stand tall. We see further into the future." Well, "indispensable" is arguable, but "vulnerable" is not. In the Egyptian opposition newspaper *Al-Sha'ab*, less than two weeks after September 11, columnist Khaled Al-Sharif wrote, "Everyone was in a state of shock because of what happened, and all were surprised to see America, which controls the world, collapse, and the Satan that rules the world, burn. The patron of terrorism was burned by its own fire."

This, of course, is the hate-filled rhetoric of Islamism, the poisonous speech that in hundreds, perhaps thousands, of mosques throughout the Islamic world, is being used to rouse the world's Muslims into a war to the death with the United States. From the point of view of the Islamists and their followers, it is a legitimate jihad, a struggle with the forces of unbelief that stand in the way of the advance of Islam. But more clearly than anything, the call articulated by Bin-Laden is a fight to the death not just with the United States and Israel, but to any mode of commerce or discourse or creativity or social life that does not fit into the pinched, medieval mindset of a utopian campaigner for a universal, coercively imposed, brutally reactionary, theocratic dictatorship.

A Golden Opportunity for Diplomacy

Two major perceptions of the events of September 11 seem to have crystallized all over the world. One is that if the United States can be terrorized and devastated by the newest network of international assassins, no nation on earth is safe. The second is an almost intuitive understanding that the United States is the only power on the planet with the resources, the credibility, and the overall respect to lead a global assault on the deadly virus of terrorist fanaticism.

It is hard otherwise to explain the astonishing offers of intelligence collaboration, with no *quid pro quo* suggested, from powers normally as suspicious of American motives as Russia and China. The willingness of some of the "stans," the formerly Soviet Central Asian states, to make their airfields available for U.S. tactical sorties into nearby Afghanistan is additional evidence of the global sea-change. So is Russian consent to this, and acquiescence to U.S. military overflights. As for the traditional close allies of the United States, the Germans have been overwhelmingly cooperative, and not since World War II has a British prime minister rallied so unhesitatingly to America's side in time of trouble.

We should understand the point clearly: the very magnitude of the anti-American atrocities of September 11 has presented the United States with the greatest opportunity to lead and indeed reshape the global security system in its history.

First, the sense that world civilization itself, not just the United States came under attack September 11, along with the desperate carnage in Manhattan, has helped erase in many countries previously critical the image of the United States as either pushy and arrogant on the one hand, or — contradictorily — selfish and aloof on the other. To a remarkable degree, the most important parts of the world seem to really want the United States to win this conflict.

Second, so broadly based — at least for now — does the global popular sympathy seem to be in many countries that the United States would be downright negligent not to move in rapidly to develop that sympathy further. What the world is surely ripe for is a major re-ordering of security relationships that could provide a basis for stability among the major powers — the U.S., Russia, China, the European Union, and Japan, in particular — possibly for the next few decades.

Should the major powers join in a grand security system — perhaps called the Global Concert — opposed to global anarchy, its existence might help stabilize some politically vulnerable Third World states, such as India and Pakistan. This global security system would make it clear that all the world's major powers had undertaken mutually not to exploit domestic unrest anywhere in the world for their own national purposes.

The Middle East, of course, is likely to remain tense with or without the Global Concert, though the opportunities for Israel's front-line Arab neighbors to exploit overall global tensions would be lessened. A new global security network might dissuade muscle-flexing powers like Iran or Iraq from pursuing their own regional and global agendas through the medium of Israeli-Palestinian tensions. It might also dampen any hopes among Palestinian radical Islamic elements that outside forces would eventually intervene on their behalf in the conflict. If this turned out to be the case, the incentive for the Palestinian authorities to accept less-than-perfect peace terms with Israel, and thus actually bring an end to the conflict, would be very strong.

Yet one of the main challenges of the Global Concert in the short and medium-term will be informational. Huge efforts — and on the U.S. side there is much catching up to do — must be made to refute Islamist contentions that the U.S.-led war against terrorism is a war against Islam. Wherever they can be found and assured of protection from reprisal (a pre-requisite even with the United States) prominent moderate Muslims must be brought forward and encouraged to explain, on-camera and in print, why every element of the Bin-Laden ideology is incompatible with core Islamic values of charity and peace. Relatives of Islamic victims of the New York bombings should be interviewed in a way that evokes powerful emotions of sympathy for bereaved families. U.S. government information services, meanwhile, must work overtime preparing documentaries that portray the freedom and sense of fulfillment of Muslims living in the United States. For the United States to win globally the war against Bin-Laden and his fanatical followers, it must prevail in the global war of ideas. For the Global Concert to last beyond this war also, it must share in that struggle. It will become increasingly important in the years ahead, independently of the war on the Bin-Ladenites, to convince the world's poor that no answer to their economic or cultural needs is ever going to be found in a religious conflict waged against the West.

V.S. Naipaul, named as Nobel laureate for literature barely a month after September 11, 2001, and author of two books on Islamism (*Among the Believers* and *Beyond Belief*) soberly articulated just how huge the stakes are in America's — and the world's — struggle to undo the terrorist network of al Qaeda. "We are within reach of great nihilistic forces that have undone civilization," he said in a talk in Melbourne before the terrorist attacks in the United States. "Religion has been turned by some into a kind of nihilism, where people wish to destroy themselves and destroy their past and their culture . . . to be pure. They are enraged about the world and they wish to pull it down." The Taliban have offered their own small contribution to this assault on civilization by reducing Afghan women to the status of indigent misery and by demolishing through artillery fire and dynamite two of the great artistic achievements of Asia, the Bamiyan statues of Buddha. But al Qaeda, hell-bent on acquiring weapons of mass destruction such as systems of chemical and biological warfare, is intent on destroying more than merely the emblems of human culture. They would like to pull down, all over the world, civilization itself. "We tremble," wrote Charles Krauthammer in the *Weekly Standard* in commenting on Naipaul, "because for the first time in history, nihilism will soon be armed with the ultimate weapons of annihilation. For the first time in history, the nihilist will have the means to match his ends. Which is why the war declared upon us on September 11 is the most urgent not only of our lives, but in the life of civilization itself."

Krauthammer is right, and President Bush is right. This is civilization's fight. And we must win it.

FRANK GAFFNEY is the founder and president of the Center for Security Policy in Washington, D.C. In 1987, Mr. Gaffney was nominated by President Reagan to become the Assistant Secretary of Defense for International Security Policy, the senior position in the Defense Department with responsibility for policies involving nuclear forces, arms control, and U.S.-European defense relations. He acted in that capacity for seven months, during which time he was the chairman of the High Level Group, NATO's senior politico-military committee. He also represented the Secretary of Defense in key U.S.-Soviet negotiations and ministerial meetings. From 1983–1987, Mr. Gaffney was the Deputy Assistant Secretary of Defense for Nuclear Forces and Arms Control Policy under Assistant Secretary Richard Perle. From February 1981 to August 1983, Mr. Gaffney was a professional staff member on the Senate Armed Services Committee, chaired by Senator John Tower (R-Texas). In the latter 1970s, Mr. Gaffney served as an aide to the late Senator Henry M. "Scoop" Jackson in the areas of defense and foreign policy.

The Arab-Israeli Conflict — the Key to Fighting International Terrorism

by Frank Gaffney

The idea of building peace on truth should be so self-evident that it oughtn't need saying. And yet we have seen for so long exactly the opposite approach — trying desperately, in fact, increasingly more desperately, to build peace on falsehoods, or downright lies. I happen to subscribe to the notion of peace through strength.

I must tell you that I learned a lot, about both the importance of truth and the importance of strength in dealing with threats to our freedoms, from my long-time friend and mentor, Richard Perle.

I want to talk about the Arab-Israeli conflict as a key element of the war on terror. That conflict is a front in a global war on terror. I happen to think, however, that it is more instructive to think about this front seen through the prism of the larger war — what I would call, actually, one war — on international terror, rather than look at that war through the prism of this microcosm.

I think clearly America and Israel confront the same enemies. And one of my abiding frustrations with this whole thing is that we've been very reluctant, certainly in the United States, to talk about who the enemy is. In fact, the whole notion that we're fighting a war on terror seems to avoid the discussion of who is the enemy — who is using terror's courses and instruments against us. And I think we should be clear about this. The enemy is by and large, not exclusively, but by and large, radical Islam, or as I prefer to call it, Islamists who have, I would argue, hijacked a religion and seek both to dominate it and the rest of us, through their perversion of the religious faith that they purport to hold.

This may be a somewhat controversial view. I know there are others who believe that it is absolutely inherent in the nature of Islam that it must be radical, that it must be violent, that it must dominate others — other faiths. I hope that's not true.

We are confronting a very determined effort on the part of those who believe in the jihadist strain, whether they're the Wahhabis of Saudi Arabia, or the Shiite extremists of Iran, or various other sects associated with them, benefiting from their help or otherwise. They will, left to their own devices, compel the rest of the Islamic world to be every bit as much our enemies as these sects are today. They have to be fought effectively. That means not only dealing with the symptoms, it means dealing with the sources. Some of those sources of greatest concern at the moment are those that are using immense wealth, most of it drawn from the West's dependence on oil, to fund international efforts to dominate the faith and assault those who stand in the way of its triumph worldwide, whether they are Jews in Israel, Americans in the United States and elsewhere around the world, or more generally, those who are committed to modernity, to liberal democracy, to freedom.

A particular problem with which we have been very much consumed in the United States is the presence of these Islamists, and their growing influence inside the United States itself. For too long we thought of this as a problem that was more or less confined to the Middle East.

Well, unfortunately it's a presence in our own hemisphere as well, even inside the United States. One of the particular concerns that we must reckon with if we are to prevail in this war on terror, is to understand both the extent of the Islamist penetration of our country and even our government, which I think has contributed to this reluctance to call the enemy what it is, let alone to counter it effectively.

If we have the same enemies, I think we have the same reasons for the enmity of our foes. We, like the people of Israel, and like free people elsewhere around the world, stand against the aspirations of the radical

Islamists, to dominate the faith and their world. Everything about us, let's be clear, is anathema to them. How we treat women. How we exercise our individual liberties and freedoms. The very fact that we respect and are tolerant toward other religions. The fact that, of course, we don't believe that religion is the principal function of the state, and the state is the principle vehicle of the religion. If we fail to appreciate that intractable hostility, we are absolutely going to get it wrong when we think that we can appease our way into some form of accommodation with them. This sort of behavior only encourages in such people the conviction that their philosophy and aspirations are correct, that we are weak and they will prevail inexorably, if not in the very near future.

We face the same dangers in this war — the dangers that fundamentally arise from the inherent vulnerability of free societies. Here in Israel, in the United States, elsewhere in the free world, we have open societies — the very nature of which lends themselves to attacks. Murderous attacks. And we confront the reality that we can only diminish the danger of those sorts of attacks by making ourselves less free, less open, less the way we are. Less the way our values demand that we be. This is a very unpalatable proposition, needless to say. And nobody knows it better than the people here confronting day in and day out the shahids, of which we've heard so much of late. Needless to say, the dangers that these shahids represent obliges us to wage this war, as Alan Keyes so eloquently says, without any accommodation, and with no goal other than victory.

It follows from all of the above that Israel, and indeed free people elsewhere, must have the same latitude, the ability to use the same techniques and tactics that we in the Unites States are employing, to counter this horrific thought and to mitigate the danger posed by their destructive potential. This means, of course, taking the war to the enemy — an offensively oriented campaign. It means, just as the United States has been trying to do, in the words of the Deputy Secretary of Defense Paul Wolfowitz, draining the swamps — going after the infrastructures of terror that enable radical Islamists, and, to be clear, those who are secular allies or at least those who hope to benefit from the jihadist efforts to weaken (if not to destroy) us.

One of the reasons I was very unhappy about the "Roadmap," was when President Bush said on June 24, 2002, that a pre-condition of the United States even contemplating, let alone actually recognizing, a Palestinian state, was that the terrorist infrastructure had to be dismantled in the Palestinian community, in addition to new leadership and so on. The swamp had to be drained before it was possible for the United States to support the creation of a Palestinian state. This was thrown over the side in the pursuit of a Roadmap.

In addition to these offensive operations, clearly in this one war we must appreciate the importance of doing what we can, within our commitment to free and open societies, to secure our own homelands. And in this respect, I must say I think American efforts, to say nothing about the world community more generally, to compel Israel to weaken itself, to make its homeland less secure, are abominations.

It is important to remember that back in 1967, after the Six Day War, the Joint Chiefs of Staff of the United States were asked to evaluate what it was Israel required in the way of territory to assure its own security. The concern of that moment, of course, was the prospect that its Arab neighbors would once again do what they had done several times before, and of course did subsequently in 1973, namely trying to use conventional forces to destroy Israel. And our Joint Chiefs of Staff, in, I think, a professional and objective analysis said Israel needs to have the high ground of the West Bank. It needs to retain control of the Golan Heights. These are simply essential barriers to, once again, any effort made by Arab neighbors to bring force to bear through such territory for the purposes of liquidating the Jewish state. I believe that remains true today. Some say it no longer applies in an age of missiles. I think that's not correct. And while the nature of Israel's enemies and their relative military capabilities may be different, creating a terrorist state on the high ground of the West Bank and the Gaza Strip, and relinquishing control of the Golan Heights, I think would invite certainly the conviction that the Phase Plan is working and the Palestinians will be emboldened to believe that the liberation of the rest of "occupied" Palestine is just a matter of time. But I think it will also, almost certainly, induce others in the Arab world to believe that the opportunity for joining in the destruction of Israel again is at hand.

> The Phased Plan, the Arab strategy adopted after the shattering defeat in the 1967 Six Day War, called for a process for eliminating the state of Israel. Rather than confront the Jewish state in a single military campaign, the Arab nations would work through diplomatic and political channels to shrink Israel through territorial concessions, finishing with an optional, quick war to retrieve "Palestine."

Winston Churchill wrote in, I believe, roughly 1933, about a very different time of course and a very different set of circumstances, but a similar proposition. He talked about the folly of Great Britain pursuing a policy that deliberately weakened its ally — at the time, France — in the hope of appeasing what was then the nascent threat from Nazi Germany. And I think he was correct, and it is no more sensible for the United States or, for that matter, the rest of the free world, to be participating in any effort that would have the practical effect, whatever its intent, of reducing our important ally in this front in a global war on terror to our own detriment, as well as the detriment of that ally.

Let me just emphasize a point that I think has not been made perhaps as much as it should. Because this is one war, I would argue that successes in various fronts have a synergistic effect on the prospects for success on other fronts. I am very hopeful — and I had the privilege of being in Iraq in the fall of 2003 — that the work that has been done to liberate that country — not complete yet, but well advanced — will have very palpable and very long-standing benefits for us in this larger war on terror. Specifically, I think the very fact that we have indeed, I guess the biblical verb is "smitten" our enemies, eliminating a regime that was indisputably a source of terror, a sponsor, an enabler of the murderous sorts of attacks by Islamists or secular organizations bent on our destruction . . . will be very beneficial. We've changed the correlation of forces, as the Soviets used to say, by eliminating that Iraqi threat. We have cut off funding; certainly that was materially benefiting the families of shahids in Israel, and we have indeed begun to create a model for a very different Middle East. We're a long way from seeing this to completion. Indeed, this is a long-term war which will probably take a generation or two to prevail in, but I am confident that if we recognize these realities, these truths, and we maintain and we utilize effectively the strength that we have at our disposal, particularly as a community of free nations, and we don't work to undermine each other in the course of fighting this common war, we will indeed prevail — and God help us if we don't.

ALAN KEYES spent 11 years with the U.S. State Department. He served in the U.S. Foreign Service and on the staff of the National Security Council before becoming Ronald Reagan's ambassador to the United Nations Economic and Social Council, where he represented the interests of the United States in the U.N. General Assembly (1983–85). In 1985, he was appointed Assistant Secretary of State for International Organizations (1985–88). Keyes was president of Citizens Against Government Waste (1989–91) and founder of National Taxpayers' Action Day. As the two-time Republican nominee for the U.S. Senate in Maryland, he challenged liberal Democrats Paul Sarbanes (1988) and Barbara Mikulski (1992). In the 1996 Republican presidential campaign, Alan Keyes eloquently elevated the national political debate. With his unequivocal pro-life, pro-family message, he forced the GOP leadership to address America's moral crisis. His political views are consistently based on America's founding ideals, those in the Declaration of Independence and the U.S. Constitution.

Moral Clarity in Fighting Terror

by Alan Keyes

I guess my learning process started when I was thrown in, head first, at the United Nations in the role of the political troubleshooter who had to deal with all the efforts going on in different forums to destroy and undermine and criticize and otherwise make more difficult both U.S. policy in the Middle East and our relationship with Israel during the Reagan administration. So I come to it with the sense of someone who's had some experience, but who is still at the stage where I get to scratch my head about what appears to me sometimes to be the blindness of the so-called experts.

I believe that it is vitally important that in our present environment we understand the situation in the Middle East and the Arab-Israeli conflict. We understand it in the context of war on terror. Because if we are clear and are willing to look at the facts, we would acknowledge that war on terror is at least in part — and perhaps in large part — a consequence of the situation in this region. And I'm not sure that that's something folks care to acknowledge, and I'm not sure why.

For instance, how many of us remember and take seriously the fact that when Osama Bin-Laden went to justify or explain or otherwise put into context the attack on the World Trade Center, he did so on the basis of ascribing his action to a desire to strike out against America for its support of Israel and its willingness to aid and abet the oppression of his Palestinian brothers. All we could say was, "Well that was just a convenient excuse on his part, he really just wants to kill us." I think we're missing the point. And the point is very clear, if we take it seriously at face value, as I often think we ought to take the pronouncements of people like this. What he is telling us is that there is a direct relationship between what has happened and gone on in the Middle East with respect to terror and the globalization of that phenomenon of terrorism to the extent that no one is safe. We should have recognized this long ago, but if we see it now in retrospect, then perhaps we would have to take a second look at the whole course of the history and situation of the region and see it not in terms of this or that stage in the so-called process or in the so-called dialectic between the Arabs and the Israelis, but see it instead for a moment as the process in which the culture of terror was incubated and grew. If we look at it in that respect, what do we see? Well, sadly, I think what we see is that the environment for the incubation of terror was largely and greatly contributed to by the response of the United States and other countries in the world to the practice of terror as a legitimate instrument of policy and negotiation by the leadership of the Palestinians.

Over the course of the last several decades, from the very beginning of that practice of terrorism by Yassir Arafat, through every stage of the so-called negotiating process, I think one would be clear in seeing that each progressive stage in the implementation of the practice of terror was rewarded by a new stage in the development of the so-called negotiating process, that gave to the terrorist Palestinian leadership greater legitimacy and greater scope for their actions. That has been particularly true in the last ten years or so.

When Yassir Arafat said that Oslo represented a new epic, and so forth, we would naturally interpret that, wouldn't we, in the context of all the lovey-dovey, let's-have-peace sort of themes that were going on in the media. What if Yassir Arafat was thinking, *Yeah, we wanted to get here all along. We wanted to get to that epic where you Westerners would finally be stupid enough to accept the creation of a platform from which we can launch the next and perhaps final stage in our effort to destroy the state of Israel.*

We have seen that in a formal way, a major shift occurred in the declared policy of the United States government. That formal policy shifted in such a way as to accept as the legitimate basis for further progress the idea of a Palestinian state on the West Bank. That had not been done before. I think one could seriously argue that that looks like a concession to terror.

Now, of course, we avoid that impression, because we want to pretend that the Middle East is over here, and the war on terror is over there and somehow these two things can be dealt with separately; but from the point of view of the participants on the other side of the chessboard, that's a lie. From the point of view of the legitimization of the terrorist leadership in the Arab world, it turns out to be a very dangerous lie.

Yet, that is how we insist on looking at it, as if these two things are separate entities. There has been a lot of talk about the clarity in which the president of the United States responded to 9/11 and declared an implacable war against terror. He declared it in terms that assumed that the attack had represented the violation of a clear and universal principle of human conscience and decency. That's the only way you can justify the statement that you are either with us or against us. You're either going to join us in this war against terror, or you are going to be part of the enemy. There will be no in-between. No Switzerlands this time, no neutrality, nobody trading with both sides: if you facilitate terrorism, you have made yourself our enemy. That was, and still is as far as I know, our declared policy.

What gives us the right to make such a declaration? Obviously, that's not the way that a war usually goes, the mere fact that one country goes to war with another doesn't imply that a third must be involved in that war — it never has before! Why does it now? Well it does now, on the premise that all of humanity ought to be engaged in that which is a violation of the fundamental premise of human community and human conscience and the possibility of co-operative human interaction. Something about that attack and what it represented deeply violated the possibility of our common humanity. And, therefore, we stand before the world to declare that this assault on our community ought to be of concern to all who have a decent and conscientious interest in maintaining that possibility.

But that does lead to a problem, doesn't it? Because if that's true, then we would have to look first at the nature of that evil, and what is it? What is it that was so clear and recognizable? Some people are confused about this, because they talk as if it was the use of violence and so forth and so on that was the problem — that's not true, and we all know it.

Violence is sadly sometimes a necessary instrument that nations use in order to defend themselves. And there is even a difference between what happened on September 11 and what we have grown used to calling and ought to call "aggression." At the end of World War II, a certain progress was made, I think, in the fragile understanding of the limits of human depravity — by an agreement that was probably the most important thing that was represented by the existence of the United Nations. It wasn't all the other palaver and possibilities and this and that, but what was represented by it was this — the simple notion that if Country X committed aggression against Country Y, everybody in the world would be implicated in the stand against that aggression and that that would now be the presumption of the international situation. And that was a step forward. It essentially meant that, as an instrument of pure policy, aggression was no longer acceptable. It meant in point of fact that, as an instrument of pure policy, war as such was not going to be acceptable, it would only be acceptable under certain terms and those terms were clear — there had to be an attack, or there had to be a response to a clear and direct threat to your peace and security, to the peace and security of a region or to international peace and security. Now that doesn't necessarily preclude the possibility of preemptive action. But it does require that all war-like action be justified on the basis of defensive security concerns. Not on the basis of the securing of positive strategic advantage that has nothing to do with defense. It eliminates a lot of plausible and good-sounding pretexts.

The plausible and good-sounding pretext that, for example, was used by Hitler and others to justify their aggressions at the beginning of World War II — we forget that, don't we? That Hitler never said, "I'm a mean nasty guy, and I'm going out to act like the devil and conquer my neighbors." He didn't say that. He was always filled in his speeches with the redirect that he was going to deal with those who are heaping oppression upon the ethnic German minorities and doing things that were inexcusable and that had to be stopped and that would be stopped by the intervention of the German people. This was a good-sounding redirect. And I think at the end of World War II, in the light of the knowledge that evil people can turn good-sounding redirect to extremely evil purposes, we kind of excluded that good-sounding redirect from the acceptable justifications for war. It doesn't matter how good it sounds: if you have acted without response to a threat to your security, then your war is unjustified, and we will react against it as a community. That is essentially what the U.N. security arrangements were supposed to represent.

But even that act of aggression is different from terror. Why? Well, because by and large you can commit an act of, yeah, I can send my military forces into somebody else's country without any provocation. That doesn't mean I'll storm through it and start killing women and children, does it? No, I could direct my blows at their military forces with a view to securing control of their land and resources; but, following the normal rules of war, I could exclude noncombatants as targets, and so forth and so on. As a matter of fact, the wars of aggression can certainly be conducted in ways that respect those norms. Aggression is not the same as terrorism. What is the difference? Well, I just hit on it, didn't I? The difference is the conscious use of violence. The conscious use of violence against the in-nocent — read: "those who are in a position to do no harm, the unarmed, those who are not part of a supportive of or implicated in the military structures of a country and who therefore can do you no harm." The para-digm of such innocence is, of course, children. Unarmed babes like the babe sleeping in the crib in northern Israel taken out by terrorists — there is no way that one can doubt that when I creep into someone's home and slaughter a child sleeping in the crib, I have killed an innocent. And that becomes the paradigm for the heart, the true meaning of terror. Why did I go through all of this? Because I think we have to. We have to realize that in dealing with terrorism we are not dealing with normal warfare. We are not dealing with "normal" violence. And even in the context of a war of insurgency against a perceived oppressor, there can be limits to the nature of the means that are employed to inflict damage on the so-called enemy.

Now what is clear — what was clear in 9/11 — and had been clear long before that, as we all know, is the way in which the Palestinian leader-ship conducted their operations against Israel. Decades ago, in fact, they crossed the line between legitimate war, even insurgent war, in that sense still within the boundaries of our understanding of how war can be con-ducted — they crossed the line into that terrorism which is in and of itself a violation of the most basic and elementary sense of human decency that we have sought to implement in our modern times.

We should have seen this all along, shouldn't we? This is one of the sad truths of human life, that evil is evil all along, but sometimes people don't get on their hind legs and declare it to be evil until it hits them. And in many ways I have to declare with a certain sadness that this does appear to have been true of American policy. Because terrorism was around long be-fore the World Trade Center fell. And we were fighting it long before, but we dealt with it as a strategic threat, as a security threat. Did we deal with it as in the post-9/11 period? Did we stand up and deal with it as a moral reality? As a moral threat? No, we didn't. But, thankfully, in the wake of 9/11 that changed, and in order to involve the conscience of all humanity, we invoked that moral understanding that allows us to see in terrorism that which stands outside the circle of what is acceptable to decent human conscience. If this is true, though, and we have declared that if you're for terrorism, you're against us, the war on terror therefore should involve the decent conscience of people everywhere, in every region, in every area, and so forth. What does that imply for the Middle East?

Well, it implies something that we have not seen and yet that we should see if the war on terror is to be consistent. And I don't say what I am about to say by way of criticizing, though I guess criticism is implied. I say it just by way of observation, because it's a natural and, I think, quite logical consequence of the declared policy of the United States government on the war on terror. We have said that we're fighting this war, an implacable war against this phenomenon that violates the most basic and elementary premises of human conscience and decency. Wherever it rears its head, we will smack it down and everyone who is part of it, directly or indirectly, becomes implicated as the enemy in our war. Now somebody would need to explain, and I'm sure all of us have asked ourselves this question, if that is in fact the basis of and the nature of the war on terror, how can it be that you read in the *New York Times* that Palestinian *militants* have killed 19 Israeli civilians?

Something in that statement ignores the distinction between terror and other uses of violence and war. In this context, we will look at a terrorist and call him a militant. In this context, we will see the implementation of terror and act as if we are in presence of a legitimate instrument of policy.

In order to understand who the enemy is, we must keep our clarity about what constitutes the evil of the phenomenon we find. Once we have lost that clarity, we have moved into a realm of confusion that ultimately threatens the possibility of prosecuting the war.

And that is where we are. Because that means that if we can't recognize a Palestinian terrorist as a terrorist, then we have destroyed our ability to maintain clearly the distinction between terrorists and other warriors. And once that distinction is lost, the war on terror loses its moral universality, and becomes instead just a particular response of a particular nation to a particularly egregious attack upon its people. It requires no special moral determination from all the other nations of the world.

Now if we can't, and by "we" I mean the United States in this case, what would that imply for our policy in the Middle East? Well, it would imply that since September 11, we should have taken a very different stance from the one we have taken. And what I am about to say will seem to some people to be harsh and maybe excessively limited and I don't know what else, but I think it's also clearly necessary.

In the wake of September 11, we should have taken a stand clearly and unequivocally, that, if you practice terrorism, you lose your claim to legitimate participation in all and any international processes whatsoever.

We should have taken that stand, we should be taking it, and we should hold on to it, come what may. What does that mean? What it means is that the first priority must be to deal with terrorism. If there is a process that exists in the world as the so-called peace process, whatever may be the state of play, if there is a process in which there is as part of that process the participation of elements that engage in an ongoing way in the practice of terror, then that process should come to an end.

That would mean that, for the time being, there can be no peace process in the Middle East.

There can be none, no. People say, "Well, that's harsh. We need peace! We want peace!" Of course we want peace. I want peace just as much as anybody else! But the first thing we have to recognize is a fundamental truth, that I think we talk around and deal around and in other ways get around, but peace doesn't start until it has been introduced into the heart and conscience of everybody at the table. You cannot have a discussion of peace with those who remain committed to, not only war, but to the most illegitimate and evil and immoral form of warfare known to humankind. And until we are willing to recognize this as a fundamental premise of policy, I think two things are true. There will be no peace but the war will also not be prosecuted effectively. And this is the second point I would like to make.

When you are at war, what is the objective? Today, it is popular to answer, "Our objective is peace."

Well, I'm sorry. Logically speaking, this can't be so. Why? Because in the midst of most situations, you can get peace anytime you want. Just give up! Surrender! Let the enemy have his way! And you will have peace, be it the peace of the grave and oblivion and destruction — but you'll find it! When engaged in a war, particularly a war forced upon you by those who will not stop their acts of terrorism or aggression, peace cannot be the objective of your war. Peace is a secondary objective that will hopefully be produced as the byproduct of achieving that which must in such a war be your main objective, and that is to defeat the enemy.

We do not want peace with terrorists! We want an end to their existence. Since our aim in the war with terrorism is not peace, it makes no sense to negotiate peace with terrorists.

Terrorists have taken up the instruments of war in a way that suggests that their consciences are immune to the usual categories of persuasion. And that I think is particularly true in the case of the form in which terror presents itself and has presented itself in this region — the homicide bomber, the suicide bomber, the person who has clearly declared that they don't mind dying so long as they take the enemy with them. Something about that defies the usual logic of those people who stand up and act as if we don't have to treat negotiations as a zero-sum game. When somebody walks into a room with a bomb strapped around them, determined to set it off, guess what? Negotiations are a zero-sum game. There is no win-win situation there. If they win, that is to say achieve their objective — you're going to lose. And anything else is simply soft-headed, stupid, self-destructive response to whom and what they are. All you need to know is that you're dealing with someone who has only one objective in mind — to kill you, and who will not be stopped because you ask them to.

That laughable idea has actually been built into the so-called negotiating process we've been faced with for the last several months. Why? Well, because when everybody was fawning over Abu Mazen, and he was going around making a good impression on people, he seemed sincere, but then he'd come out and he would say that he was against terrorism, they ought to stop that nasty terrorism, but that he wasn't going to engage in civil war in order to end the terrorism. You see, the minute he said that, I stepped back and said: "This guy's a phony."

Why? Because people who are out to kill other people and who have gained advantage and adopted a strategy based upon the killing of others, are standing there, all armed and ready to do the killing, and you've created a negotiating process that creates capital for them every time they kill. Because every time they kill, they prove that you better deal with them, because the killing won't stop until you do.

So in the context of such a negotiating process, for him to stand there and say he doesn't want a civil war with them, means *he doesn't want to stop them*! They are obviously not going to stop just because you ask. As a matter of fact, every time you ask, there is going to be an incentive for them to kill somebody else. Because then you'll ask more seriously and more earnestly and put more on the table when you ask, so that the response will be more advantageous to them. We in fact created a process, the so-called Roadmap to peace. I don't care what you call it. At the moment, any negotiating process whatsoever creates capital for terrorism. Creates opportunities for terror to show its power and prove its might.

And that's exactly, I think, and sadly, what happened, what happens, what is happening on an ongoing basis. We end up with the result that, far from leading in the direction of peace, actually makes the war being waged more implacable. It makes those who are waging that war more certain of the advantages that they will derive from it. Now, you would be naturally thinking, *Well, okay, this is all well and good, but what is the alternative?*

Step number one, I think, for the immediate future, is to be clear-eyed and tough-minded about the situation that we're in. And I address this to both Israel and the United States because I think now, though some people would like to think otherwise, we're pretty much in the same boat. It will take the forces of terror longer to galvanize themselves for another blow against the United States, but the fact that it takes them a longer time doesn't necessarily mean it's not going to happen, does it? Or that it won't be devastating. It's just going to take them longer to prepare. Meanwhile, they will practice on Israel and whoever else is a more convenient target. Since we are in Iraq, they'll start practicing on us in Iraq, too — you are noticing that already, I think. No end to the mentality of terror, no end to the war of terror — just different ways of expressing it, and that is going to be an ongoing reality. We are at war. The proper objective in war is not peace but victory.

I think it's time that people, people in every country affected by this threat, begin to stand up and demand from their leaders and from their government a clear commitment to an articulation of this objective. We must stand with a famous general in American history who may or may not have been right when he said it, but it would certainly be right today: "In this context, in this war, there is no substitute for victory. We shall win it or we shall be destroyed."

Now, that does require that we define what it is, right? And I think that is also relevant, though, to the situation of defining what constitutes for the immediate future a clear and proper objective for states like Israel and the United States that are the victims of this war. I hope that someday in some way there will come to the Middle East an era of peace and co-operation and economic interchanges. It's going to be so much better for everybody.

You know, for a good part of my career in the government I worked in Africa. I used to sit down sometimes and, based on what I have learned about the continent, I would think about what a wonderful future people in Africa would have if countries in Africa would just get together and co-operate and join to exploit the amazing natural resources of the region. If they would not be engaged all the time in tribal bickering and ideological warfare and greedy governments and nasty militarists and all this sorry stuff. It's nice to dream about such things, and maybe someday one will see the realization of those happy hopes. However, wishing for such a day and hoping for such a day is no basis for policy.

Policy must be based upon an effort to understand what confronts us today in light of the history that produced it in order to realize objectives that will secure for our people today the necessary requirements of their life and security. And that's what I think ought to be on the minds of both Israel and the United States right now.

I think it's time that for a while we end the preoccupation with peace in the Middle East, and I say that quite advisedly. If you want peace with those people, they've got to say yes. And if they won't, what then?

Well, if they won't, your preoccupation with peace makes them *the master of the situation*. See? I think it's time that we declare to the Arabs, the Palestinians, and to all of those who might seek through the strategy of terror to impose their will upon Israel, upon America, upon the world — that we will not talk peace, we are not preoccupied with peace, that if you want war, we shall make more effective war!!

And I know this goes against the current thinking, where everybody goes, "Well, I dunno, we should do both things, we should have the two-track policy," and so forth.

I think there are cases where something like that might work, but it has to be based on the presumption that somewhere behind it all there is actually a common element, a common commitment to some understanding that the cessation of hostilities will be beneficial. I don't think you're going to reach that point with the Arabs, and I won't say just the Palestinians. I don't think we are going to reach that point with the Arabs and with others, by the way, who support the strategy of terror incubated in the Islamic Arab world, until they have come up against a solid wall of failure in terms of their strategy of blood. It must fail. And it must be clear that we are going to pay the price, bear the burden, fight the fight by all effective means, until they get the point that down that road lies nothing but their destruction. That's a hard saying, but frankly, I think it's a hard saying that's going to make the world safer for peace — not even the long term, but I think in the medium term. It's going to be like riding a bronco in the Old West. You just had to hang on to that beast, no matter how hard it tried to throw you, you just had to make sure you stayed in the saddle until its will to fight was broken. And I think that we have no alternative now. People always like to talk as if we do, but we don't. We're in one of those situations where we've got no alternative. We don't want this war. And I'm not speaking now just of Israel, I'm speaking of America and others. Do you know why we don't want this war? We don't want this war because we know how good peace is! We know what to do with peace! We know what its joys and pleasures are. We know how to satisfy our ambitions and aspirations by the ways and means of peace. We know how to envision the conquests of things that don't require that there be blood in the street and slaves serving our every need and people oppressed by our desires. We have devised a world in which all of the hopes and dreams and aspirations of our lofty human spirit can be realized in ways that result from the effective cooperation of human hope, instead of its destruction.

But the fact that we can understand peace in this way doesn't mean we're dealing with a world of people who do. And whatever the reason, and I'm not saying that the reasons are necessarily all the fault of the Palestinians or the Arabs or anybody else, but for whatever reason, I think we are at a time now where the scope of their understanding of peace is simply not sufficient to produce a true desire for it. That's hard, but we must recognize it because that means that all the talk and all the negotiations are not going to end it.

I want to say one final word, because a part of me feels really badly speaking this hard language of war. I am not, by and large, a person who prefers war as an instrument. As a matter of fact, a good part of my life is spent thinking about how we can stop folks from killing innocent babes in the womb, killing each other in the streets, killing over money and greed. Killing, I think, is one of those great banes of humans. We need to figure out how we stop that violence, and I think that ought to be a prime objective. But you don't figure that out by hoping for it, dreaming of it, or wishing for it. Sometimes you have to be fairly tough-minded in order to make sure you do not encourage the phenomenon of violence and the reality of violence out of your longing and hope for peace.

In order to do that, though, you have to remember what's really at stake. What's really at stake goes beyond peace, because peace, like a lot of other things in human life, like money and power — peace is just an opportunity. In and of itself, it's fine, but it also depends a lot on what you do with it, doesn't it?

There are many different ways of understanding peace, and some of them are quiet as the grave. And that's where, I think, especially when we're dealing with Israel we have to remember the heritage and the background, so that we keep in mind that we are not only engaged in a war on evil. That ought to be especially true when we deal with Israel. Why? Well, sometimes it's hard for me to put this into words, but I think it has a lot to do with the context from which Israel emerged into the world, into the modern world. And by that context I mean quite clearly World War II, the Holocaust, the experience of one of the most clear and extensive assaults by evil upon a people ever known in the history of humankind. One of its characteristics, of course, shows its similarity with terror. One of the most poignant things about that assault was that it reached out to people who had done nothing wrong, who were simple, decent, law-abiding citizens in the countries where they lived, who were productive people, making great contributions to the society and to the culture, and it disregarded utterly their lives, their worth, their dignity, their heart, their hope, their contributions, and, simply because they were Jews, it reached for them, crushed them, disregarded their humanity, and snuffed out their innocent lives.

But you see, the interesting thing about the birth of Israel, in my opinion, was that in the truest sense its birth was not, as one might have expected, a simple reaction to that evil. It had a root that was born before that experience, as the quest for a Jewish homeland was born before the terrors of the holocaust, but it also had a spirit that resisted what might have been the natural propensity of the human heart, after such a terrible ordeal — a propensity, by the way, that sadly is clear in the way that the Palestinian leadership has led the Palestinian people. Because when you consider yourself oppressed, when you see and feel the weight of that evil crushing you out — you still have a choice. You can be left with nothing at all except somewhere in yourself your unwillingness to give up on your own belief that there is still something righteous, something decent, something good that is left both in you and in the universe.

The thing that has impressed me over the years about Israel, not just in my understanding of its founding and my reading of that history, but in my experience of Israel and the Jewish people I have come to know around the world, is that while, yes, there was surely as a result of that terrible Holocaust a temptation to let the soul go sour, to embrace the vision of revenge and hatefulness that can be the natural consequence of that kind of experience — though there was that temptation, it was never embraced as the destiny of the Jewish people or the state of Israel. Now, instead, this state was born with an understanding that it was not in response to evil but in the hope for a future in which children could be raised without the shadow of that evil, in which they would reach for the fulfillment of their potential, in which the hope and heritage and righteousness and faith and that spirit that says, "Come what may, do evil what it will, God is God and I shall stand for him." This, I believe, is a moral heritage that transcends any struggle for evil. And it is for the sake of this heritage that we — all of us — must join together to assure that our souls shall not be soured and our hope shall not be dimmed. Not by the struggle against evil, not by the triumph of terrorism. We shall fight the fight as it is necessary in the world, but we shall win it first in our own souls and spirit. So that at the end of the day we shall stand not as people who have defeated evil, but as people who have once again vindicated the truth that come what may, you cannot crush that faith which holds on forever.

CAL THOMAS, with a twice-weekly column appearing in over 550 newspapers nationwide, is America's most widely syndicated op-ed columnist and is one of the most highly regarded voices on the American political scene. His weekly television show "After Hours with Cal Thomas" appears on Fox News Channel on Saturday nights. Thomas also hosts a daily radio program syndicated to more than 300 stations nationwide.

The Roadmap:
Another Folly?

by Cal Thomas

I have this television show on the Fox News Channel on Saturday night at 11 o'clock in the evening, Eastern Time, 5 o'clock in the morning at the current rate of exchange of time zones, in Israel. This is something that has not been done before, so far as I know, on American television, and it's an entire half-hour from Jerusalem presenting equal time. I have this little segment called "Caltoons" which my producer came up with, a play on "cartoons," and we usually use cartoons from American newspapers, but recently we used cartoons from mostly the Arab and the Palestinian media.

I want the American public to understand the unbelievable racial stereotyping that is being done in the Arab press. They never see this on "Nightline," they never see it on "Nightly News" or the CBS evening news, or World News Tonight with Peter Jennings. They've seen it on my show.

I have a platform and I intend to use it as long as I have it. God has prospered my newspaper column beyond my wildest dreams. It's in 550

American newspapers and several overseas; nobody is more amazed at this miracle than I. There are far better writers than me, there are certainly greater thinkers, but there is no one who out-hustles me. I learned that from basketball.

This is a model that I think we need to perpetuate among ourselves and to the wider planet. We have to hustle this story; we cannot take it for granted. I've said to Morton Klein on more than one occasion, whenever he pulls out that map, I think all of us ought to be carrying that map. And we ought to be carrying it around like sandwich boards proclaiming the message to anyone who will listen, and to those who will not.

Israel is not some great Goliath, oppressing people who also live in this region, surrounded by weak people who want to live in peace with it, but in fact is a tiny little sliver of land, one eighth of one percent of the Arab land mass.

I want to say a little about Yossi Beilin's latest proposal. He has the benefit of being consistent. Consistently wrong in all of his proposals.

And this latest one [Geneva], I must say, goes beyond all of the previous ones. The deal as I understand it is that if the Palestinian side gives up the right of return, they can have the authority over the Temple Mount. Now this begins with the faulty premise, once again, that there is somehow some great combination lock on the safe behind which exists peace, that if we just get the numbers right — 22 to the right, 13 to the left, 47 to the right — a great miracle will occur and the safe will be open and peace and everyone will live in harmony and understanding . . . sympathy and trust abounding . . . the age of Aquarius, remember that? People sitting around, smoking dope in their ashrams! Right?

The formula is wrong, and the only thing I learned in math class before I flunked Algebra 2, was that if the formula is wrong, the answer can never be right. So let's stop fooling around with these wrong formulas and get to the real problem. The Roadmap contains what should be unacceptable concessions by Israel in exchange for meaningless assurances by the Palestinian side.

These concessions include Israeli withdrawal from land it captured for its own security in the 1967 war, which was started by Israel's neighbors with the expressed intent of wiping Israel off the Roadmap, or any map. A goal that remains unchanged. These concessions would put Israel in great peril from her enemies, which now possess more sophisticated and lethal weapons than they used in each of the previous wars.

In the past, Israel has said it would start implementing the Roadmap only after Palestinians cracked down on the militias. Terror got the Palestinians to the brink of their objective, so why would they give it up now when total victory seems so close? Hamas has said it intends to continue killing Israeli civilians regardless of any agreements. Many on the right in Israel and the United states hope the acceptance of the Roadmap is merely a feint by Prime Minister Sharon, who should know better, given his experience in war and in politics. He has seen and heard the sermons, editorials from the Arab press, television programs, Palestinian textbooks and classroom videos, all of which express hatred of all things Jewish, Christian, Israeli, and western, and uphold martyrdom as the highest calling of any and all Palestinians! Now given such a history, why would any reasonable person not believe them?

A dangerous game is being played by the U.S. State Department, extending over several administrations. Ignoring or downplaying Palestinians' terrorist acts and choosing to pressure Israel into making dangerous concessions while accepting empty and unfulfilled promises from Israel's mortal enemies, American officials have laid the groundwork for Israel's destruction on the installment plan. In his memoir, *The White House Years*, former Secretary of State Henry Kissinger says something that is so unbelievable, I couldn't believe it when I first read it, but it's true.

> Washington ignores or minimizes evidence of Arab violations of peace agreements.

He continues,

> Israel, with her survival at stake, cannot afford to take chances.

Well. That is a good beginning. But it gets bad from here on:

> The nature of the Israeli situation is bound to influence their interpretation of ambiguous events.

Ambiguous events.

> We, on the other hand, have an incentive to minimize such evidence, since the consequences of finding violations are so unpleasant. Violations force us to choose between doing something about them and thus risk the blowup of our initiative, or doing nothing, and thus renege on our promises to Israel, posing the threat of her taking military action. Accordingly, we tend to lean over backward to avoid the conclusion that the Arabs are violating the cease-fire unless the evidence is unambiguous.

Now that philosophy continues to be practiced and believed in the State Department. In his autobiography, *Warrior*, Ariel Sharon writes about peace:

> A widely acceptable formula must somehow be found so that Israel can take the initiative in the peace process rather than be relegated to responding to the demands of others. Then, after we had the most nearly bipartisan approach that we could come up with, we should if possible attempt to get American support on substance. At that point, when our house is in order and our allies are with us, then we can approach the Arab Nations.

Sharon adds that two prerequisites must be in place before progress can be made. The first, he says is that peace must be equally important to both sides, Arabs as well as Jews; the second prerequisite is that the peace process cannot be rushed. Sharon wrote that in 1989. Nothing has changed except the peace process is being rushed and the Roadmap has not been widely accepted. Other than that. . . .

Communism had its useful idiots, too. These were people who believed whatever Communists said, and were helpful in advancing their cause. In the Middle East, the enemies of Israel, the United States, and all things Jewish, Christian, and Western have far more useful idiots than Communists ever counted on. These are the people who refuse to believe what they are repeatedly told and see in bloody streets, in mosques, in political literature, and in schools where children are taught to hate and to be martyrs before they are potty trained.

In the matter of "the Roadmap to peace," all of which is in quotes, between Israel and her mortal enemies, we are seeing the usual "razzle dazzle." Remember that movie *Chicago*, and the play before it? Where Richard Gere does the "razzle-dazzle 'em" song? That's not just about lawyers, that's what's going on in Israel and in the United States. "Razzle-dazzle 'em."

Elected Israeli prime minister Ariel Sharon stood a few months ago next to appointed Palestinian Prime Minister Mahmud Abas. Now they [Palestinians] have another one who promises only to save 30 days, who mimics Sharon in his Western-style suit. Both men — it doesn't matter who's standing there at all — both men make pronouncements required of them by their American puppeteer, and the useful idiots think Abbas and his band of bloody brothers will play the lion lying down with the Israeli lamb.

In the midst of all the photo ops and feel-good diplomacy comes a sober and welcome word from someone the useful idiots no doubt will regard as a skunk at their party. Uzi Landau told Israeli radio, just a few months ago, that Israel should set a timetable with dates or clearly define a measurable Palestinian course of action regarding security. These would include, he said, collecting weapons, outlawing terror organizations, unifying Palestinian authority security groups in one group, and ending propaganda against Israel, which requires among other things the removal of regional maps that do not show Israel on them and elimination of anti-Israel text books from Palestinian schools. My, how intolerant, how insensitive can you get? Actually desiring and demanding performance!

These seem like reasonable requests from Uzi Landau. If the Palestinian side is sincere about ending decades of war, more than words and signed documents ought to be required, don't you think? Israel is being pressured to give up more land. When it has done so before, the gestures have not brought Israel closer to peace, but allowed for more war to be made! From the relinquished territory in order that more territory might be gained on the road to Israel's obliteration! Such remains the stated goal oozing from every Palestinian pore. The German philosopher Hegel said, "What experiences in history teach us is this — that people and governments never had learned anything from history or acted on principles deduced from it."

Useful idiots continue to accept new promises built on a foundation of previously broken promises. This is what makes them useful! It is also what makes them idiots. Israel has waited in vain for Palestinian deeds to live up to their words. Agreements, covenants, promises, and pledges! At what point should it be concluded that the Palestinians leadership and so many of their people have a definition of peace that begins and ends with the annihilation and elimination of Israel? In the States, we hear a lot about the enemies of peace, who would destroy the peace process — like happiness is not an objective to be pursued. Peace and happiness are by-products of nations deciding they will study war no more and lay down their arms and hostile intentions.

The Bush administration unbelievably proposes to pay protection money to the Palestinian Authority in amounts that would make even the Mafia blush with embarrassment. Now why should the enemies of Israel and America disarm, when they can get the United States to subsidize their murderous ways? This makes the United States the biggest and most useful idiot in history if they continue in this line, which in its secular mindset does not understand the depth of the Palestinian religious mandate, or their commitment to fulfilling a prophecy of their own making.

The dismantling of the terrorist infrastructure, the ending of incitement, and the election of a new leader not compromised by terror, as well as the embracing of democracy and free market economies, were all conditions laid down by President Bush on June 24, 2002, if the Palestinian side wanted American support for the creation of its own state. Not one of those conditions has been fulfilled, but the United States continues to pressure Israel to give more, thus encouraging terrorists to kill more. Why compromise when your murderous policies are working? Former national security advisor Brent Scowcroft, an ally of Jim Baker and the rest of that bunch, repeated the miscalculation of those who support the so-called Roadmap when he wrote in the *Washington Post* that the Israelis and Palestinians must take steps "in parallel rather than sequentially in order to increase the prospects for building and sustaining momentum." Otherwise, he says, "there will be renewed violence."

Now what in the world is he talking about? Violence as an instrument of policy by the Palestinian side has not stopped; it ebbed and flowed as a strategy for extracting the maximum possible concessions from the Israeli and American side before the coming all-out war to eliminate Israel. Any cessations are pauses that the terrorists merely use to re-arm. Despite all of the gestures and hand wringing by well-meaning Westerners, eradication of Israel has been the objective of the Palestinian and Arab states since modern Israel's creation in 1948. Nothing that Israel's enemies have said and done in the last 55 years has done anything to change their minds.

Now, I want to say a few words about the media in Israel, because I've been a part of it all of my professional life. I don't think that there is any kind of conspiracy going on against Israel, but I do think there is an enormous amount of ignorance in my profession.

We don't teach basic historical truths in American schools anymore. If you watch Jay Leno's show, he does these "Jaywalking" segments where he goes out and asks people things, and the most incredible, outrageous, stupid things are said. Most people couldn't find Israel on a map, and if they did, they would be surprised at how small it is. When I spoke in a synagogue a couple of year ago in the Washington area, Morton Klein was there and he carries this map around, and it just struck me, as he held up the map, and the 22 Arab states and tiny little Israel — this is so obvious to all of us. It is entry level, grade school stuff to all of us. But to overwhelming numbers of people, they don't have a clue. Most people are people of good will. If you explain things properly to them and show them, hopefully we can still get them to reach the right conclusion. But most of the American media don't do that.

Somewhere around Entebbe in 1976, something switched in the minds of the media. They were happy to portray Israel up to that point as little David overwhelmed by the Goliaths of the region who wanted to eliminate her. But after Entebbe and that incredible, brilliant rescue that we celebrated along with our own freedom, because we identified with Israel's freedom, a beacon of democracy in a sea of dictatorship — something happened. It began to change. It wasn't overnight; it was very slow, and all of a sudden Israel became the big Goliath.

It was fueled in part by a subtle kind of anti-Semitism that no right-thinking individual would openly express any more than we would express today racism or homophobia, because it would come back to reflect on us as un-modern and bigoted and backward, and magnify things of the past and the Klan and all of those other horrible images. We prefer now to do it more subtly. We are more sophisticated and the anti-Semitism that is reflected in so much of the media now is obscured, not with a sheet but with a phony intellectualism and a phony appeal to equality.

Well. Wouldn't that be nice? Israel is willing to get along but its enemies are not. And so what we have to do in my judgment is to begin to tell the story in the media and we do that in several ways:

> • About the failure of the Roadmap — it has no possibility of succeeding, because it is based on a flawed formula. First we begin to identify those friends in the media who will tell the story, and we begin to support them by supporting their programs that are on and watching them and spreading the word, writing letters to the editors which are often read more than the columns that inspire them, I am sorry to say. And making sure that the papers that do the best job of supporting the things in which we believe are subscribed to by us, and if we have businesses or friends in businesses, patronize the newspapers by advertising in them, and doing just the opposite, of course, to those who do not do those things. Everybody else is doing that. Why aren't we more sophisticated in doing that?

> • Secondly, I think we need, as a start, to develop friends outside the so-called mainstream media. This is the way to get your message out. Find a friendly journalist or one you can meet with who has an open mind or doesn't know the truth yet in Des Moines, Iowa! In Charleston, South Carolina! Now why do I pick these places? Because these are places where radical Islam is establishing chapters! They are doing it funded by the Saudis. The Hamas front is setting up chapters of radical Islam around the country. They are putting in the libraries their story of the history of Islam, which is a perverted story and is filtered on its

own. Why aren't we doing that? Why aren't the friends of Israel doing that? Why aren't the friends of freedom doing that? Because we think that the inertia begun by our founders is going to continue without being renewed! Each generation must renew the truth and embrace and endorse and live the principals that were handed down to it, because it takes only one generation for those to expire. Just one. That's all. We need to start doing this aggressively and regularly.

People say, "Why do you write about this subject so much?" I say, "Because I know there are so many others who are not."

Richard Cohen had a piece in the *Washington Post* recently. It was basically about, you know, the failure of Israel: it's never going to work, basically you've got to give in and surrender, that kind of thing. I'm oversimplifying, but that's basically what it was. You've got Anthony Lewis, thank God, now retired from the *New York Times*! You know, he actually wrote, after Reagan's tremendous Evil Empire speech about the Soviet Union in the early eighties: "Debunk the idea of evil as a proper metaphor and concept for sophisticated diplomatic discourse." And I remember writing in response at the time: "Well, what was Hitler then, in need of a behavior modification course? Maybe, but first you had to stop him from killing people!"

I think that we can prevail in this battle, but only if we tell the story. We've got to go out and tell the story. Every day, every hour, every minute, and every second. You have to be a living testimony to that which has been passed down to you in a wicked and adulterous generation (to dredge up an old biblical statement) about who we are. It's not going to be easy, but freedom never is. It has to be bought and paid for with the blood and the sweat and the intellect and the commitment of people like us. We've got to go out and tell the story. And we must reject every formula, every Roadmap, every idea that comes down the pipe that is not based on truth and that is not based on history and that has not a prayer, voluntary or otherwise, of succeeding. We have to tell why the formula is wrong. It's not about giving Israel's enemies what they say they want, because they want it all. It is about defeating them.

Germany is at peace today because Hitler was defeated. Communism is less a threat, except in China, because it was defeated. Not in war, but intellectually and economically. And people breathe free for the first time in nearly a hundred years because they were defeated. There is nothing wrong with victory.

Let's go out and tell the story, and let's do it with new vigor and new hope and new encouragement for being together. Let's network, let's support people in government, in the media, in schools — we're on the right side. They don't call us right for nothing! We ought to have right wing and wrong wing, forget left wing! The wrong wing! Let's come up with new language. The other side has language that they use against us, let's come up with new language that tells the story that's ideologically loaded, that reflects the truth, and let's do it with humor, and let's do it with conviction, and let's do it with passion. Because we have the truth on our side, we have nothing to be ashamed of! Let's go out and do it!

Richard Perle is Resident Fellow, American Enterprise Institute for Public Policy Research, Washington DC (1987–), where he has directed its commission on future defenses. Mr. Perle is a member of the Defense Policy Board. He is a leading authority on national security, military requirements, arms proliferation and defense, and regional conflicts. Mr. Perle is co-chairman, Hollinger Digital, and a director of Hollinger International, Inc.

Accepting Senator Henry "Scoop" Jackson Award for Values and Vision in Politics

by Richard Perle

To be in Jerusalem in Sukkoth, in this magnificent city, is a joy. To be here to receive an award in the memory of Scoop Jackson is a joy and a humbling honor. I'm enormously proud to be the recipient of this award, and I'm very pleased that the Jerusalem Summit has chosen to honor this great man, not just now and today, but in its future activities, as this award is given on an annual basis. Scoop was a man who had an absolute commitment to the core value of individual liberty. Whenever there was a choice to be made, whenever there was a conflict between that value and any other value, you knew on what side Scoop would come down. He believed in the universality of human rights. No people, he believed, should be consigned to life under a dictatorship, and he was ready and eager to help those who fought for freedom.

This belief in freedom, and this willingness to join with those who fought for it, explains Scoop's commitment first to the establishment, and then the protection and the security of the State of Israel. And it explains his fervent and untiring effort to help liberate the Jews of the Soviet Union. They were willing to fight for themselves, and he wanted to be part of that fight. And then, many people in this room were a part of that battle, and the relationship between those brave individuals in the Soviet Union who risked everything for their own freedom was the inspiration for Scoop, and Scoop in turn became an inspiration for them.

All of this together helps explain an extraordinary relationship between Henry Jackson and two people he never met: Andrei Sakharov and Natan Sharansky. You know, Sakharov was a Nobel laureate, a man of such distinction that despite the problems he caused the Soviet leadership, he was safe in a physical sense, exiled to Gorky. But Natan was not safe; he was a young mathematician, with no protection. He became Sakharov's trusted confidant, and a leader in the movement for freedom for Soviet Jews, and he took enormous risks. And in the end, he went to jail, went to the Gulag for a decade, in large part because of his support for the Jackson Amendment, for speaking out at a time when speaking out could produce a decade of hard labor. So their lives were inextricably bound up. Scoop worked hard for Natan's release when he was in the Gulag, and sadly he didn't live to see the day that Natan was freed. But Natan was the first recipient of the Human Rights Award from the Jackson Foundation, conferred by Helen Jackson in Washington, shortly after he was released. Even heroes have heroes. Scoop was a hero, and his heroes were Sakharov and Sharansky.

The Jackson-Vanik Amendment was a huge accomplishment, and there are people in this room who are deeply and essentially involved in it. Morry Amitay is sitting there. I'm not sure we would have had that amendment without Morry's tireless and effective efforts. Amos Yoran, who was in the Israeli Embassy at that time, pretending to be the labor attaché. In fact, that was your title, wasn't it, Amos? In fact, Amos became then, and to the best of my judgment since, the most effective lobbyist on behalf of his country that I've ever seen, and they still talk about Amos on Capitol Hill. When he left, after some years of service, I think 40 senators turned out. It was an extraordinary accomplishment, and Amos was with us every minute, on Jackson-Vanik and on other crucial legislation. And let me just say, it wasn't always clear that the government of Israel, or any other government, would support the things that we were trying to do. There were always conflicts, there were always trade-offs. There were always practical considerations. But for some people, the absolute commitment to the value of individual liberty became decisive when choices had to be made, and that was true of Scoop for sure, and that was true of good friends like Amos and Morry.

Then, in 1972, the Soviet leaders imposed an education tax on persons wishing to emigrate. Scoop understood that if they could impose this tax, that would be the beginning of closing the door. And he knew something had to be done about it, and his [inaudible] in about that time. The Nixon administration decided to confer some trade benefits on the Soviet Union, in the form of most favored nation status and access to credits which Mr. Brezhnev hoped would be available for the development of the oil and gas resources of the Soviet Union. And Scoop saw an opportunity. There was something the Russians wanted from us, and there was something we wanted from them. They wanted trade benefits, they wanted credits, and we wanted freedom for those people who stood up and fought for the opportunity to leave. And so the amendment was the result. And it said simply that no country can receive the benefits that the Soviets were looking forward to, if that country denies its citizens the right and the opportunity to emigrate. So, in June of 1972, after endless meetings (that Morry was in most of them, and occasionally we had Amos looking on us), that legislation was offered, and it eventually passed, and passed overwhelmingly, despite very substantial opposition in a number of places.

Amos will remember the occasion on which Golda Meir visited Washington. And President Nixon, who was not happy with the Jackson Amendment, decided he would try to persuade her to abandon it. And he was well briefed by Henry Kissinger and others, and had to present the case against the Jackson Amendment to the Prime Minister of Israel. And he did, in the Oval Office. And Prime Minister Golda Meir listened to what he had to say, and looked at President Nixon, and this was, by the way, at a very difficult moment. Israel always feels dependent on the United States, but at that sensitive moment it felt particularly dependent. She looked up at President Nixon and she said, "Mr. President, do you want me to take this message to the Jewish people?" And that was the end of the discussion.

Scoop's desire to help those who were prepared to help themselves in the cause of freedom explains his lifelong involvement and commitment with respect to the security of Israel. Amos will remember well a piece of legislation, almost obscure at the time, Section 501 of the Defense Act of 1970 — a piece of legislation that provided Israel with the first Phantom jets that came here, essentially paid for by the government of the United States. Until that moment, Israel had taken great pride in its ability always to pay for the defense equipment it received from the United States, but it was clear that because of the involvement of the Soviet Union on the side of Egypt and Israel's other enemies that Israel could no longer sustain that burden by itself. And so, a half billion dollars of Phantom aircraft arrived in Israel for the defense of this country, and he was enormously proud of that achievement. Scoop's abiding belief in democracy would have made him an advocate of an important argument made by his hero, Natan Sharansky — an argument about the relationship between peace and democracy. This argument seems to me to be entirely appropriate to discuss in this setting and in this forum, which is all about values. Democracies don't start wars. Leaders who have to go to voters and gain their approval find it very difficult to animate those voters to spend massively on defense, or to initiate conflicts in which their sons and their daughters may die. Dictators, by contrast, must have wars. They must have enemies — internal enemies and external enemies. We will not find peace with dictators, and that is why we will not find peace here, until there is on the Palestinian side a democratic entity with whom one can negotiate. And negotiations before that time will fail.

I believe President Bush recognized this in the speech he gave on June 24 last year. And it may even not be a coincidence that in the days preceding that speech Natan Sharansky was in Colorado with some of us, including the vice president, discussing this very point, about the relationship between democracy and peace. And in that speech, the president put forward a simple proposition, but one that represented a radical break with all previous American diplomacy. He said, "If the Palestinians want American support for a state of their own, they must do three things: They must first end the corruption that is characteristic of the Palestinian Authority. Second, they must end the violence; the acts of terror against men and women and children. And finally, they must establish democratic institutions, because it is only a Palestinian democracy that is a worthy candidate for statehood, and a worthy interlocutor at the negotiating table."

I would have hoped that this would have been greeted with much greater enthusiasm than it was among our European allies, for example. They preferred to continue down the well-worn path of diplomacy, skating on the surface, without dealing with the fundamental and underlying causes of this conflict. I would have hoped that there would have been support elsewhere, among Palestinians, even support within the Israeli government, for an approach that put the challenge exactly where it belonged. I understand the reservations of many people, including many in this room, and share many of those reservations, about the creation of the Palestinian state. If that statehood is to be conferred on a dictatorship, then those reservations are wholly understandable. They're right.

It may take a long time before we see the emergence of democratic institutions among Palestinians, but the point about June 24 that I think is so important is that the democratization on the Palestinian side was a precondition, not something to be done in parallel — a precondition. The Roadmap confuses that issue. I hope that in the course of contemplating where we go from here, we return to the fundamentals of June 24, and insist that it is a precondition not to appoint the prime minister and make some other gestures, but to establish proper democratic institutions on the Palestinian side.

While doing that, we have a right to insist that if there is to be a process that can truly lead to peace, the Palestinians have to stop celebrating suicide bombers as heroes. Those posters have to come down. We cannot have peace, we cannot have a reliable peace with an interlocutor who celebrates those who are prepared to kill Israelis, and until we see a change, a fundamental political and social and cultural change, until we see the emergence of democratic institutions, I'm afraid there's really no alternative, but to depend for the security of this country and the people of Israel on its very formidable military capability. There's a role for diplomats, but diplomats cannot overcome. They'll never be able to overcome the fundamental underlying social and political contamination of the existing leadership of the Palestinian Authority.

Let me conclude with a quick word about Iraq. Scoop, of course, was not alive when decisions had to be taken about whether to go to war with Iraq, and I know he would have been on the president's side on this. This was a war of liberation. As we search for weapons of mass destruction and struggle to understand the programs for the production of those weapons that we know were in place, as we debate the establishment of new political institutions in Iraq, and as we read the stories about casualties we are suffering in Iraq, we mustn't lose sight, and he wouldn't have lost sight, of the fact that 23 million Iraqis are now free, free from one of the most brutal dictatorships of modern times. And the situation there is vastly better than the press would lead you to believe. Almost every Iraqi town, village, and city, now has a governing council. It's not perfect democracy, it's not the Knesset, it's not the Senate of the United States, but it's a lot better than orders from the Baathist thugs in Baghdad, which is what passed for governance until the liberation of Iraq, and it's moving in the right direction. Every school in Iraq is now open. Every child from kindergarten through university who wants to be in the classroom is in the classroom. The infrastructure of that country was protected by the manner in which the world has fought: the bridges, the dams, the hospitals were protected from American precision bombing, and yet we destroyed a government, a brutal dictatorship in 21 days, with very few losses, either on our side or on the Iraqi side. It was an enormous achievement, and people who worry about the current dissatisfaction — things are not moving fast enough — can even suggest that the president may be in difficulty as a result of that — let me make a rash prediction: On election day, which is a year away, if Iraq is an issue, it will be an issue in the president's favor.

A word about Iran. I'm certainly not going to give a lecture on Iran, but I want to tell a story. A friend of mine, a French scholar, was in Tehran recently, and he gave a lecture at the University of Tehran. He shared the platform with one of the mullahs who runs the university. There were 400 students present, and when he finished his remarks, the floor was open for questions. A young woman student got up, and she said, "Monsieur Capel, we Iranians have only one friend in the world." And Professor Capel told me he expected some very kind words about Jacques Chirac. And then she went on, and she said that that one friend is the United States of America. And turning to that French scholar, she said, "The United States liberated you in 1945. Why won't you support them in liberating us now?" I don't know what happened to that brave young student, but I think it's a sign, it's a sign of the enduring belief in human freedom. I know that if Scoop were alive today, he'd be involved in the liberation of Iran, as he was involved in the liberation of the Jews of the Soviet Union, and as he was involved in protecting the security of this great country.

He's fighting the war on terror, and from the beginning, from the 11th of September, he said, "We Americans will not distinguish between the terrorists and the states that sponsor them." That is the underlying basis of the war on which we are now embarked. And I'm quite sure he's right. I'm quite sure we will not be able to cope with people who want to destroy our civilization, unless we can persuade those governments that give them sanctuary and support that it's not in their interest to do so. We've started that process, first in Afghanistan, then in Iraq. I was happy to see that a similar message was delivered to the Syrians the other day by the Israeli Air Force, and I hope it's only the first of many such messages.

This is a war we'll win. I have no doubt about it. It will be long and it will be costly, but we have settled on the first critical principle, and that's what counts.

Let me conclude. I had an opportunity, yesterday, to visit an extraordinary place, a school not far from here. Marcia Weiss, who built this school, is here. I can't tell you how gratifying it is to go to Marcia's school and see young children from Ukraine, from Russia, children from broken homes, children who've been abandoned by their parents, in some cases, children whose parents saw that their only opportunity was if they could come to

Israel. A group of enormously dedicated people worked tirelessly to give these kids an opportunity. Their parents needed permission to leave, and they struggled for that. They need someone to help them survive, now that they're here, and Marcia is doing her best. If Scoop were here, he'd say, "Thank you, Marcia."

Let me say thank you. Thank you to the Jerusalem Summit for conceiving of this award. I'm delighted you've done it. I look forward to honoring the future recipients of it. You're good to honor the memory of a great man, and I'm grateful to you.

Dr. Uzi Landau is a veteran leader of Israeli politics and consistently high-ranking member of the Likud party, He is currently the minister responsible for overseeing Israeli intelligence services and the U.S.-Israel strategic dialogue in the prime minister's office.

A member of the Israeli Knesset since 1984, Dr. Landau has held a series of central positions including Minister of Public Security during the current conflict, as well as chairman and member on several defense, finance, and international relations committees. Dr. Landau is a member of presidium of the Jerusalem Summit.

Finding the Right Road to Peace

by Uzi Landau

Israel is an isolated island of democracy, of rule of law, of human rights. It's a lonely host of Western civilization and its values in the rough sea of terrorism, of dictatorships, of corruption, of human enslavement. The Jewish state continues to build and continues to enhance its democracy, its economy, its social fabric, while we continue to fight for our independence against terrorism.

Ours is not the only war in the Middle East. In the past few years we've had a couple of them: one in Afghanistan, in our vicinity, another one in Iraq. The United States and Britain were involved in that war (which, by the way, had nothing to do with Israel).

We had a number of chains of activities of terror in which Middle Eastern citizens were associated, such as the bombing of the twin towers, the Pentagon, the embassies in Tanzania and Kenya, the USS *Cole*, the resort area in Bali, and the theater in Moscow. None of them had to do with Israel, as well. All the strings of those terrorist actions led to Middle Eastern countries like Iran, Iraq, Saudi Arabia, Libya, and Afghanistan — countries that provide shelter, finance, training, intelligence, and many more things to those terror organizations. This global game has a name — a fundamentalist part of Islam is challenging the very existence of Western civilization.

They want to destroy us and to come in our stead. And the method is to break our spirit and our will, and thus bring economic collapse and the collapse of our social fabric by instilling terror in our hearts. They deliberately are targeting whole families. Kids on their way to schools, babies — and by the use of TV, they are terrorizing the many by the killing or the murdering of the few. And please note, the type of war which they are running from within ourselves is a war that has no armies, no frontier, no uniforms, no tanks, no guns — it is taking place — the frontier is — on the corner of the street, in the disco, in the bus, in the station, in the restaurant, in the malls, just wherever we live. It's not an army against an army. It's a society against a society, a culture against a culture. And this war is going to take place quite a number of years ahead of us. Their methods are methods of killing. This is genocide, it's not just crime against a few, this is crime against humanity and we don't speak here about actions of war but rather war crimes. And for us of the free world who are involved in this struggle, in this war — it must be crystal clear to us what the moral essence of this war is.

We are the citizens of the free world, fighting for our life and for our beliefs, for our values of the rule of law, of democracy, of human rights, of human lives, for the very principle that no cause justifies terror. And this is done against the civilization of dictatorships that despise the rule of law, democracy, human rights, and if there are no constraints whatsoever, on the use of whatever means to promote its political objectives. In this war, Israel is considered to be the small Satan. We are not the main or the prime target of fundamentalist Islam. We are a target. The real Satan, the real target is America and the West. But we are here on the front line. And we are viewed by them as a testing ground, as a laboratory — what's the method by which they could bring to its knees a democracy? And please make no mistake, if terror will not be defeated here, its methods will move to the United States and to Europe, and the enemy will continue from here to hit deep at the heart of freedom as they did on that terrible day of September 11. Therefore, the war of Israel is the war of all of the free societies in the world against tyranny and terror.

A number of years ago, Ze'ev Jabotinsky (the ideological patriot of the political right in Israel politics) wrote an article in which he spelled out what should be the way to develop the chance for peace in the future. He called this article the "Iron Wall" and he said something which is very simple. He said that there is no chance that the Arabs will come and sign peace with us of their own will. He said they are going to do whatever they can to expel us from here and to destroy us. They see us as a foreign culture. From their point of view, we are invaders. From their point of view, this place is theirs. And in spite of the fact that many naives among the Jews, perhaps fools, who are saying that what we are doing here, by coming to this area, is something that the Arabs are going to benefit from, that we are going to bring here modernism, jobs, high standards of living, technology, lavish economic assistance — they are going to perhaps support us in signing a peace agreement with us, because if we are not going to be here, they are going to lose something, and that's why they'll sign.

Jabotinsky said, "This has no chance because Arabs have dignity, self-respect, pride, and as long as they continue to have this hope of destroying us, they will continue and fight until they fully oust us."

But, he has asked, "When will be the first time that there will be a chance for peace? This will take place only after they give up any hope for victory. And the peace which they will then come to sign won't be done because of their free will, but because of no other alternative. No hope to destroy us. That is, the reality of living together will force them to sign an agreement with us, and therefore what we Jews have to do is to build this Iron Wall of strength. Of moral clarity, of military strength behind which we will be able to build the state, and this unshakeable wall will bring them, perhaps, to abandon their war against us."

Let me say that I believe this Jabotinsky formula applies also beyond the shores of Israel. I think that it is critical that the free world build today — I shall not call it an iron wall — a shield, a shield of freedom, against terror. This is the minimum. Unlike, however, the iron wall of Jabotinsky, this shield of freedom will not lead to peace with terror, because there will never be peace with terror. This is the main message: we'll have to combat terror, until it is totally eradicated. Terrorists must know they have no hope whatsoever to win.

These days there are some problems in this process of building this shield of freedom in the democratic world. While there are some in the free world who work hard to build this shield against terror, and many of whom are here today with us, still many are trying to destroy this shield. This shield of freedom is built when there is moral clarity, when leaders have the courage and the inner conviction to speak in clear terms about good and evil. This shield is destroyed, however, when we place terrorists and their victims on the same moral footing and when leaders speak about them in a language of moral equivalence. This shield of freedom is enhanced when we defeat and when we hurt the cause which terror is trying to promote and this shield is weakened when terrorists are promoting their goals, in particular when we give in to terror and its promotion of its goals.

I think that this shield of freedom is enhanced when the international community holds terror-sponsoring states accountable and it is hurt when these countries believe that they can go on in promoting terrorism, supporting it and being unpunished. In this point, I believe it's important to highly appreciate President Bush for his contribution to the war on terror in the world — to his vision, his leadership, and his tenacity. He introduced moral clarity into this war against terrorism, and he is also proving that he will hold regimes accountable for whatever their support in terror. By doing this, President Bush helps build this shield of freedom.

There are Arabs who wage war against Israel to destroy us. There is fundamentalist Islam that wants to destroy the free world. There is no confrontation; there is no equal moral footing. There are good and there are bad. Unfortunately, there are those among us who fail to differentiate between actions which mean to save the lives of citizens and perhaps sometimes unintentionally kill civilians used by terrorists as protective shields — from those actions that deliberately target civilians. The damage caused by this failure to differentiate is tremendous because it provides a ray of hope to those terrorists that they can break us apart; that they can weaken and destroy our society. I should add that we are also not really demanding the full price from those regimes like the PLO that fully support terrorism. We, for example, have said to the Palestinians that if you don't fight terrorism, we'll fight it. It's good, but I think Israel should have said to the Palestinian authority exactly what the United States has said to the Taliban and to anybody else who supports terror: "Either you fight terror, or we fight you."

I should add that since Oslo, the United States and Israel haven't really succeeded in conveying this clear message to terrorists. The message that you terrorists have no hope, that you'll never succeed. That your political goals will be defeated.

On the contrary. In particular after the Roadmap, terror organizations here believe that they won a great victory.

Let me add a third facet, a third point which I think is important for this shield of freedom. And this is international cooperation among free countries in the world. No one country alone could really fight terrorism. Cooperation is of essence in exchanging intelligence and in developing doctrines.

The victory over terror and the road to peace in the Middle East are paved with this shield of freedom against terror. We shall not come to peace immediately. It's not waiting just around the corner; it's going to be a process. It's going to take some time. But this process will again be built by us building this shield of freedom, of this combination of moral clarity, of force, national force and international cooperation. It must be clear that every round of killing or of terror must be finished by a clear victory by us. It cannot be misunderstood who won. And each such wave of terror must be finished when they pay a disproportional price on all of their aspects of life. And we should speak about detailed specific peace plans before terror is totally defeated, because as we start to speak about detailed peace plans, those concessions that they see in those plans are going to be the first line for future negotiations when we sit with them at the table. So negotiation for peace is possible, but only after the war has been fully and clearly decided and Muslim fundamentalist terrorism has been totally eradicated.

There's a necessary condition that must take place for such a peace agreement to hold water and hope in the future.

First of all, a Palestinian leadership must be new, must be different, and must want to have peace. They must teach peace in their school system from a very young age. When we first signed the Oslo agreement, in Israel, a whole year was termed "the year of peace" and we taught every kid in our schooling system that Arafat is no more a terrorist, he's a partner. And the Palestinians are no more enemies, they are neighbors. I want to see the Palestinians doing that in every school. Before that, it's a non-starter. They have to give up their demand for the return of the refugees. Returning the refugees is a recipe for destruction of the state of Israel. I think Israel has to adopt the game, this principle by the late Mr. Begin who said that peace in the Middle East will be in the future, and the Palestinians will enjoy a generous self-government — but Israel will be fully responsible for all of the security aspects. Of course, a Palestinian sovereign independent state in addition to Jordan cannot come into being. It does not have any moral or historic justification, it cannot economically survive, it will endanger immediately the very existence of Israel and Jordan — it will be a host to terrorism and therefore it will become yet another terrorist state, another rogue state, in addition to Iran and Syria in the Middle East. Of course, it is possible to have intermediate agreements. But all those agreements must be done within the constraints that I have mentioned.

Israel, too, must combat terrorism with moral clarity and hold those regimes who support terror accountable for their action. I must say that, unfortunately, Israel as a society hasn't adopted lately and fully these two principles. There are still those among us who speak about occupation in our own place.

Some live near Bethlehem. I don't think that in the Old Testament, King David was born in Bethlehem in the West Bank; I think he was born in Bethlehem, Judea.

We'll have to be committed to build this shield of freedom against terror, insisting that each democratic state adopt this policy of shield of freedom, and let me go back to the previous term, the Iron Wall. Israel has basically used this policy, regardless of the different government, socialist or non-socialist that was running the show here, until ten years ago. Basically, what we were doing was that we were trying to get closer to peace if this was possible, and without peace we were simply enhancing ourselves as we did all these years.

We have had always those Jews who have been asking "What will there be? How shall we be able to make it in front of all the difficulties that are ahead of us?" And this question was asked during the pogroms of '20 and '21, that started here in Jerusalem by the mufti of Jerusalem. How many Jews were here in the country? 50,000, perhaps? And then we had the pogroms of '28 and '29, and the entire Jewish community of Hebron, of generations destroyed, and the pogroms of '36 and '39, and the Jewish community grew stronger. And then we came to the war of '48 with 600 Jews, with a small army, with a minute economy, and then we had the war of '56, and the war of '67. In the war of '67, we were already around two million Jews! And we had the war of attrition, and the Yom Kippur war, and the Lebanon war, and please note — after all those questions of "What will happen?" we had peace with Egypt. Egypt came to peace with us because they lost the wars of '48, '56, and '67, the war of attrition, the war of '73 when they got us by surprise. And in '77 we had this new Israeli government with Menachem Begin, the "great warmonger, " and all of those generals, General Dayan and General Weitzman and General Sharon. Why did Sadat need to have any problems, any risks about sitting with the Jews and signing an agreement with them, and then see 50 years from now what will be. And then we had the peace agreement with the Jordanians who wanted to do it before. But they just waited for a chance to do it. And as we are today, in this country, over 6 million citizens, over 5.3 million Jews with a very strong army, with a strong and sound industry, with science and technology that touches the frontiers, with a satellite in orbit, and we still have those people who accompany us all the time and ask, "What will there be?" Just hang tough and continue to believe and maintain our moral clarity and inner conviction. What will there be?

It'll be fine for our people and for our country and for democracy and freedom. So help us God.

BENJAMIN "BIBI" NETANYAHU is the former Prime Minister of Israel (1996–99) and at present Israel's Minister of Finance. He is a world-renowned spokesperson for Israel, a global commentator on current Middle East affairs and a much-in-demand speaker on the international circuit. He was first elected to the Knesset in 1988 and has since served as Prime Minister, Foreign Minister, Housing Minister and as a member of the Foreign Affairs & Defense Committee.

The Failure of the U.N. in Dealing with the Global Moral Crisis

by Benjamin "Bibi" Netanyahu

America does not want a new terrorist state to emerge. How to prevent it? Introduce the concept of limited sovereignty. In our quest for peace with the Palestinians, three imperatives unite Israelis: *Terror must end, our borders must be secure, and the Palestinians must abandon the goal of destroying Israel.* That is why we insist that the terror organizations be dismantled, that we not return to the indefensible 1967 lines and that the Palestinians give up their claim to a "right of return" — a euphemism for destroying the Jewish state by flooding it with millions of Palestinians.

Genuine Palestinian peace partners will accept these elementary conditions for peace. But what will happen when Israel finds such partners? What kind of agreement can we reach?

We are told that Israel is faced with only two options: either continue to rule over millions of Palestinians or cede them full sovereignty over Judea, Samaria, and Gaza. Yet both options are unacceptable.

Israel does not want to rule the Palestinians. The only reason our forces are deployed in Palestinian cities and towns is to prevent the savage terror attacks being launched from these places against us. As the terror subsides, we will be able to gradually withdraw those forces.

As for ceding full sovereignty over Judea, Samaria, and Gaza, this is doubly wrong. First, most of Judea and Samaria is barren and empty. The combined Palestinian and Jewish populations live on less than one-third of this territory. But the empty swaths of disputed land, comprising the heart of the Jewish ancestral homeland, are vital for Israel's security.

Second, full Palestinian sovereignty over Judea, Samaria, and Gaza would so weaken Israel that it would tempt the Palestinians to roll back the peace and use the strategically placed territory as a base for even more lethal terror attacks on the shrunken Jewish state. Every time Israel was forced to cross the border to root out terror, it would be accused by the United Nations of invading a foreign country and would be threatened with sanctions. Thus, neither Israeli control over the Palestinian population nor full Palestinian control over Judea, Samaria, and Gaza is acceptable.

But there is a third option, one that offers hope for a realistic and responsible solution for Israelis and Palestinians. The guiding principle is this: The Palestinians would be given all the powers needed to govern themselves, but none of the powers that could threaten Israel. Put simply, the solution is full self-government for the Palestinians with vital security powers retained by Israel.

For example, the Palestinians would have internal security and police forces but not an army. They would be able to establish diplomatic relations with other countries but not to forge military pacts. They could import goods and merchandise but not weapons and armaments. Control over Palestinian daily life would be in the hands of the Palestinians alone, but security control over borders, ports, and airspace would remain in Israel's hands. Prime Minister Ariel Sharon expressed these ideas last year, and most Israelis support him. Indeed, those Israelis who support a Palestinian state are in effect calling for limited Palestinian sovereignty with Israel retaining control of vital security powers.

The greatest danger to peace and security in the world today is the notion of unlimited sovereignty applied indiscriminately. In many flash points around the world, the right to self-government must not include unlimited security powers. Otherwise, every ethnic group with a grievance will seek to establish its own army, its own weaponry, and eventually its own weapons of mass destruction.

Since September 11, 2001, the dangers posed by unlimited sovereignty applied indiscriminately are becoming better understood. People increasingly recognize that in the 21st century, resolving conflicts in many trouble spots will require modifications in the concept of sovereignty. Stability in the Middle East and elsewhere will depend on our ability to free ourselves from the mistaken assumption that we must either rule over hostile populations or grant those populations unlimited sovereignty. There is another way.

Do those in the free world calling for a Palestinian state really want unlimited sovereignty for the Palestinians? Do they really want to have a Palestinian state with its own army, free to dispatch suicide bombers all over the world? Certainly not. They want the Palestinians to govern themselves, but not to threaten others.

But unlimited sovereignty will produce just that: a fanatical, dictatorial, armed terrorist state in the heart of the Middle East. This state will threaten Israel, America, and the entire free world. It will become a university for suicide bombers with departments for every terror organization imaginable — from Hamas to Hezbollah to al Qaeda.

After toppling terrorist regimes in Afghanistan and in Iraq, America surely does not want a new terrorist state to emerge. I believe all those who seek a durable peace will support the safeguards I have outlined here. By insisting on these safeguards, we will not be thwarting peace but enabling the emergence of a genuine peace that is stable, secure, and ultimately successful.

Ehud Olmert is currently Vice Prime Minister of Israel and Minister for Industry, Trade, Labor, and Communications. This follows 12 consecutive years as the dynamic mayor of the city of Jerusalem in which he resides. Olmert is a much sought-after lecturer and commentator on matters pertaining to Israel, Jerusalem, and world affairs.

The Crisis in Morality and International Policy; How Israel May Be the Solution

by Ehud Olmert

I don't want to talk about Jerusalem as a moral alternative, but rather Jerusalem as a moral basis, and I hope that the difference is clear to everyone. I think that the time has arrived to make a clear and strong statement that will be heard the world over about certain basic parameters regarding the present situation, and where we are heading.

In all the years that I was mayor of Jerusalem, I never believed that there can be any future political process that can be established on the notion that at any point in the future this city will be divided or that any part of this city will ever be under the sovereignty of any other nation but the Jewish nation — and I haven't changed my mind.

I firmly and profoundly believe that there can be no future agreement that will be of any value on the basis of dividing this city. And I think that the time has arrived, not just for us, the Israelis — I think the government of Israel on this particular issue is very clear and very strong — but I think the time has arrived for all those who care for peace in the Middle East to understand that there will never be peace, there will never be reconciliation, there will never be a genuine process between us and the Palestinians if they believe and the world believes that there is a possibility for the division of Jerusalem. Because if the Palestinians indeed believe that there can be a political process on that basis, then they will understand that no principle, that no fundamental belief of the state of Israel and the Jewish people will ever be strong enough and consistent enough to oppose the pressure of the Arabs and their supporters. And that will lead to almost eternal war between us and them, rather than to convince them that there is a point beyond which no pressure, no political influence of any kind, can be of any consequence as far as the state of Israel and the Jewish people are concerned. If there is one issue upon which we can build this position, this is the unity of Jerusalem, which has never been a capital for any Arab or Muslim entity and will never be any part of a capital or any Muslim entity.

This is not just a practical political issue of great consequence. It is first and foremost a moral question. I can understand that in their campaign for statehood, the Arabs are fighting to have a territory which they will be the sovereigns of. What is this territory, where it has to be, and so on and so forth, is a different question.

But when they talk about Jerusalem, they don't talk about some municipal boundaries that were defined at a particular time because of some political convenience. You know, when we talk about Gilo, we talk about Jerusalem. It is true, because Gilo is a neighborhood within the framework of Jerusalem today. And when we talk about Ha'anot and Ramot and Talpiot, we talk about Jerusalem, because they are defined now within the boundaries of the city. But with all due respect to all these important neighborhoods of the modern city of Jerusalem, Jerusalem is one place. First and foremost is the Temple Mount.

Jerusalem is the Temple Mount. Why? Because for two thousand years, when Jews were praying for Jerusalem, they were praying for the Temple Mount. They were not praying for Gilo! They were not praying for Ha'anot! Not that these neighborhoods are unimportant. They are very important, and I'll do everything in my power in every capacity, and I'll be serving the people of Israel to make sure that all of these neighborhoods will continue forever to be part of the city of Jerusalem, of course. But the basis of Jerusalem is the Temple Mount! And I said once to a former prime minister of Israel, twice in our history we lost the Temple Mount. In those two times that we lost the Temple Mount, we lost it in spite of our bitter fight to prevent it, because we were too weak to be able to defend it. That's why we lost it. In all the history of the Jewish people, there never was a Jewish leader in any position of leadership who voluntarily agreed to pull out from the Temple Mount and give it to others. We were forced to do it. We fought to prevent it. We died fighting to prevent it. We never volunteered this precious place, the most significant, the most important — the heart of Jewish existence in Jewish history — we never offered it voluntarily to anyone. And I said to the former prime minister, "Don't be the first Jew in history to want to do it." We have ambitions, we have desires, we have political philosophies, but no one knows how accurately the political process will develop. I know one thing: There never will be a Jewish government that will have the moral authority or the political power to give up any part of the Old City and the Temple Mount, which is the heart of Jewish existence. Not only this, but I firmly and wholeheartedly believe that the claims and the rights that the Jewish people have for the Temple Mount and for the old city of Jerusalem are the essential ingredient for any political solution that will emanate from this situation in the future. And I happen to think — I certainly believe so and hope — that the present leadership of the United States of America, even if it doesn't spell it out in explicit terms at this point in time, fundamentally believes that this is the destiny of the city of Jerusalem, that this has been its role in history, and that there can be no other future for the city but as one united and undivided capital of the Jewish people.

I'm not talking about secretaries in American government. I'm not talking about assistants. I'm not talking about advisors. I'm talking about the leadership of the United States of America, the one that was elected by the people of America, who sets the direction and inspires and leads the people. This leadership, I believe, understands and feels precisely what I said. Therefore there can be no other basis for future political developments, but this basic principle that there is only one city, that this city is united and that this city is forever, and that it has to be capital of the Jewish people and only of the Jewish people. It can't be shared in any form or manner.

I want to make another point, about the war against terror. I think that in the last three years, more and more Americans understand that perhaps the greatest challenge that our civilization has today is the war against terror, but not only the immediate war against terror — also the war against the principles, the attitude, the state of mind, and the philosophies from which terror is generated. This is the real confrontation that we have today. It's not just against the killers, the terrorists, it's not just the military aspect of it, it is not just the political battle — it's the confrontation between the values of the civilizations of the Western world, and the values that dictate the use of these measures against our civilization.

I know it is delicate and sensitive, but one can't escape the inevitable conclusion that wherever you go in the world, where you find terror, you also find Muslims. That's the proof. I don't say that there haven't been extreme unrestrained, violent, and aggressive groups in different parts of the world. In different periods, there were. But when you look at the world of today, wherever you see brutal, murderous terror, you find Muslims. I know there is always a danger that when you spell it out in these terms, you are in danger of being accused of sponsoring or inspiring or encouraging a religious confrontation, which is certainly something that no one wants.

I don't say that the Muslim religion creates a natural tendency toward terror — I say the opposite! I don't think that Islam encourages terror or the use of such measures against other civilizations, God forbid. No. But there are groups of terrorists, across the world, that are giving extreme, violent, intolerant interpretations of the orders of their religion in order to fight the basic values of our societies. And no one can escape this conclusion.

I think that for quite a long time, it was somehow thought by various countries, including the best friends of Israel, that maybe we can somehow find a pattern whereby we don't need to do what I think is inevitable when you fight terror in order to stop it. In the course of this, all kinds of political solutions were offered to us as ways to perhaps quiet down these voices of terror within the Palestinian community, and to reach an agreement with them. I think that by now it is most obvious that all of these illusions have failed and all these, in a way, artificial attempts to make agreements with the terrorists in order to stop terror are not working. I hope that at this time it is well understood that there is only one way to fight terror, and this is to fight against it. When you fight against terror, you can't impose upon yourselves restrictions which will make this war ineffective. You have to take the risk of using the measures which can stop terrorists without any political restraints.

I know it's not simple and I know that sometimes there are political forces that are prepared to use almost every possible hypocrisy and double standard in order to criticize you, but that should not be considered a major consideration of shaping the policy of the state of Israel in fighting terror. I think that what President Bush said is something that should be remembered in all the future situations that we will encounter. I think that he spoke from his heart, and he is always very effective when he speaks from his heart. He said, "Had I been the prime minister of Israel, I would have done the same." Had he, the president of the United States of America, been in the same similar position, he would have done the same as I did. Why? Because you can't fight terror with words. You can fight terror if you reach for the terrorists, if you reach out for their supporters, if you reach out for those who finance them or orchestrate these operations, who make the supplies — and you do what you need to do, including killing them!

Sometimes, when I use these explicit words, people say, "Oh, come on — you know, it's not civilized, you can't speak like this."

You better speak like that — and do it — rather than fool yourself and fool others. Because when you fool yourself and you fool others, you create a state of mind that may encourage terrorists to believe that they can carry on and that ultimately the other side will surrender. And when you do what you need to do, there can be no chance of any misunderstanding, and there are better chances.

Now I don't suggest that there is a simple and quick solution for the war against the terrorists, and unfortunately it will take a much longer time than what we would desire. But I believe that at the end of the day, there will not be any measure of success unless we carry on this battle without any restraints against the terrorists, against those who are directly involved in the violent and aggressive actions, against their leaders — and there should be no immunity. I repeat, there should be no immunity to political leaders that sponsor terror, that encourage terror, that finance terror, and that protect terrorists.

And I hope that the same will be true about the nations that play host to terrorist organizations. There can be no immunity for anyone who is involved in helping terrorists in any possible way and there should be no immunity for countries that are playing host to terrorist organizations, within which terrorist organizations can operate and influence the actual violent action against innocent people in our country. What should be done, how it should be done, and with what measures we should deal with it are things we need to be very careful about, and we will be. But no nation that plays host to terrorists should feel that it is always safe and always protected and always immune from the actions that Israel may take in order to defend its citizens.

I think that there was a great hypocrisy in the criticism against the Israeli action in Syria in the fall of 2003. There was no intention to start a war against Syria and we are not interested in a war against Syria. But we are interested that Syria stop supporting the terrorist organizations which are perpetrating actions against innocent Israelis in our cities. And finally,

I don't think that I have to convince anyone here that I was against Oslo, and I never changed my mind, throughout these ten years, about Oslo. I was happy to vote against Oslo agreements when they were originally voted in the Knesset in September of 1993. At that time I was a member of Likud, and we were in opposition. And I never thought that Oslo was a prescription for peace, and therefore, for me, Oslo was not dead, because it was never born as a viable and valid political process that may have led the state of Israel and Palestinians closer toward reconciliation and peace.

What I want to say basically is this: what Israel has to do must not be calculated on the basis of political pressure from the outside, not from false and artificial moral principals that are repeatedly spelled out from all kinds of hypocrites from Europe, but by one thing: What are the best long-range interests of the state of Israel? What kind of a society do we want to have, what kind of a country do we want to have? This is something that we have to decide on the basis of our needs, our perceptions, our principles, and our desires. What kind of a country do we want to have? How many non-Jews do we want to have living as part of our country? In what way do we want them to be part of our country, if they are forced by circumstances to be citizens of our country or residents of our country, and whether they may help us decide to what degree we want to make compromises. Again, not because we recognize their right to any part of our land, but based on what is the best in terms of our long-range interests, how we want to live our lives as an independent nation, on what part of the land of Israel we want to have our independent state, and so on.

This approach is entirely different from the one that some countries are trying to dictate to the state of Israel and I think that, based on the developments and the assessment of forces that are operating at this part of the world now, I am inclined to believe that, sooner or later, we will have to decide on a unilateral process that will not be based on any agreement but will be based on the accurate definition by us of what are the interests of the state of Israel.

Congressman Eliot Engel, a Democrat, represents the 17th Congressional District of New York covering areas of the Bronx and Westchester and Rockland counties. He was elected to Congress in November 1988, and is currently serving his eighth term in the House of Representatives. Congressman Engel serves on the House Committee on Energy and Commerce and the International Relations Committee. He previously served on the Committee on Economic and Educational Opportunities.

Congressman Engel is also a member of the Congressional Human Rights Caucus, the Democratic Study Group on Health, and the Long Island Sound Caucus. He co-chairs the Albanian Issues Caucus and is an Executive Board Member of the Congressional Ad Hoc Committee on Irish Affairs. During his political career, Mr. Engel authored landmark housing and education legislation, led battles to gain increased funding for fighting crime and keeping our streets safe, and is recognized as a leading advocate for improved mental health services. As a member of Congress, he has written innovative bills dealing with U.S. trade policy, education reform, long-term health care, and domestic terrorism. He was the prime sponsor of the congressional resolution recognizing Jerusalem as the undivided capital of Israel.

U.S. House of Representatives — Syria Accountability Act

by Eliot Engel

When you look at the situation in the Middle East today, it is just absolutely unconscionable that 55 years after Israel was established, of all the nations founded in the 20th century, Israel is the only one that still has to constantly fight to justify its existence. It's absolutely a disgrace. And yet to this day, when an Israeli gets up at an international conference, the United Nations, or any of its committees, delegates from the Arab countries walk out. If Israeli journalists ask a question of an Arab figure, they're ignored and treated as a non-entity, as if they don't exist. All of this is obviously part of a conscious effort to deny Israel its place among the community of nations.

This past year, the head of the U.N., Kofi Annan, had the gall to actually ask, "Is it possible for the entire world to be wrong and Israel to be right?"

What a telling and silly question. Just as the minority in the world who once said the world is round, when all believed it was flat were right, just as those who said that the earth revolved around the sun and not the other way around were correct. So, too, are we right to support Israel. How about the masses that joined the Third Reich and the Nazi regime when Jews were in the minority there? Maybe, according to the secretary's perverted way of thinking, they were right as well?

Ostracized by the international community, Israel is not allowed to sit on the Human Rights Commission. The body delights in passing resolutions affirming the legitimacy of armed struggle against Israel. And it is currently chaired by Libya. Can you imagine? And Kofi Annan wonders if the world must be right, since they are all against Israel. Well, when you have the Human Rights Commission chaired by Libya, and you have a country like Syria sitting on the Security Council of the U.N., is it any wonder that we scratch our heads and wonder if the world has gone mad?

We hear a lot about terror. And that discussion leads up to the Syria Accountability Act [which Engel wrote]. It's not poverty that leads homicide bombers to act. That is a phony argument. It's fanaticism. The bomber in August 2003, who took the lives of religious Jews returning from the Western Wall, was a Muslim Imam with two children of his own. The woman who blew herself up in Haifa and murdered 21 innocent people was a law student. These are not impoverished people acting out of desperation. They are the product of the system which hates Jews — let's call it the way it is — and admires and rewards violence and views as heroes those who take innocent lives, and it hates everything Israel represents.

Novelist Cynthia Ozick writing in the *Wall Street Journal* this summer commented about the depravity and sickness of a society which produces children who are "taught to die and to kill from kindergarten on, via song and slogan in praise of bloodletting," and of how despicable Hamas leader Abdel Rantisi is, a physician, who is supposed to heal children, but instead recruits them for suicide bombing missions.

An article in a recent *Wall Street Journal* by the former head of the Rumanian intelligence service detailed the role of the Soviet KGB in setting up Arafat and creating his persona. The forces at work against Israel are so much more sinister and complex than any of us can imagine.

Now we know that Israel is constantly being singled out among all the nations of the world, and I believe that is obviously a clear evidence of anti-Semitism. I speak out about Israel in order to condemn the hypocrisy of those morally bankrupt, non-democratic, corrupt, oppressive, repressive, despotic dictatorships who actually have the gall to criticize Israel. In fact, it's more than just hypocrisy. We know what's behind their actions, and we shouldn't be afraid to call it what it is. Motivated by hatred and anti-Semitism, attempting to cloak themselves in the guise of respectability, as if they are only critics of certain policies or of a country, and not

Jews. How many times have you heard someone say, "Well, I'm anti-Zionist but I'm not anti-Jewish"? We all know that being anti-Zionist is being anti-Jewish. It's bigotry, and we must not allow it to go unchallenged! How interesting that the world is indifferent to the slaughter of thousands of Kurds, the eradication of tens of thousands of Shi'ite Arabs in Iraq in the 90s, the brutal occupation of Tibet by China, the killing of Chechens by Russians, the human rights abuses throughout Africa, Asia, and the Arab world, the selling of blacks into slavery by Arabs in Sudan, but if one Israeli soldier at a checkpoint happens to question a seemingly pregnant Palestinian woman to be sure she's not packing a bomb, it becomes an international incident befitting a Security Council motion and calls for international investigation.

The world seems incapable of being able to distinguish between those who commit terror, and the nation which has the legitimate right to defend its citizens — between the nation that's giving up land conquered in a war of self-defense, I might add, something no other country has ever done, and those who seek to destroy it. They fail to distinguish between the side which constantly takes risks for the possibility of peace and the aggressors who seek her destruction. The world makes no distinction between those who, at the risk of their own lives, attempt to limit the loss of innocent non-combatants and those who wantonly and indiscriminately dispatch murderers seeking to kill and maim civilians and to inflict as much damage as possible.

Let's talk about terrorism. That's what we're trying to get at with the Syria Accountability Act. President Bush put it very simply — you're either with us, or you're with the terrorists. There are people who thought that was overly simple, I think it was actually a great statement. Because you can't have it both ways. Similar to the Jewish experience throughout the millennia, we know that what happens to Israel will eventually happen to the rest of the world. When terrorism first reared its ugly head in the 1970s, the world was virtually silent, for, after all, the victims were Jews and Israelis. But now we see that, allowed to get away with impunity, they have accelerated their attacks. Now terrorism hits a night club in Bali, the most populist Islamic nation in the world, and even in Saudi Arabia and elsewhere. The reality is, as my friend Daniel Pipes has pointed out, that the problem is not really with terrorism but rather Islamic fundamentalism. Terrorism is the weapon they use, but the ideology is behind it, whether in the Philippines, Malaysia, or the Middle East — it's predicated upon radical teachings. It's clear that each of us has to choose, as President Bush said, which side we are on and where our sympathies in this conflict lie. It is beyond me how any decent, moral person cannot sympathize with the plight of Israel in its efforts to live a normal life and to defend itself.

If people think that terrorism is going to only be confined to the Middle East or to Israel, they are sadly mistaken. As a New Yorker, I'll never forget September 11, and neither will anyone else. Now a couple of years ago, when Israel retaliated to defend itself, I took to the House floor and I said, "If the United States was right to go halfway around the world to destroy the Taliban in Afghanistan — and we were — then Israel surely has the right to get at terrorism and destroy terrorists in its own backyard." The hypocrisy of people who say the United States has the right to act and other nations have the right to act, but somehow or other tiny Israel has to show restraint. . . . If I hear one more word from the State Department about Israel using excessive force in putting down terrorism, that's enough to make me scream. *There is never excessive force in putting down terrorism.* And as President Bush said, Israel has the absolute right to go after terrorists wherever they rear their ugly heads. And Israel, like any other country, doesn't have to wait till terrorists strike. Israel has the absolute right to go after terrorists — anyplace, anytime, anywhere.

Regarding Iraq, we hear people cry that the United States should somehow cut and run. It would absolutely be the worst thing that the United States could do. Regardless of how one feels or felt about the war in Iraq, cutting and running is not something you do; it would give the terrorists great pleasure to think that they drove the United States out of Iraq. That's what terrorists are trying to do in Israel.

Several years ago, the Congress passed a law called "ILSA," which is the Iran Libya Sanctions Act. At that point I wanted to offer an amendment in Congress that would have included Syria in the Act. You know, it's really galling to me that back in 1979 the U.S. State Department for the first time put forth a list of countries which aid terrorism — terrorist countries. In 1979, Syria was a charter member of that list. Syria has remained on that list unabated for 24 years. And yet, today, Syria is the only country still on that list with which we have normal diplomatic relations. It has never made sense to me why the United States ought to have normal diplomatic relations with a terrorist country. And so I decided it was time to get tough with Syria. If you look at the track record of Syria, I believe that country has an even worse record than Saddam Hussein's Iraq. After September 11, for me as a New Yorker and as an American, the equation changed. We can't sit back anymore.

This is going to be a long fight. This is going to be a costly fight. You begin the fight and you fight the fight going after nations which harbor terrorists. Now, it's no secret that Syria has a stranglehold on Lebanon. It's no secret that the people on Lebanon's southern border, the terrorists, are wreaking havoc and causing all kinds of destruction, and could be stopped tomorrow if Syria wanted. This is Hizballah, the group which blew up over 200 U.S. marines in 1983. This is the group that goes out not only to destroy Israel, but would destroy the United States as well.

The Syria Accountability Act was written in my office, with my chief of staff, and was put forward two years ago in the United States Congress. We were told at that time that the administration would not support the bill because the United States had impending moves in Iraq and they didn't want to do anything that might hurt the effort in Iraq. But this year I redoubled my effort because I thought there was no longer a reason for the administration to oppose the bill.

Let me tell you what the bill does. It's very simple and very easy. It calls on Syria to do four things. Number one — first and foremost, stop its support for international terror. Number two – get out of Lebanon. Stop occupying Lebanon. Number three — stop its programs of weapons of mass destruction. And number four — immediately stop aiding America's enemies in Iraq. We know that people and armaments are going through Syria right now into Iraq. So it calls on Syria to do those four things.

If Syria does those four things, there are no sanctions. But if Syria does not do those four things, then sanctions kick in and, immediately, all dual-use items such as computers are blocked from going to Syria. And the president of the United States has a pick of at least two of the following sanctions: freezing Syria's assets, stopping trade with Syria, restricting Syrian diplomats, restricting Syrian air flights, and pointing out, even more importantly, that Syria is a terrorist nation and the United States will do everything in its power to end it. That's the bill, simple and clear and concise. [In the fall of 2003] the bill passed the International Relations Committee by a vote of 33 to 2, so I think that is certainly a vote that shows strong bi-partisan support. The administration no longer opposes the bill, and Secretary John Bolton came to the International Relations Committee and told us so.

I guess what I want to say is, I really believe that we can make progress in the war on terrorism. We are making progress in the war on terrorism. Yes, it pains us greatly when we see horrific things, but I believe that the United States and Israel and other nations of the world, when they understand the fact that terrorism can rear its ugly head any place, and it's not something that just happens over there, it is something that can happen everywhere, then, perhaps, the nations will join with Israel and the United States in fighting terrorism. It's not just the fight for the survival of Israel, for the survival of the Jewish people, for the survival of the United States, for the survival of democracy — it's the fight for decency and moral clarity, and the fight, actually, for world civilization.

Morris J. "Morrie" Amitay currently serves as Vice Chairman of the Jewish Institute for National Security Affairs (JINSA), and leads its annual visit to Israel of retired U.S. generals and admirals. He is an original board member of the Center for Security Policy and has been an adviser to presidential candidates of both major political parties on Middle East issues for more than 30 years. Morrie is also founder of the Washington Political Action Committee, which has contributed generously to so many of Israel's supporters in the U.S. Congress.

Israel Endangered: A Threat to the Free World

by Morris J. "Morrie" Amitay

What happens in Israel in the coming months and years goes far beyond Israel's struggle against Palestinian terrorism. It will have ramifications that extend far beyond this tiny area between the Mediterranean and the Jordan — and far beyond the Middle East. The war against terrorism and Islamic fundamentalism has become a worldwide battle. The struggle against the terror masters, as my good friend Michael Ledeen calls them, is taking place every day — in the streets of Jerusalem, along the roads in Yesha, and, tragically, in the restaurants and shopping malls of Haifa and Netanya.

It is a war that is being fought in Jenin, Gaza, and Hebron. But to win this war, it must also reach into the entire Muslim world — to Iran, to Syria, and to Saudi Arabia — a true axis of evil. Israel cannot win this war alone. And we can be thankful that despite receiving bad advice from the State Department, my president is on the right track.

President Bush had it exactly right after the raid on the terrorist camp in Syria when he said, "Israel's got a right to defend herself, Israel must not feel constrained in defending the homeland."

This is surely not a time for "constraint" or for the restraint the U.N. always calls for after another atrocity perpetrated against Jews.

Israel's fight against the terrorists is no different than the fight American soldiers are waging against the terrorists in Najaf, Fallujah, and Tikrit and in hunting down the al-Qaeda murderers who planned 9/11. Some still maintain, even here in Israel, that there can be no military solution to this conflict. But while we all want peace, there are times when there is no alternative to the use of force. There have already been too many victims of diplomacy. There is no substitute for the total defeat of a cruel enemy who follows no norms of civilized behavior — and who interprets concessions as weakness.

Around the world, there is insufficient understanding of the threat of militant Islam or of Israel's geopolitical reality.

If forced back to its pre-1967 borders, Israel would be some 8,000 square miles — the size of New Jersey. How could it be expected to defend itself, with neighbors such as Egypt armed to the teeth with the latest U.S. weapons; Syria, with almost 400,000 regulars and in control of Lebanon; and Iran with its ongoing development of nuclear weapons and missile delivery systems? If you add to this mix the establishment of an irredentist sovereign Palestinian state with a border only nine miles from the sea, you have an invitation to disaster for Israel. Given these realities, it is fair to ask, considering the track record of Yassir Arafat and the PLO, whether the creation of yet another authoritarian terrorist-led state in the Middle East serves the interest of the world's democracies, much less of peace.

There are still those who deny that there is a clash of civilizations. They either have no understanding of radical Islam, or choose to ignore it. Militant Islam seeks to impose its will on all unbelievers. Their leaders say it openly — and we should take them at their word.

We already have seen since Oslo what years of concessions to terrorists have brought. We have witnessed the utter futility of demonstrating good will and peaceful intentions to those who simply want you to disappear. This is the ugly truth. At this point, the formula of "land for peace" is a cruel joke on the families of the victims of the terrorists.

PART II

THE DEATH PROCESS

Land of a Tiny Democracy for Words of Huge Tyrannies

Prof. Talia Einhorn is adjunct professor of law at the Tel-Aviv University Faculty of Management, and professor of law at the Sha'arei Mishpat College of Law in Hod Ha-Sharon, Israel. She is the former editor in chief of the European Business Organization Law Review (2000–2002). Her numerous writings published in international, European, and Israeli law journals and books, cover various aspects of the Arab-Israeli conflict.

The Status of Palestine/Land of Israel and Its Settlement Under Public International Law

by Talia Einhorn

I want to discuss the establishment of Israel, the state of the Jewish people, west of the Jordan River. It shows that the Arab claim that there is a legal right to a separate Arab state to be established in Judea, Samaria, and the Gaza Strip (in Hebrew, the acronym YESHA), whereas Jews are forbidden by public international law precepts from settling there, and the further claim that all Arabs who can trace their origins to pre-1967 Israel have a right to return to Israel, have no basis in international law.

Nonetheless, Israel has been put under incessant international pressure calling on it to recognize the "rights" of the Arab people and to uproot the Jewish towns and villages in Yesha by deporting hundreds of thousands of Jews to the territory of tiny, pre-1967 Israel. The international pressure is supported by internal pressure coming from Israeli citizens, who have been educated to prefer international comradeship and universal values — even when those are shattered in the face of reality — over the basic needs of Jewish national existence. The pressures from within and outside Israel have caused part of the Israeli public to lose faith in their just cause. The Oslo agreements and their difficult consequences are testimony to that.

Under public international law, Israel is not obliged to accept or support the establishment of a sovereign Arab state west of the Jordan River. Indeed, the dangers emanating from such an Arab state should make all peace lovers wary of such a "solution" to the Arab-Israeli conflict. This does not mean that there is no peaceful solution that both Israelis and Arabs would find desirable. But such a solution requires political will as well as a serious law reform, some major aspects of which will be mentioned.

1. The establishment of Israel, the state of the Jewish people

"If I forget thee O Jerusalem, let my right hand forget her cunning," declared Mr. Charles Malik, the Lebanese delegate to the United Nations, immediately after the U.N. General Assembly adopted its plan of partition. Mr. Abba Eban, the Israeli delegate, retorted, "If you keep saying this for two thousand years, we shall start believing it." Jews can trace their roots in Jerusalem back to the days of Abraham. Jerusalem has been in the hearts and minds of Jews throughout the history of the Jewish nation, who physically turn toward Jerusalem when they pray. Throughout history, the Jewish people have maintained their ties to their Promised Land (according to the promise made by God to their patriarchs, Abraham, Isaac, and Jacob), from which they had been expelled by force.

> By the rivers of Babylon, there we sat down, yea, we wept when we remembered Zion. Upon the willows in the midst thereof we hanged up our harps. For there they that led us captive asked of us words of song, And our tormentors asked of us mirth: 'Sing us one of the songs of Zion.' How shall we sing the Lord's song in a foreign land? If I forget thee, O Jerusalem, let my right hand forget her cunning. Let my tongue cleave to the roof of my mouth, if I remember thee not; if I set not Jerusalem above my chiefest joy (Ps. 137:1–6).

During the two millennia of diaspora, Jews retained a clear, direct link to their Jewish heritage through language (Hebrew), religion (Judaism), and culture (practices common to Jews all over the world). Jewish settlement in eretz Israel has not ceased for even a single generation after sovereignty had been lost. The return of Jews to Israel has intensified and turned into waves of immigration since 1882.

No other people has ever turned eretz Israel into a separate, sovereign, thriving entity to which they had unique spiritual and cultural links. The biblical curse — "I will scatter you among the nations, and keep the sword drawn against you. Your land shall remain desolate, and your cities shall be a waste" (Lev. 26:33) — has been vindicated. After the Jewish people lost their sovereignty over the territory of Israel in 70 C.E. (Christian Era) the territory was governed in turn by the Romans, Byzantines, Arab Moslems, Christian Crusaders, Mamluks, and Ottomans. Contrary to current popular thought, there was no Arab "Palestinian" state prior to the establishment of the state of Israel. Jerusalem fared no better under Islam. Whereas Mecca and Medina are mentioned many times in the Koran, Jerusalem is not mentioned even once.

When Moslems controlled the city, they never turned it into their capital. During its occupation by Jordan from 1948 to 1967, no foreign Arab leader came to pray in the Al-Aqsa Mosque on the Temple Mount.

It was in acknowledgement of the special ties of the Jewish people to their homeland that the international community recognized Israel as the state in which the Jewish people had the right to regain their sovereignty. This right was enhanced by the further acknowledgement that Jews in the diaspora were in constant danger of persecution and annihilation, their precarious status culminating in the Holocaust. The right of all Jews to immigrate ("return") to Israel has been an inherent characteristic of the Jewish state, whose *raison d'etre* is to provide a safe harbor for Jews worldwide who wish to practice Judaism openly and undisturbed, living in a state that, *inter alia*, celebrates the Sabbath, rather than Friday or Sunday, and where life is free of anti-Semitic attacks on Jews, or, if such attacks nonetheless take place, they are capable of actively defending themselves.

2. Sovereignty over eretz Israel under public international law

The Arab nation has accomplished self-determination and is represented by 21 states, controlling 99.9 percent of the Middle East lands and all its natural resources. Israel represents only 1/10 of 1 percent of the lands. Yet, the Arabs claim that they have a right to another state between the Jordan River and the Mediterranean Sea. As aforementioned, there was no such Arab "Palestinian" state prior to the establishment of the state of Israel. The claim to Arab sovereignty in eretz Israel west of the Jordan River has no basis in public international law.

2.1. The Palestine Mandate of the League of Nations

In 1920, the San Remo Conference of the Allied Powers assigned to Great Britain a mandate to establish the Jewish national home on a territory covering Israel, Jordan, and part of the Golan Heights. The preamble to the mandate specifies that "recognition has thereby been given to the historical connection of the Jewish people with Palestine."

- Article 2 of the mandate made Britain responsible for placing the country under such political, administrative, and economic conditions as will secure the establishment of the Jewish national home in Palestine.

- Article 6 required Britain to facilitate Jewish immigration to Palestine and encourage close settlement of the land, including state lands and waste lands not required for public purposes.

- Article 11 required Britain to introduce a land system that would promote the close settlement and intensive cultivation of the land.

- Article 7 made Britain responsible for enacting a nationality law that would facilitate the acquisition of Palestinian citizenship by Jews who take up their permanent residence in Palestine.

- Shortly prior to its ratification, Article 25 was added, empowering Britain, with the consent of the Council of the League of Nations, to postpone or withhold application of the mandate provisions to the territories lying between the Jordan and the eastern boundary of Palestine.

The Palestine Mandate does not mention Arab national or political rights in the land of Israel. It only states that the civil and religious rights of all the inhabitants of Palestine, irrespective of race and religion, must be safeguarded. The reason for that is clear, since the object and purpose of the mandate was to reconstitute the political ties of the Jewish people to their homeland.

Arab pressure and riots in Palestine (supported by British officials favoring the establishment of a homogenous Arab empire, affiliated with Britain, in the whole of the Middle East) brought about Churchill's White Paper of 1922, that reiterated the right of the Jews to a homeland in Palestine, but detached (permanently!) from Palestine all of the area east of the Jordan River (constituting almost 80 percent of the territory), and gave it to the Hashemi family, brought by Britain from Arabia, first as an emirate subject to the British mandatory and, since 1946, as an independent kingdom. The mandate was approved by the League of Nations on July 24, 1922. During the entire period of the Palestine Mandate, the British who were entrusted with ensuring its fulfillment, in practice acted to frustrate its very purpose, wishing thereby to appease the Arab and Moslem world. They did so by limiting Jewish immigration to Israel, by restricting the sale of land to persons who were not Arab residents of Palestine, as well as by poorly administering state lands, allowing the Arab population to seize them freely. The Palestine Citizenship Order-in-Council, 1925, contained no provision that would facilitate the acquisition of Palestinian citizenship by Jewish immigrants, as provided in the Palestine Mandate.

2.2. The U.N. Partition Resolution

The U.N. Partition Resolution of November 29, 1947 (General Assembly Resolution 181 (II)), regarding the partition of Palestine into an Arab state and a Jewish state linked by an economic union, was accepted by Israel's Jewish population but rejected out of hand by all Arab states. Under public international law such resolutions are mere recommendations without binding effect.

2.3. The "green line" and the armistice agreements

In any case, it was not a U.N. resolution that established the state of Israel. Had Israel not defeated all Arab armies that invaded the newly born state upon termination of the British Mandate, Israel would not have come into being. Truly, the Arab states did not declare war on Israel, since such a declaration might have implied recognition of Israel's existence. However, each of the Arab states that attacked Israel declared thereby a state of war in an unequivocal manner. The Arab states' attacks were illegal acts of aggression, since in public international law war may not be used to settle international conflicts. Those must be settled peacefully (subject to the "self defense" exception). Israel's War of Independence ended with the illegal occupation of the Gaza Strip by Egypt and of Judea, Samaria, and East Jerusalem by Jordan.

The 1949 Armistice Agreements signed between Israel and its neighbors provided expressly that "[t]he Armistice Demarcation Line is not to be construed in any sense as a political or territorial boundary." The element of "defined territory" as a condition for statehood has always been unclear in the case of Israel. The Armistice Agreements specified that they were intended to facilitate the transition to "permanent peace" and the end of military aggression.

No sooner had the ink dried on the Armistice Agreements than Israel had to suffer Arab violations thereof. Syrian snipers frequently shot Israelis working in the valley underneath or fishing in the Lake of Galilee, and Syrian artillery shelled Israeli settlements. Numerous terrorist acts of sabotage, murder, robbery, looting, and plunder, were launched from the territories of Egypt and Jordan and deliberately promoted by those states in violation of the armistice agreements. Israel was repeatedly condemned by the Security Council for its limited retaliatory actions (which were, in fact, acts in self-defense, designed to prevent future acts of terrorism), whereas the Arab states were protected from condemnation by a Soviet veto.

Under public international law, states are held responsible for terrorist activities launched from their territory against other states, and the state invaded is entitled to use force to protect itself from those. In addition, in violation of international law, Egypt occupied the island of Tiran at the mouth of the Gulf of Aqaba and imposed a naval blockade of the Straits of Tiran, thus preventing Israeli shipping from reaching Eilat, the Israeli port at the head of the gulf (Egypt had, since the early days of the state of Israel, closed the Suez Canal to ships traveling to Israel or coming from it, another blatant violation of international law). These activities caused Israel to join France and Britain in the Sinai Operation (October 25 – November 5, 1956), in the course of which Israel captured the Sinai Peninsula, from which it withdrew later on, as the United Nations deployed its Emergency Force (UNEF) in the Sinai.

2.4. Security Council Resolutions 242 and 338

In 1967, Egypt's President Gamal Abdel Nasser poured seven divisions of the Egyptian army into the Sinai Peninsula. At his behest, the U.N. Secretary General U Thant removed UNEF two days later, precisely when it was supposed to prevent the escalation of hostilities into war. President Nasser further made declarations that left no doubt regarding his imminent intentions to wage war on Israel. Israel's diplomatic efforts to stop the aggression and remove the threat to its existence failed. In international law, no state is expected to be a sitting duck and wait until bombs are actually dropped on its territory. The state that engages in aggressive activities and statements is itself considered the one to have launched an aggressive attack in violation of international law. After weeks of mobilization, which paralyzed the Israeli economy, Israel was finally forced to act in anticipatory self-defense, and on June 5, 1967, it struck the Egyptian air force, destroying its aircraft on the ground. Syria and Jordan, totally unprovoked, attacked Israel on that same day, opening fire all along the armistice line. Contingents supporting the Arab attack arrived from Iraq,

Algeria, and Kuwait as well. The war ended with Israel's victory. The Sinai Peninsula, the Golan Heights, the Gaza Strip, Judea, and Samaria (also known as the "West Bank"), and the Old City of Jerusalem came under Israeli control.

U.N. Security Council Resolution 242, passed in the wake of the Six Day War, was aimed at establishing the guidelines for a "peaceful and accepted settlement" to be agreed by the parties. Accordingly, it affirmed that the fulfillment of charter principles requires the establishment of a just and lasting peace in the Middle East which should include the withdrawal of Israeli armed forces [not necessarily all Israeli armed forces] from territories [not necessarily all territories] occupied in 1967 as well as the "termination of all claims or states of belligerency and respect for and acknowledgement of the sovereignty, territorial integrity and political independence of every state in the area and their right to live in peace within secure and recognized boundaries free from threats or acts of force."

U.N. Security Council Resolution 338 which dates to the 1973 Yom Kippur war waged by Egypt and Syria on Israel without any provocation, reiterates Resolution 242 (1967) and declares that "immediately and concurrently with the ceasefire, negotiations start between the parties . . . aimed at establishing a just and durable peace in the Middle East."

Although not expressly mentioned in these resolutions, there is no doubt that they were adopted under Chapter VI of the U.N. Charter which authorizes the Security Council to make non-binding recommendations for the peaceful settlement of disputes (unlike the Security Council's powers to adopt binding resolutions and enforcement action under Chapter VII to deal with threats to the peace, breaches of the peace, and acts of aggression, the recent resolutions adopted against Iraq being a case in point).

2.5. The peace treaties with Egypt and Jordan

According to the peace treaty with Egypt (following the Camp David Accords), Egypt regained the Sinai Peninsula and an international border was fixed by consent between Israel and Egypt. The peace treaty with Jordan fixed the international border between them. Israel does not have an international border with Syria and Lebanon. Such a border can only be fixed by agreement between Israel and these countries.

2.6. The status of Yesha in public international law

Judea, Samaria, and Gaza were all part of the Palestine Mandate territory until 1948. During Israel's War of Independence, Egypt occupied (unlawfully, under public international law) the Gaza Strip, and

Jordan occupied (likewise, unlawfully) Judea and Samaria (the "West Bank"). Egypt has never claimed title to the Gaza Strip. By contrast, Jordan purported to annex Judea and Samaria in 1950. The annexation was not recognized under public international law, Britain (with a reservation regarding East Jerusalem) and Pakistan being the only states to recognize the annexation, which was also vehemently opposed by the Arab states.

In 1967, following the Six Day War, the territories of Yesha, which had been originally designated for the Jewish national home according to the Mandate document, returned to Israeli rule. Leading international law scholars opined that Israel was in lawful control of Yesha, that no other state could show better title than Israel to Yesha's territory, and that this territory was not "occupied" in the sense of the Geneva Convention, since those rules are designed to assure the reversion of the former legitimate sovereign which, in this case, does not exist. Israel was therefore entitled to declare that it has exercised its sovereign powers over Yesha. In practice, however, for political and other reasons, Israel exercised its sovereign powers only with respect to East Jerusalem. Regarding the rest of Yesha, Israel's official position was that Israel was entitled to annex them, and that, since they had not been taken from a legitimate sovereign, the Fourth Geneva Convention and the Hague Regulations 1899/1907 were inapplicable there. Nonetheless, Israel chose voluntarily to observe and abide by the humanitarian provisions included therein.

In 1988, King Hussein declared that Jordan severed its legal and administrative ties with the West Bank.

In 1993, the PLO signed the Declaration of Principles which states that Resolutions 242 and 338 should provide the basis for negotiations with Israel. In 1994, in accordance with the agreements made with the PLO, Israel handed over to the Palestinian Authority extensive powers — regarding both civil and security affairs — over a substantial part of Yesha in which the Arab population was concentrated. Resolutions 242 and 338 do not mandate the establishment of a separate Arab state in Judea, Samari, and the Gaza Strip. Neither have the interim agreements entered between Israel and the PLO determined the question of sovereignty over these territories.

3. The Jewish settlements in Yesha under public international law

3.1. The rules of public international law regarding "occupied territories"

Even had Israel been an occupant in Yesha, Jewish settlement there would have been permitted under public international law. Article 49 of the Fourth Geneva Protocol only prohibits the occupying power from deporting or transferring parts of its civil population into the territory it occupies. It does not prohibit civilians from acting on their own, purchasing land in occupied territories, and settling there among the existing population of that territory. This prohibition is aimed at preventing the occupant from introducing a fundamental demographic change in the structure of the population of the occupied territory. In addition, the occupant may actively establish civilian settlements for its citizens in the occupied territories, if such settlement is warranted by security needs of the occupant, and concerns territories in which its presence and control are deemed necessary. This does not mean that the land must be used to serve the army's own needs. It suffices that the military considers: (i) that the land should not be left in the hands of the enemy, for fear that it would be used by the enemy for its purposes, and (ii) that the land is important from a military and security perspective.

With respect to public land, Article 55 of the Hague Regulations provides that the occupying state shall be regarded only as administrator and usufructuary of public buildings, real estate, forests, and agricultural estates belonging to the hostile state, and situated in the occupied country. The occupying state must safeguard the capital of these properties (subject to reasonable amortization), and administer them in accordance with the rules of usufruct. Among others, the occupying state is entitled to rent out such land or cultivate it.

Regarding private property, the situation is different. According to Article 46 of the Hague Regulations, the occupying state must respect private property and it must not confiscate it, that is — expropriate it without consideration for an illegal purpose. The occupying state may, however, assume temporary possession of private property, against consideration, for the purpose of establishing civilian settlements that serve its security needs.

As aforementioned, with respect to Yesha, Israel was not obliged, under international law, to apply the Hague Regulations or the Fourth Geneva Convention. However, in the cases brought before the Israeli courts, the state declared that, although not legally obliged to apply these rules in Yesha, it will nonetheless apply the humanitarian provisions included in them. As far as the court was concerned, it accepted the state's position and abstained from deciding it on its merits. This is the background against which one must read the decisions of the Israel Supreme Court, according to which private property can be seized (against consideration) for the establishment of civilian settlements only to the extent that such settlement is necessary for security reasons, whereas confiscation of private property for the establishment of settlements which is not motivated by security considerations is prohibited (the "Elon Moreh" case). In another case, the Court allowed the seizure of land, despite the claim of the applicant that the area concerned was all very quiet and posed no threat to the peace. The Court's reply (Justice Witkon) stated that "there is no better cure to a malady than its prevention at onset, and it is better to discover and thwart a terror act before it has been committed. . . . One does not have to be a military and security expert to realize that terrorist elements operate more easily in an area inhabited only by a population that is indifferent or is sympathetic toward the enemy than in an area where there are also persons likely to look out for them and to report any suspicious movement to the authorities. Among the latter, terrorists will find no hideout, assistance, or supplies."

In other cases, the Supreme Court declined to address the legality of Jewish settlement beyond the green line, since the status of the settlements will be determined definitely in the peace treaty, when such is signed, and "until then it is the duty of the respondent [in casu, the Israel Defense Forces (IDF) Commander of the Gaza Strip — T.E.] to protect the civil population (Arab and Jewish) in the area within his military control."

3.2. The settlements in Yesha

Israel is not a foreign occupying power in Yesha, and therefore there is no rule in international law to prevent Israel from establishing civilian Jewish towns and villages on state lands. The initiative to establish the settlements may be taken either by the state or by private persons. Insofar as private property is concerned, Israel is entitled to expropriate such land (against consideration) for a range of public purposes, according to the standards existing in democratic states (including "tiny" Israel — that is, pre-1967 Israel within the green line — itself).

3.3. The agreements with the PLO

The Interim Agreement of September 28, 1995, entered between Israel and the PLO for a period of five years from the Gaza-Jericho Agreement of May 4, 1994, provides that Judea, Samaria, and the Gaza Strip (including state lands) will be handed over to the Palestinian Authority in stages (Art. 16 of Annex III — Protocol Concerning Civil Affairs — of the Interim Agreement). Therefore, in areas handed over to the Palestinian Authority its authority extended also to state lands for an interim period of five years. But the Interim Agreement does not apply at all to those issues which will be discussed during the final status negotiations, including the issues of Jerusalem and the Jewish settlement in Yesha (Art. XXXI[5] of the Interim Agreement). Moreover, the Interim Agreement provides that the parties agree that the results of the final status negotiations will not be influenced and not be adversely affected by the interim arrangements, and the parties will not be deemed to have waived any of the rights, claims, and positions that they allege, as a result of their entering the Interim Agreement (Art. XXXI(6)). The interim period is over by now. Truly, Article XXXI(7) provides that the parties are prohibited from initiating activities that will change the status of Yesha prior to the final status arrangements. However, had this provision been capable of preventing the establishment of new Jewish settlements, it would have rendered Article XXXI(6) devoid of meaning and therefore redundant. The Palestinian Authority has not applied such an interpretation to its own acts, since that would have prevented the Arab population, too, from building in the land handed over to the PA under the Interim Agreement. In any case, the interim period has elapsed and this provision is not valid any longer.

In conclusion, the Interim Agreement does not restrict the Jewish settlement of Yesha. The existing settlements may be expanded, and new settlements may be established.

4. The refugee problem

As a result of the 1948 war, Israel absorbed some 600,000 Jewish refugees from all over the Arab world, and about the same number of Arabs left Israel. Every war in history has yielded its share of refugees. The novel aspect of the Jewish-Arab conflict has been provided by the Arab countries' deliberate refusal to absorb and integrate their refugees, despite their vast territories and their rich oil resources. Israel, on the other hand, absorbed the Jewish refugees without any compensation being received for the property that they had to leave behind and without any help from international organizations. Had the Arab countries only used the property that they had expropriated from the Jews who had fled to Israel there would have been no difficulty whatsoever to absorb the people whom they openly declare to be their brothers. Indeed, there is no parallel in history to an everlasting refugees' problem, since in the normal course of events every state absorbs the people who share the ethnic origin in common with its citizens. Moreover, according to data provided by the Palestinian Authority, there are nowadays more than 5 million such persons. Their admission would mean that Israel, with its 6.4 million citizens (which include a substantial minority of almost 19 percent of Israeli Arabs) would cease to be the state of the Jewish people.

U.N. Security Council Resolution 242 does not mention the Palestinians. This was no omission. The Resolution calls for "a just settlement of the refugee problem" in acknowledgment that both sides had their share of refugees. Indeed, the fact that there were both Jewish and Arab refugees cannot be ignored when a final and just settlement is contemplated.

In recent years, a claim has been advanced that the Palestinians are a separate people and therefore no exchange of populations could have taken place. However, there is no "Palestinian" language and no distinct "Palestinian" culture. Palestinians are Arabs, indistinguishable from Jordanians, Syrians, Lebanese, Iraqis, etc. The statement made on September 29, 1947, by Mr. Husseini, representative of the Arab Higher Committee, to the Ad Hoc Committee on the Palestinian Question makes this point clearly:

> One other consideration of fundamental importance to the Arab world was that of racial homogeneity. The Arabs lived in a vast territory stretching from the Mediterranean to the Indian Ocean, spoke one language, had the same history, tradition, and aspirations. Their unity was a solid foundation for peace in one of the most central and sensitive areas of the world. It was illogical, therefore, that the United Nations should associate itself with the introduction of an alien body into that established homogeneity, a course which could only produce new Balkans.

Before 1967, Palestinians living in the West Bank and in Gaza did not demand a separate right of self-determination.

5. The risks posed by an Arab sovereign state west of the Jordan River

The promoters of the Israel-PLO Agreements expected them to improve the economy in the territories controlled by the Palestinian Authority (the "territories") and enhance security and peace in both Israel and the territories. Such a development has not taken place. Instead, the Palestinian Authority (PA) has given Israel a preview of the risks posed by a terroristic entity established alongside Israel.

The killings of innocent Israeli citizens through harsh and gruesome, well-planned attacks by Arabs who could then escape to safe havens in the PA-controlled territories, has become part and parcel of the "peace process" since its inception. The Palestinian "police" (in effect, Chairman Arafat's regular army) established under the Oslo agreements, did not turn the guns provided by the Israeli government to defend themselves against the "enemies of peace" from within, but rather against the Israel Defense Forces (IDF) and Jewish civilians.

In the Israel-PLO Interim Agreement, the parties committed themselves to foster mutual understanding, abstain from incitement, and prevent incitement by any organizations, groups, or individuals within their jurisdiction. In reality, however, the Palestinian Authority's television and press have never ceased to broadcast and publish incitement of the most virulent kind. The books and programs present the whole Jewish people, past and present, as the source of evil, using classic and modern anti-Semitic libels.

The worst of all is the cynical use made of children in active warfare. Rather than protect them as the Israelis do, Chairman Arafat and his people place them in the front line and encourage them to throw stones and ignite explosives, and create a live shield behind which adults fire with guns and rifles at Israeli positions. Daily, television and newspapers praise *jihad* (holy war). Children are taught that to be a *shahid* (martyr) who murders Jewish men, women, and children indiscriminately, is a virtue. The Protocols to the Geneva Convention of 1949 set the age below which children may not be recruited into the armed forces at 15 years. Article 38 of the U.N. Convention on the Rights of the Child provides that "State Parties shall take all feasible measures to ensure that persons who have not attained the age of fifteen years do not take a direct part in hostilities."

The Interim Agreement provided specifically (Art. V and Appendix 4 of Annex I — Protocol Concerning Redeployment and Security Arrangements — and Art. 32(3) of Appendix 1 — Powers and Responsibilities for Civil Affairs — to Annex III — Protocol Concerning Civil Affairs) that Jews would be ensured free, unimpeded, and secure access to the "Shalom 'al Israel" Synagogue in Jericho and Joseph's tomb in Shechem and freedom of worship and practice there. Shortly after the agreement came into effect, the synagogue was torched and looted. Later on, Joseph's tomb was destroyed and desecrated.

The peace process and the economic agreements made between Israel and the PLO (including the establishment of a customs union between Israel and the territories controlled by the PA) should have yielded "dividends of peace" to the Arab population. Instead, the standard of living of ordinary Palestinians has substantially deteriorated, despite billions of dollars poured by donor states (mainly the EU, the USA, and Japan). PA corruption has squandered and mismanaged the funds. Substantial funds from the donor states were channeled through personal accounts of PA officials. The aims of the customs union were frustrated. Instead of promoting the establishment of a functioning and thriving economy, the PA established more than 100 exclusive importing agencies, or monopolies, controlled by persons with close contacts to Chairman Arafat, some of them serving simultaneously as PA officials.

Independent Palestinian entrepreneurs lost a substantial share of their Palestinian market. The PA-controlled monopolies thus served to transfer income from the poorer classes to a new economic class that used some of the money to pay a self-serving bureaucracy which, in turn, helped that class become ever richer. The legal system established by the PA was a sham, providing only a facade of justice, another tool to serve the Authority rather than the population. In the absence of a proper rule of law and the necessary legal infrastructure, investors were not attracted, industries were not created, and employment and trading activity have deteriorated.

Israeli citizens have suffered serious economic damage, too, resulting from deliberate sabotage of equipment and countless thefts by Arabs residing and taking refuge in the PA. The Israeli economy has suffered from the direct and indirect implications of the war against terror, the extra costs imposed on the Israeli economy by the ever-growing security expenditure, and the insecure climate which scares away investors. Yet, blame for the poverty and frustration of the Palestinians has been put on Israel. Moreover, human rights organizations have turned a blind eye to the grave transgressions committed by the PA, which has shown no respect for the basic human rights of the Arab population (e.g., total repression of criticism, public executions of people suspected of cooperation with Israel, the use of ambulances to carry explosives, and suicide bombers) while making every effort to detect, and often invent, "crimes" committed by Jews.

6. The possible impact of the International Criminal Court

The International Criminal Court, established under the Rome Statute (in force as of July 1, 2002) to try people who have committed the crime of genocide, crimes against humanity, war crimes, or the crime of aggression (yet to be defined), poses yet another grave risk to Israeli citizens, their leaders, and soldiers. Whereas the Rome Statute does not even mention well-established crimes, such as airplane hijacking, the taking of hostages, and attacks on internationally protected persons, the Statute includes (Art. 8(b)(viii)) "the transfer, directly or indirectly, by the Occupying Power of parts of its population into the territory it occupies," a crime inserted at the initiative of the Egyptian delegation, in order to render the Jewish settlement of Yesha a war crime, and make all those who live there or fight to protect them be considered war criminals, even if the settlements were not established by the state of Israel, even if the initiative came from the settlers, even though their establishment has not violated the Fourth Geneva Convention (irrespective of the issue of its applicability in Yesha, dealt with in para. 3.1 above) or any existing rules of public international law. Had Israel ratified the International Criminal Court (ICC) Convention, it would have made it possible to charge with war crimes Jews living in Jerusalem, the ancient capital of the Jewish people, in Hebron, the site of the tombs of the matriarchs and patriarchs of the Jewish people, and in any other part of Judea, Samaria, and the Gaza Strip.

Settlements in occupied territories, in general, could hardly be considered "the most serious crimes of concern to the international community as a whole," as defined in the preamble of the ICC Rome Statute. Their inclusion in it and the grounds for that are cause for deep concern.

Moreover, unlike the World Trade Organization (previously GATT), which only admits states having a market economy, the Rome Statute admits states which have no regard whatsoever for fundamental freedoms and basic human rights. The judges and prosecutor will be appointed by all contracting parties on a regional basis. Israel is capable of shielding its citizens from prosecution by not ratifying this international treaty. The jurisdiction of the court is limited to acts committed on the territory of a contracting party and to nationals of contracting parties.

But, should an Arab state be created west of the Jordan, it will have the right to ratify this treaty and thereby put every Israeli leader and every Israeli citizen at the risk of being prosecuted for any of the crimes mentioned therein. The U.N. Conference against Racism in Durban (Summer 2001) and the numerous condemnations of Israel by the U.N. General Assembly, the Security Council, UNESCO, the U.N. Secretary General, and the U.N. Human Rights Commissioner, may provide us with insight into what Israel may expect from this new institution created by the United Nations. Although every state has a right to self-defense under public international law, Israel has been condemned time and again by the international community for acts taken in self-defense. Political and other reasons have made the international community, the international media, and human rights activists, apply double standards to Israel. The fear alone from such prosecution may paralyze Israelis, their political leaders, and their army commanders, from defending Israel as they should. Israel must prevent such a risk from materializing.

7. The preconditions for a peaceful solution

The above legal arguments notwithstanding, the Jewish population of Israel has at all times wished to make peace with their neighbors. Since 1947, Israeli leaders have, one after another, agreed to accept programs that would bring peace in the Middle East. Israel has had an ever-growing peace camp. The late Prime Minister Menachem Begin ceded Egyptian territories captured during the Six Day War, the whole of the Sinai Peninsula, in return for a peace agreement, calling for "No more bloodshed. No more tears." Upon signing the Declaration of Principles with the Palestinian Liberation Organization (PLO), Prime Minister Yitzhak Rabin declared on the White House lawn, "We have had enough of blood and tears. Enough." Israeli children are brought up to understand the viewpoint of the Arabs, a task hardly ever taken up by nations in times of conflict. Prime Minister Barak attempted to go the extra mile toward a lasting peace by dividing Jerusalem and giving up the Temple Mount, the heart and soul of the Jewish people.

But whereas in Israel people were rallying and demonstrating in the hundreds of thousands in support of the peace process, the Arab perception of the so-called "peace process" turned out to be a very different one. Indeed, the very term "peace process" is a contradiction in terms unless and until the following, elementary pre-conditions are met : Arab democratic institutions must be established; Arab governance must become transparent and accountable; the Arab reformed legal system must protect individual rights and subject its authorities to open criticism; private law being the charter of a free society, private sector initiative — the key to economic prosperity — requires legal rules that govern property rights, their transfer and the settlement of disputes by an independent judiciary. The rules must be transparent, stable, and enforceable in a fair and efficient manner; violence must be renounced and outlawed; Arab leadership must engage in education to peace and relinquish incitement and anti-Jewish hate propaganda.

8. Conclusion

The Jewish people's historical right to eretz Israel had been recognized by the international community and upheld by the rule of public international law. Israel is not obliged to support the creation of an Arab state west of the Jordan River alongside Israel. The Oslo Agreements were made with a view to enhance "a just, lasting, and comprehensive peace." Yet, since their coming into effect, the Middle East has witnessed not peace but violence of the worst kind in recent history. The establishment of the Palestinian Authority should serve as a "guide to the bewildered" of the grave risks posed by such an Arab state, which may eventually lead to the destruction of the Jewish state. Under public international law, Israel is entitled to diligently encourage and promote close Jewish settlement of eretz Israel, thereby realizing the principles set out by the League of Nations in the original Mandate document.

This speech was first published as a policy paper by the Ariel Center of Policy Research, 2002, and appears here by the courtesy of the ACPR publishers.

Dr. Mordechai Nisan holds a Ph.D. in Political Science from McGill University in Montreal and settled in Israel in 1972. Dr. Mordechai Nisan teaches Middle East Studies at the Hebrew University of Jerusalem (primarily in the Rothberg International School) and is affiliated with both the Ariel Center for Policy Research and the Jerusalem Institute for Western Defense. He has published extensively in Hebrew and English, and his latest books include *The Conscience of Lebanon: A Political Biography of Etienne Sakr (Abu-Arz)* (London: Frank Cass, 2003); *Minorities in the Middle East: A History of Struggle and Self-Expression*, second edition (London & Jefferson, NC: McFarland, 2002); and *Identity and Civilization: Essays on Judaism, Christianity, and Islam* (Lanham, MD: University Press of America, 1999).

A Radical Approach to the Arab-Israeli Conflict

by Mordechai Nisan

Prologue

Following the extraordinary Israeli military victory in June 1967, the Arab summit meeting in Khartoum in late August categorically rejected negotiating, recognizing, or making peace with Israel. The infamous "Three No's of Khartoum" represented Arab militancy and obstructionism, while Israel continued to voice her diplomatic refrain in favor of direct negotiations as the mechanism for resolving the impasse with the Arab world. While Israel was proposing and the Arabs were opposing, each side was confident it understood where its national interests lay. Might it not be the case, however, that each side adopted a policy that was in fact incompatible with its interests? Direct negotiations can be the effective political venue for Arab gains, but for Israel a prescription for territorial loss and a large gamut of disabilities and ailments.

In this essay, we shall confront and challenge the conventional opinion regarding the importance and utility of Arab-Israeli negotiations. We put aside "politically correct" notions of conflict resolution, and raise the banner of truth according to the record of history and as the foundation for a realistic policy proposal.

Israelis, both the left and others, while knowing little of the history of nations and less of the fickleness and fragility of international political commitments, have an abiding single goal and obsession: to withdraw from territories and sign a piece of paper known in their world of textual legalism as a "peace agreement." This untamed zeal disregards the profound Islamic contempt for Jews, the irrefutable Arab opposition to a Jewish state, and the savage Palestinian campaign of terror directed against Zionism and Israel for a hundred years. In consideration of which, the Israeli passion for peace appears pathetic, perhaps pathological, and excessively hazardous. Peace could traumatize Israel, unleashing instability and vulnerability on a grand scale, with the ink on the agreement with the Arabs dissolving into blood. It is therefore worth pondering that a status quo situation, without peace and withdrawal, is a moment of historical grace for the state of Israel and their besieged and battered people.

While negotiations are considered the effective vehicle for resolving conflicts and inaugurating peaceful relations among states, the Israeli case suggests otherwise. Negotiations with the Arabs have proven to be a source of anxiety and tension, whose results have been burdensome and worrisome. Perhaps, therefore, the path to peace does not pass through the conduit of negotiations, but rather by avoiding them. This radical thesis is buttressed, as we shall show, by the record of Arab-Israeli diplomatic history.

PART ONE
Competing Views on the Value of Negotiations and Agreements

Barring the elimination of one side, conflict and war between states will eventually produce a readiness for efforts at peacemaking by conducting negotiations between the rival parties. In order to induce trust and good faith in an otherwise conflict relationship, the negotiation process aspires to a give-and-take compromising ambiance designed to overcome the stated incompatible positions dividing the sides. By talking and negotiating, tension will be reduced and the path to accommodation opened, leading then to understandings and agreements.

Examples abound in international relations from the recent decades concerning this subject. To build mutual confidence, the United States and the Soviet Union arrived at the Hot Line Agreement in 1963 to assure direct communication between the two superpowers. The Non-Proliferation

Treaty (NPT) in 1968 was designed, though failed, in regard to India, Pakistan, and Israel, to prevent the expansion of the elite nuclear club, thereby reducing the danger of a nuclear conflagration in the world. In 1972, the United States and the USSR signed the bilateral SALT strategic accord, though later the Soviet Union admitted its guilt in failing to observe time limits for dismantling ICBM launchers of older types. In 1975, the Helsinki Conference on Security and Cooperation in Europe was launched to reduce mutual uncertainty and create a security regime between Eastern and Western Europe. The Stockholm Agreements of 1986 continued the effort toward accommodation among the countries of Europe. Changing the thinking of enemies or rivals is the objective of such accords. It was not, however, apparent that the negotiating mechanism itself was the key factor, perhaps just the framework, to these developments. The central and operative strategic factor was the superpower balance and containment over European affairs.

Pursuing the diplomatic enterprise of conflict resolution has evoked a variety of specific formulae. Charles Osgood introduced the notion of Graduated Reciprocation In Tension Reduction (GRIT), while the more current terminology regarding Confidence Building Measures (CBMS), such as addressing issues of non-proliferation of nuclear weapons and disarmament, was a similar prescription toward creating a political atmosphere of calm and security. These ideas consider conflict as due to a lack of dialogue and contact between rival sides. The fundamental obstacle to peace does not lie with radical ideologies or a disruption in the balance of power, but rather with the lack of a constructive learning process to bind the enemies into a community of trust. Therefore, according to this mode of thinking, the wall of distrust can be cracked by initiating meetings, launching gestures of goodwill, and thereby reshaping the interests and goals of the respective sides.

A different outlook on negotiations considers the process marred by deception and the outcome threatened by violation. In fact, the negotiation encounter itself constitutes a forum for political warfare. Of special mention is the lack of trust deemed to characterize diplomacy. As it is, so the remark goes, the job of the ambassador to a foreign country to lie, so it is the task of the prince to seek power and defeat adversaries like a fox, as Machiavelli advised in the 16th century. The 17th century French statesman Richelieu proposed and practiced politics according to the dictum that "the state is above everything. The state is the value that permits all means." This position was and is called *raison d'etat*. No moral scruples were to stand in the way of pursuing and assuring the national interest; that interest, we may suggest, was the primary moral value.

The place of cunning in politics was for Machiavelli a general proposition ruthlessly applicable in the context of diplomacy. In *The Prince* he wrote that a "prudent ruler ought not to keep faith when by so doing it would be against his interest, and when the reason which made him bind himself no longer exists." To follow a virtuous path of honesty will bring ruin upon a prince and his state, while employing his vices will bring security to the realm. There is, in this view, a clear sense of the precariousness of agreements with the likelihood that, from the very start of the negotiating mechanism, a dissembling party feigned his commitment for some advantage. The prince should preach peace and good faith but be an enemy to both.

Countries would be wiser not to base their national security on treaties than to blindly rely on the word of an adversary. Norman Angell, the well-known pacifist in the period of World War I, pointed out examples of European states setting aside signed agreements with impunity. He nonetheless believed that peace should be pursued, not so much among the politicians, but by teaching the children the value of commerce and money, and the fruitlessness of aggression and war, which disrupt the economic wellbeing of the average citizens.

American Secretary of State Henry Kissinger, serving under presidents Richard Nixon and Gerald Ford, was endowed with a profound sense of history while he engaged in conducting global diplomacy. In 1975, he invested great time, effort, and skill in trying to bridge Israeli-Egyptian differences in order to reach a second Sinai disengagement agreement. He waxed impatient with Israel's demand that Egypt commit itself to non-belligerency in return for a partial withdrawal. And then mused, "What penalty has there ever been for revoking a peace agreement or for disregarding a proclamation of non-belligerency?"

Undeterred, Kissinger continued his diplomatic endeavors between the parties, perhaps with a mixture of cynicism and pragmatism.

Principles of Islam and Insights from Middle Eastern History

The first foundation of Islam is the Koran, considered by the Muslim believing community as the holy word of Allah, offering dogma and direction for the conduct of all aspects of life.

Muhammad, the prophet of Islam, serves as the inimitable human personality of perfection whose words and actions constitute a binding model for emulation. As the transmitter and messenger of Islam, Muhammad teaches his followers that "the party of Allah will triumph" over the enemies designated as the infidels — Jews and Christians — whose friendship the Muslim believers should not seek.

The Koran conveys a view of deep hostility toward Jews, who received a revelatory text but betrayed it, breaking their covenant with God, implacable in their enmity to the Muslim believers *(Al-Mu'minin)*. Noteworthy is the fact that the term "believers" is reserved generically solely for the Muslims inasmuch all other ostensible people of faith possess but an aspect of belief, whose fullness and completeness descended only with the appearance of Islam. It becomes incumbent upon the Muslims to make war against those "to whom the Scriptures were given [but] believe neither in God nor the Last Day; who do not embrace the true faith [Islam]." Jews, obligated to pay tribute and suffer humiliation under Muslim rule, are targeted by Muhammad and his militant followers in an endless struggle until Islam triumphs over them.

Inasmuch as a state of war between Islam and Jews is a fixed political situation, no permanent treaty can be negotiated unless employed as a ploy to gain the Muslims advantages until the final assault is launched. Securing the objective of *Dar Al-Islam* (the territory of Islam) as a total global Muslim religious triumph denies from the start the legitimacy of a Jewish state denigrated as a religious affront to the primacy of Islam in Palestine.

The massacre of the Jewish Arabian tribe al-Qurayza in 627 was at the same time an act of treachery on the part of Muhammad more than it was an act of war. The same judgment applies to the fate of the Treaty of Al-Hudaybiya from 628 between the Muslims and the pagan Meccans. For two years later, Muhammad executed his staged strategy and turned his diplomacy into conquest. The treaty had been exploited by Muhammad in a deceptive fashion for the purpose of attaching nomadic tribes to the expanding Muslim community, this at the expense of his Meccan rivals. The subsequent seizure of Mecca in 630 was a military takeover mediated by a truce agreement that camouflaged, so it would seem, Muhammad's conquering intent that buoyed the wave of the expanding Islamic religion.

The use of deception is manifested no less in the Koran's depiction of God. The enemies of Muhammad schemed against him, but Allah schemed even better in order to save his prophetic messenger. Indeed, declares the Koran, "God is most profound in his machinations." This crafty characteristic attributed to the Divine becomes a sacred model for the Muslims to follow in their political machinations.

The idea of feigning behavior (*tahalluq*) or posing a false identity to avoid danger (*taqiyya*) constitutes part of the cultural arsenal for Muslim cunning in problematic situations. European travelers to the East would encounter Muslim dissimulation in their daily experiences. One fascinating and humorous example was related by A.W. Kinglake in the mid-19th century during his crossing of the Sinai desert. He misplaced his trust in a band of Bedouin with whom he entered into an agreement for safe passage, only to eventually be apprised of their devious tactics.

While unlocking the cultural code of the Muslim East, Kinglake was informed of a local proverb that admonished you to "treat your friend as though he were one day to become your enemy, and your enemy as though he were one day to become your friend." Isabel Burton, wife of the daring and insightful English traveler Richard Burton of the 1850s, supported Kinglake's dictum: "In the East it is safer to treat everyone as if he might someday be your enemy." This mental convolution hardly ranks as a formula to generate trust among people.

The place of deception in Muslim diplomacy assumed a central place in Ottoman Turkish reforms inaugurated to mollify Europeans through the 19th century. Known as the Tanzimat reform period from 1839–1876, Turkish policy in need of British support in facing the northern Russian threat was especially designed to convey the impression that Muslim rule would no longer discriminate against Christian inhabitants of the Turkish Empire. But in fact, Christians in Mount Lebanon and Armenians across their historic homeland were subjected to violence and massacre despite promises of good government and religious equality. The Tanzimat, though possessing an air of political earnestness and intellectual conviction, misled Europeans who discovered that the word of the Muslims was empty of content.

The Turks violated both the Dhimma of Islamic lore that guarantees security to docile non-Muslims and the Tanzimat that offered equality and liberty in the Ottoman Empire. In 1856, popular Muslim fanaticism erupted against Christians in the towns of Nablus and Gaza; in the 1860s, Christian testimony was not accepted evidence in courts in Bulgaria and Bosnia. The Dhimmis continued to live in fear and without government protection, while the rhetoric of reform was diplomacy as deception and not policy.

Zionism and the Arabs

The Jewish pioneers in Israel, or Palestine, in the early 20th century, acquired a familiarity with the Arabs in the country, their manners and customs, and often their hostility to the Zionist enterprise. Seeking ways to elicit Arab accommodation did not blind most Jews to the extreme difficulty of achieving this objective. Moshe Smilansky from Rehovot expressed in 1914 a widespread view of the Arab: "If he senses you have power, he'll capitulate and keep his hatred of you in his heart. And if he senses your weakness, he'll rule you." No authentic or permanent understanding would logically be possible while the Arab keeps his hatred of the Jew in his heart. Yet, Smilansky refused oddly enough to draw this conclusion, believing instead that a bridge of trust between Jews and Arabs in the land could be built.

The question of negotiations with the Palestinian Arabs was calculated in terms of the Jewish-Arab power equation. Zionists shied away from pursuing talks when they were, or appeared to be, in a weak position. One Jerusalem journalist commented in the 1920s, "Whenever they [the Arabs] see our peace overtures, the Arabs think that they are the stronger ones." Skilled in maintaining good relations with Bedouin shaikhs, by means of gifts and amicability, could be more beneficial for the Jews than trying to negotiate a political peace with the Arab majority population in Palestine.

Ben-Gurion, who headed the Zionist movement in eretz Israel during the critical pre-state of Israel period, conducted talks with Arab personalities to explore the possibility of a formal accommodation between the two sides. The Zionists were adamant in demanding nothing less than a future Jewish majority in the country, which certainly made Arab assent exceedingly unlikely. In 1936, Ben-Gurion pointed out to his colleagues that Zionism cannot rely on the Balfour Declaration, which was being challenged by Arabs and the English. "The Versailles Treaty which was being torn into bits, the Covenant of the League of Nations, signed by 34 states, has been rendered valueless [with Japanese aggression against Manchuria], the Assyrians and the Armenians have been deceived [denied statehood, autonomy, or security], and the Locarno Pact [of 1925] has been nullified [by German remilitarization of the Rhineland] — a pact guaranteed by England, Italy, and France, three powerful states. Italy [in Ethiopia] has violated the law in the face of the entire world."

Treaties and agreements proved worthless pieces of paper in world affairs, prodding Ben-Gurion to stress that building the Jewish national home must advance regardless of any understandings, if achieved, written or oral, with the British or the Arabs.

Meanwhile, the attempt at negotiations with the Arabs of Palestine, conducted in the mid to late-1930s, left Ben-Gurion suspicious that the Arab interlocutors were "neither frank nor authorized." The Arab spokesmen seemed to be acting deceitfully, backing away from their initial proposals. In 1947, the Palestinian Arabs rejected the United Nations partition plan for Palestine, as they had earlier rejected the Peel Commission partition plan in 1937. Rejecting compromise, the Arabs chose war and suffered abysmal defeat.

PART TWO

The path of negotiations can fail because the positions put forward by the rival sides are incompatible, with no bridge of compromise to close the gap. In addition, negotiations fail when the two parties are culturally at odds, with no shared trust, and agreements remain empty pieces of paper. Thereby, both reasons of substance and texture can prevent reconciliation. This is the case with the Arab-Israeli conflict, and while the failure of negotiations typically highlights the conflicting positions of the two sides, we shall pay special attention to the problematic and complexities of negotiations as a medium for building a relationship of peace between Arabs and Jews in the Middle East.

The 1949 Armistice Agreements

The period of the Arab assault on the Jew community *(ha-yishuv)* in late 1947 and the state of Israel in May 1948 ended, following cease-fires and a truce, with the signing of four armistice agreements in 1949. Israel having secured her national survival on the battlefield, Egypt, Lebanon, Jordan, and Syria committed themselves to "the transition to a permanent peace in Palestine." In Article Three, paragraph 3, the parties undertook the obligation to prevent any "warlike act or act of hostility" emanating from their territory against the co-signing state. Through the years 1951–56, however, thousands of acts of hostile infiltration and murderous attacks took place from Egyptian, Jordanian, and Syrian territories.

The Israeli-Jordanian armistice agreement carried a special proviso in Article Eight calling for the "resumption of the normal functioning of the cultural and humanitarian institutions on Mount Scopus, with free access to the Holy Places and use of the cemetery on the Mount of Olives." But the Jordanian regime and King Hussein violated these provisions, condemning the Hebrew University and the Hadassah Hospital on Mount Scopus to stagnation and a moribund condition; Israeli access to the Western Wall was denied while synagogues in the Jewish quarter of the Old City of Jerusalem were destroyed; and the ancient Mount of Olives Jewish burial ground was desecrated and closed off, while the Jordanians used Jewish grave stones for paths and latrines.

For her part, Syria routinely violated the armistice by firing on Israeli farmers in the Jordan valley and at fishing boats on the lake of Galilee (the Kinneret), while permitting Fattah terrorist infiltrations from her territory. According to one scholarly authority, Syria, considered the ideological beating heart of the Arab world made it clear in the 1950s, that "she would not acquiesce in the existence of the state of Israel and would endeavor to bring about its annihilation."

Egypt initially did little to stop *fedayeen* Palestinian terrorism from the Gaza Strip penetrating Israeli territory. Later, Egypt encouraged, trained, and armed these irregular guerrillas, while at the same time violating international law by preventing Israel's use of the Suez Canal. Thereafter, Egypt further exacerbated the situation by closing Israeli shipping lanes through the Straits of Tiran to the port of Eilat.

In response to Arab provocation, threats, and attacks, Israel took decisive military action. She went to war against Egypt in 1956, then later preempted in 1967. She carried out punitive measures against Jordan, and in June 1967 responded to Jordanian aggression by capturing the West Bank and East Jerusalem. In that same June 1967 war, Israelis fought their way up to the Golan Heights and, once and for all, brought to an end Syrian bellicosity that covered the period that had begun in 1948.

There is, however, a view according to which Israel was the guilty party for armistice violations and the absence of peace until 1967. Some historians contend that in the early years following Israel's founding, King Abdallah of Jordan wanted an agreement with Israel, so too Syrian dictator Husni Zaim, no less Gamal Abdul Nasser of Egypt. The Arab desire for peace was met by Israeli intransigence after 1948, according to the revisionist historian Avi Shlaim. Benny Morris, for his part, concluded that Israel missed chances for peace.

What bears clarification are the specific Arab conditions for peace with Israel. Syria demanded that Israel agree to draw a line down the lake of Galilee, thereby ceding half of it, when Israel's water needs beyond the question of sovereignty and security were a compelling national interest. Jordan wanted a port on Israel's Mediterranean coast accessible by a direct connection through the northern Negev Desert. Egypt demanded that Israel concede the southern Negev in order to provide a direct link from the Sinai to Jordan and the Arab East. These points elucidate what would emerge in 1967 thereafter as a political pattern in Arab policy demands: peace in exchange for territorial withdrawal. Before 1967, Israel rebuffed such transparent and slippery Arab diplomacy. After 1967, however, Israel was more than once tempted to enter into this fragile framework of "territories for peace."

The Arab violations of the armistice agreements in letter and spirit demonstrated bad will for any future and serious peace negotiations. The Arab economic boycott of Israel, pan-Arab ideological warfare, and a complete diplomatic blockade of Israel, were part of the Arab campaign — always military in the making — against the isolated Jewish state.

The Agreements in the 1970s

1. The August 7, 1970, Suez Canal Cease-Fire Agreement between Israel and Egypt

The aftermath of the June 1967 Six Day War was especially marked by Egypt launching a war of attrition against Israeli forces in Sinai and along the east bank of the Suez Canal. Rejecting U.N. Security Resolution 242, which had prompted the formula of "territories for peace," President Nasser chose war over negotiations as a statement of political resolve in place of diplomatic accommodation. Nonetheless, unable to force any Israeli territorial withdrawal, and impotent to impose this task upon the United States, Nasser agreed to American efforts to bring about a military cease-fire. According to the agreement, both Israel and Egypt would distance their armed forces 50 kilometers east and west of the canal, respectively, thus freezing the location of their missile batteries.

Immediately upon the signing of the agreement, Israel reported to the United States that Egypt had violated it by deploying its missiles closer to the Suez Canal line. Though initially skeptical of this charge, U.S. intelligence sources confirmed the Egyptian violations on August 14, just a week after the agreement was signed. On August 19, the U.S. State Department further acknowledged the violations.

The United States, for her part, had successfully negotiated a cease-fire agreement between the two major regional rival powers. However, Egypt was more successful in breaking the American-mediated accord with impunity. Washington's accommodation with Arab violations would become, like Israel's political reticence, a fixed and disturbing pattern of behavior over the years.

2. The January 18, 1974, Israeli-Egyptian Disengagement Agreement

Although Egyptian President Anwar Sadat successfully launched a surprise attack against Israeli forces in the Sinai on October 6, 1973, thereby igniting the Yom Kippur War, he was reportedly guided by the objective of reaching thereafter a final peace agreement with Israel. This kind of strategic double-talk is certainly no less cunning than the elliptical notion whereby Sadat had concealed his intention to go to war by having repeatedly declared his intention to do so. Of course, he would have equally been successful in hiding his intention to go to war by saying nothing.

With the war between Egypt and Israel drawing to a finish toward late October 1973, Sadat continued to dazzle and bamboozle his interlocutors. Talking about peace, he made it clear that only the next generation could decide about normalization. He would end belligerency — but call it peace. Sadat was willing to receive "his" Sinai back, without making peace with Israel.

Then, subjected to Secretary of State Kissinger's prodding and polemics, Israel succumbed to withdraw from the swash of territory it had captured west of the Suez Canal within Egypt proper, and from a strip of territory on the east bank as well. With this, a buffer zone was established for the disengagement of Israeli and Egyptian forces. Note that Israeli withdrawal was euphemized as "disengagement" in this round of negotiations. Any Egyptian undertakings in the context of the agreement were — in the immoral oddities of Arab-Israeli diplomacy — made to the United States. Israel gave up concrete assets for absolutely nothing substantive in return. Kissinger would nevertheless argue to the Israelis that American involvement was to their benefit, yet how much more was it a great boon to Egypt.

3. The May 17, 1974, Israeli-Syrian Disengagement Agreement

Kissingerian "step-by-step" diplomacy coalesced with the Arabs' refusal to conduct face-to-face direct negotiations with Israel, with the attendant highlighting of America's essential mediating role.

Kissinger began his acquaintanceship with Syrian President Hafez al-Asad in December 1973, while pursuing the goal of convening a Geneva Conference designed to transfer the October War into the arena of conflict resolution. Despite long negotiation sessions with Kissinger, and a certain agreement to the Geneva idea, Asad surprised his American counterpart by clarifying that he yet had no intention to attend the December 21, 1973, conference. Kissinger, never concealing his manifest self-assurance, had the audacity to accuse Asad of "inexperience in negotiation" in 1974. But at the same time, Kissinger recognized the Syrian's president's own personal superciliousness, stating that "Asad sought a guarantee of the result before he would begin negotiating."

In the course of the talks that continued until May 1974, Asad settled points of disagreement, but then would re-open these points. He bartered hard to get without giving Israel anything in return. In the end, the Israeli-Syrian agreement on the Golan Heights included demilitarized zones, limited forces deployment, and a United Nations monitoring team. Expectedly, Israel was pushed to concede land — what she conquered from Syria in the 1973 war and also a small area around the town of Quneitra, captured earlier in the 1967 war. Prime Minister Golda Meir bemoaned that America had brought Israel to capitulate to Syria — which had lost both wars, and yet recovered Quneitra! The agreement was at one and the same time a Kissingerian triumph and an observable political pattern which confirmed an irking fact: U.S.-Arab negotiations were singularly preoccupied from start-to-finish with Israeli territorial concessions.

Subsequent months and years demonstrated that Syria would violate the letter and spirit of the U.S.-mediated accord. Despite the understanding discussed, Syria left Quneitra desolate rather than rebuilding it as a sign of normalization. In December 1974, Israel's Defense Minister Shimon

Peres revealed that the Syrians had stationed weapons in a reduced forces zone on the Golan in excess of that permitted under the agreement. There were subsequent infractions in the positioning of excess weaponry beyond that authorized by the agreement.

Equally pernicious was the Syrian policy of employing proxy elements, especially Hezbollah in southern Lebanon, to pursue a war of terrorism against Israel rather than reach an accommodation with her. In addition, Damascus became the home and sanctuary for a variety of Palestinian terrorist organizations, like Hamas and the Islamic Jihad, the Popular Front for the Liberation of Palestine, and the Democratic Front.

Yet, the Syrians overwhelmingly observed the cease-fire and disengagement arrangements with Israel on the Golan Heights. The UNDOF mandate providing for a United Nations monitoring station was renewed every six months. The negotiations from 1974 were an exercise in hardball diplomacy, without direct contacts between Israel and Syria. But the agreement held strong over many years. The fact that it failed to lead to a peace treaty suggests that the strategic components of the situation, rather than any political thawing in the Israeli-Syrian relationship, were the formidable reason for the quiet on the border. The Israeli army was (is) just 60 kilometers from Damascus, and this is a weighty factor of deterrence bearing on Syrian military calculations.

4. The September 1, 1975, Sinai II Agreement between Israel and Egypt

Sadat refused to make a peace treaty with Israel or declare the accord to be a commitment to non-bellicosity, that is, an end to the state of war. Prime Minister Rabin, who in the spring of 1975 balked at succumbing to an accord which offered no substantive payoff for Israel, conceded in the fall to withdraw Israeli forces from the oil fields and strategic Mitla and Giddi passes in Sinai in order to conciliate the Americans and achieve an agreement with Egypt.

Meanwhile, Sadat had expressed his view that even a political settlement would not bring a final termination to the overall conflict. Indeed, a strong intellectual current within Egypt was proposing peace as the mode of struggle to eliminate Israel in stages. Accepting the Jewish state and normalizing relations with her would impose a Cold War style of confrontation designed to ultimately drown Israel in the encompassing Arab realm in the Middle East.

5. The 1978–79 Camp David Accords between Israel and Egypt

Anwar Sadat, introspective and inscrutable, was a master of surprises. In August 1977, U.S. Secretary of State Cyrus Vance visited Egypt and heard from Sadat that Washington needed to play an active diplomatic role in the conflict. Sadat then astounded Vance and pulled out a draft peace treaty (with Israel). He then went on to say that he and Vance had agreed to form working groups before reconvening the Geneva Conference. According to William Quandt, "Vance was still not sure what Sadat had in mind." While Vance was impressed with Israeli Foreign Minister Moshe Dayan, "Sadat was harder to read."

The visit of Anwar Sadat to Jerusalem that same year, on November 19, 1977, was a stunning political performance. Sadat, the actor, was in his theatrical element. The Israelis were entranced by the Egyptian president, and hungered for political acceptance by the major Arab state. In his Knesset speech in Arabic the next day, Sadat articulated his mantra of peace, but clarified firmly, "Our land does not yield itself to bargaining; it is not even open to argument." He then delineated the parameters of the "peace with justice" he was putting on the table: "Complete withdrawal from the Arab territories occupied after 1967 is a logical and undisputed fact. Nobody should plead for that." In order to avoid misunderstanding or self-delusion on the part of the Israelis, Sadat made it crystal clear that his peace formula included a Palestinian state and the right of refugee return.

After Sadat's Jerusalem visit, Begin visited him at Ismailiya in December. The Israeli delegation was given a cold reception, a foreboding of the cold peace to come. Yet the Israeli prime minister said to the Egyptian president, "Not only will we make peace — we will become friends." Begin's dreaminess was matched by Ezer Weizman's foolishness. The Israeli defense minister ignored Sadat's dogmatic Knesset speech, saying that Sadat was "not interested in a Palestinian state." Admittedly, the Egyptian was enigmatic and dizzied his Israeli counterparts by altering his thoughts. Weizman, mystified by Sadat, grudgingly admitted that Sadat vindicated those who accused him of being changeable, reneging on undertakings. Sadat, a sophisticated political chameleon, was too wily a diplomatic master for the Israelis.

Later, during the intense Camp David summit in September 1978, Sadat demanded all the territories and Palestinian refugee return, without mentioning diplomatic relations with Israel. This hinted that even when relations with Israel would be forced upon Sadat, he would empty them of any content or warmth. Thus, even if he submitted to the rival's point, Sadat would not surrender to the other's vision of peace.

Although a formal exchange of ambassadors did take place, Egypt withdrew her ambassador from Israel from 1982 until 1985. In the period of the Palestinian Al-Aqsa Intifada beginning in 2000, no Egyptian ambassador was present in Israel. The first Israeli ambassador to Egypt, Eliyahu Ben-Elissar, and his wife suffered from social ostracism in Cairo, and subsequent Israeli ambassadors were isolated and fearful for their physical safety. Egyptian political and professional circles opposed anything resembling normalization with Israel, in commerce and contacts, while vilifying the Jewish state. Egypt continued to amass modern American armaments, and prepare its army for war, though no enemy threat existed at all. Assuming its regional power status while contending with Israel as a hegemonic competitor was the Egyptian strategic ambition. In these circumstances, then, the Egyptian-Israeli peace treaty signed on March 26, 1979, was no more than a non-belligerence truce being tested daily. What you negotiate in the Arab Middle East and even agree upon is not what you get in the end.

Arab Interlude: Broken Agreements and Promises among Brothers

Political deception toward non-Muslims is only part of the sweeping role of guile guiding Arab behavior that consumes good will among Arabs themselves as well. Pan-Arab unity schemes have abounded, but Arab scheming laid them to rest.

The Egyptian-Syrian merger within the United Arab Republic survived just three years, from 1958 until 1961. Subsequent unity talks in 1963 among Egypt, Syria, and Iraq led to a signed agreement, but failed to materialize. In December 1969, the Tripoli Charter, binding Egypt, Libya, and Sudan, came to zero. The 1970 Federation of Arab Republics, with Syria joining the Tripoli Charter states, met an identical fate. In late October 1978, Syria and Iraq signed the Charter of Joint National Action in pursuance of unity; nothing happened. In September 1980, Syria and Libya agreed on a merger; nothing happened. In February 1985, Jordan and the Palestinians agreed on a federation framework; again, nothing happened. We can only explain this pattern of rhetoric and gestures as political ritual to make an impression, in the name of sacred Arab unity, but without any commitment at all to carry out such a project. Making an impression is far more significant than keeping one's word. Here is politics as a theater of masks and roles of no inherent value.

The Arab record of false pretenses and broken agreements seems endless. In the 1970s, the PLO in Lebanon became the primary cause of warfare, as the Christian population struggled to maintain its communal integrity and political power. One commentator considered Yassir Arafat to be a pathological liar who had signed 72 cease-fires in a span of 18 months during 1975–76, and then broke each one of them. Another report maintained that from 1975 until 1982, Arafat violated 786 cease-fire agreements with the Lebanese. This was Arafat's testing ground for future negotiations with the Israelis.

The 1993 Oslo Accord between Israel and the Palestine Liberation Organization

The Madrid Peace Conference in October 1991 launched a negotiating track between Israel and Jordanians, Palestinians, Syrians, and Lebanese, respectively. These direct talks failed, however, to produce agreements among the parties. But while they were conducted, Israelis and Palestinians began to hold secret meetings which over time, through 1992–93, were transformed from semi-official contacts into official negotiations. Under the good offices of Norway, the two sides produced the Oslo Accord, called a Declaration of Principles [DOP] on Interim Self-Government Arrangements, that was signed on September 13, 1993, in Washington.

In order to rescue the PLO from financial and political annihilation following the 1991 Gulf War, Farouk Kaddoumi, heading the PLO Political Department, considered the peace process a "compulsory track." Indeed, Arafat and Abu Mazen (Mahmoud Abbas) were themselves behind the secret Oslo talks that were camouflaged by the Madrid negotiating framework. Thus, both the matrix and motive for Oslo were fraudulent.

The DOP served ostensibly as a compromise interim settlement until final status negotiations would determine the final political fate of the West Bank (Judea and Samaria) and Gaza Strip territories, and the Palestinian population therein. The government of Israel and the Palestine Liberation Organization had decided "to put an end to decades of confrontation and conflict, and strive to live in peaceful coexistence and mutual dignity and security." The accord called for Israeli withdrawal, initially from Gaza and Jericho, thereafter from other areas under Israeli control. A Palestinian Authority would govern the Palestinian territories, supplemented by a "strong police force," on the path to later resolving outstanding issues touching Jerusalem, Palestinian refugees, and Jewish settlements.

The September 1993 Declaration of Principles led to the May 1994 Cairo Accord, for implementing an initial Israeli withdrawal from Gaza and Jericho, and then to Oslo II in September 1995 for further withdrawals from Palestinian towns and rural village areas in Judea and Samaria. Although obliged to prevent terrorism and hostilities, avoid anti-Israeli propaganda and anti-Semitic vilifications, limit its police force and collect illegal weapons, the Palestinian Authority under Yassir Arafat did absolutely nothing of the kind. Hamas and Islamic Jihad were not disarmed; rather they engaged in urban terrorism in Tel-Aviv and Jerusalem, with Arafat's own Fatah and Tanzim forces adding to the sweep of Palestinian violence against Jews and Israel. Confident in Israel's capitulation and the PLO's victory, Arafat declared in November 1995 that "the struggle will continue until all of Palestine is liberated" — Haifa and Hadera included.

During the 1990s, Israel both failed to ensure the full implementation of the accords, or to cancel and bring to an end the process of Israeli concessions altogether. From the initial Oslo agreement of 1993 through the Wye River Memorandum of 1998, the PLO derisively mocked Israel, violated the agreements, and ignored its commitments, while pursuing the path of terrorism. Shimon Peres, foreign minister under Yitzhak Rabin, and after his assassination in 1995, prime minister, sang of the New Middle East that would be dominated "by banks not tanks, ballots not bullets." But the Palestinians, with Arafat at the lead, sang a different song, about "jihad, jihad, jihad."

For Arafat, negotiations were a model of strategic deception based on Muslim models. On a few occasions he would mention Mohammad the prophet of Islam having accepted the Al-Hudaybiya treaty with the Meccans in the 7th century, and Salah a-Din accepting an agreement with Richard the Lionhearted in the 12th century, only to then renew the holy war against the infidels. There was, therefore, nothing inherently honest or binding about agreements made by 20th century Muslims with the Jews of Israel.

The Palestinian political war of attrition, with talks, understandings, and agreements abounding, paralleled the Palestinian war of terrorism. During the period of September 1993 through April 2000, 831 Israelis had been killed by Palestinian terrorists. Suicide bombings, a fanatic Islamic mode of warfare against Jews, struck across Israel, blowing up innocent civilians on buses and in restaurants, in Tel Aviv, Netanya, Kfar Sava, Nahariya, Jerusalem, and elsewhere. The Jewish residents of Judea and Samaria were ambushed on the roads and attacked in their homes — in Itamar, Adura, and Elon Moreh. The Palestinian media routinely described Jews as liars, cheaters, and treacherous, in a way that this collective character assassination of the Jewish people could make Palestinian lying and cheating acts of self-defense and precaution in the face of a wily foe. Kindergarten teachers taught Palestinian children to despise Jews and take up the violent struggle at an early age. To become a *shahid* (Muslim martyr) in fighting the Israelis, in the process of trying to recover Palestine from the Zionists, was a matter of historical justice and a religious obligation.

The negotiated settlement between Israel and the PLO from 1993 became a political dead letter, though this truth seemed not to penetrate the thick mental layers of Israeli self-delusion. Prime Minister Rabin had stated after a terrorist bombing of a bus in Tel-Aviv in 1995 that Israel had no choice but to continue conducting relations with Yassir Arafat. Uri Savir, a major negotiator of the Oslo process, referred in 1996 to Israel's "Palestinian partner in peace, [with whom] we feel we can work together." The Israeli left in particular was anxious not to cut the political umbilical cord binding them with the killers of Jews.

Israeli utopianism remained irrepressible through the 1990s. The October 1994 Peace Accord signed between Israel and Jordan was evoked by King Hussein's promise of "a warm peace," unlike the cold peace with Egypt. The prominent professional associations, the Islamic movements, and the Palestinians within Jordan, however, assured that the peace with Israel would be no more than a non-war agreement at best. Normalization was taboo even though it was promised by the king himself.

With Syria, negotiations persisted through the decade but, following Asad's obstinacy in rejecting Israel's plea for open borders, embassies, and normalization, no agreement was reached. Prime Minister Ehud Barak was clearly pining for peace with Syria, but even his excessive generosity in negotiations during 1999–2000 could not adequately satisfy Hafez el-Asad's appetite to gain a foothold on the Sea of Galilee.

The new Middle East was a political phantom for the imaginings of Shimon Peres, but lit no fire of interest among the Arabs. Many in the Arab world fear Israel can overwhelm the entire region, not just militarily, but commercially and technologically as well. Israel, as the repository of modern Western ideas and political institutions, threatens the cultural integrity of Muslim societies and Arab authoritarian regimes. Thus, the regional economic conferences at Casablanca in 1994 and Amman in 1995 failed to launch substantive ties with Israel, though a few Arab countries like Morocco, Tunisia, Mauritania, and Qatar, did open interests offices with Israel. Suspecting Israeli hegemonic aspirations and capabilities, the Arabs shy away from the trappings — or trap — of normalization as an unacceptable price to pay for any political settlement with Israel.

The PLO created a police force, not to keep the peace or disarm Hamas and Islamic Jihad terrorists, but to shoot at Israeli soldiers and civilians and kill as many Jews as possible. The Palestinian Authority received billions of dollars in aid from Europe and America, not to educate children and develop the economy, but to engage in rampant corruption and the militarization of society. Arafat signed agreements with Israel, not to advance toward peace, but to simulate sincerity while conducting warfare. He formally accepted Israel's existence, while the Palestinians' propaganda and educational agencies demonized Jews and vilified Israel as a colonialist enterprise in Palestine.

But the choir of "true believers" stood their ground, despite the revelations of deception. The dream was just too beautiful to be thrown away.

Yair Evron perceived in 1995 a "political and ideological thawing in overall Arab attitudes toward Israel: Israel's political legitimacy has both spread and deepened." Avraham Sela considered in 1998 that with the decline of supra-state symbols in the Arab world, there was an "increasing acceptance of Israel by Arab states." Beyond these two optimistic Israeli assessments, Janice Gross Stein was in 1999 of the opinion that both Arabs and Israelis had learned that the use of force does not pay; therefore, they have adopted negotiations as the mode of communicating and solving their conflict. William Quandt, writing in 2001, considered that the achievements of the past could be lost "if radical Palestinian sentiment gained ground" — as if that was a possibility rather than a reality — while he called upon future United States administrations to wield "both carrots and sticks as incentives" to extract concessions from the Palestinians. Such was the conventional wisdom on Israeli-Palestinian peacemaking by those who still believed that negotiations were an authentic method to resolve a conflict mired in mendacity and stymied by stratagems without end. Meanwhile, Christopher Barder came to the conclusion in 2001, that Oslo created a Palestinian terrorist entity whose significance was that a future Palestinian state would be fatal to Israel's existence. Here was a sober reckoning with the faulty equation of "territories for peace" because, in truth, the Oslo process churned up the diabolical potion of "land for war."

PART THREE
Conclusions

Israel's historic call for direct negotiations was traditionally interpreted through Arab cultural inversion as a Zionist ploy for Arab capitulation. To sit with the Israelis in political discourse was to virtually recognize the Jewish state, which since 1948 the Arabs refused to do. What was for the Israelis a mechanism for dialogue signified for the Arabs submission to the Jewish national movement in the modern Middle East.

But when the Arabs finally agreed to sit down in a negotiating ambiance, as at Camp David in 1978, Madrid in 1991, Oslo in 1993, and Sharm e-Sheikh in 1999, this did not constitute a compelling concession to the legitimate right of a Jewish state's existence. Rather, the question of negotiating had been redefined from being a matter of principle to a matter of pragmatism, in order to extract concrete land resources from Israel. Inasmuch as agreements concluded from such negotiation arenas were violated by the Arabs, this rendered more than doubtful if in fact negotiations were the venue for conflict resolution at all.

An alternative path to ending the Arab-Israeli conflict, or containing its more major levels and forms of violence, was available for consideration. Israel's Six Day War victory offered borders with strategic depth to buttress a doctrine of deterrence. Alongside the Suez Canal, astride the Jordan River, and atop the Golan Heights, the Israeli army would be a permanent threat to Cairo, Amman, and Damascus, respectively; risking war with Israel could wreak havoc on vulnerable Arab countries. Therefore, a strategic environment dominated by an Israeli regional power could induce Arab accommodation which Israeli territorial puniness would never evoke.

It is interesting to note in regard to these thoughts that Israel's quietest border was in fact with Syria: without a peace treaty, without recognition of Israel — and without Israeli withdrawal from the Golan. The Syrians preserved the Disengagement Agreement from 1974 without the textual accoutrements of normalization which, in any case we can assume, Syria would never have observed. In this way, Israel paid less but received more by non-negotiations with an Arab adversary.

We have hereby uncovered an allusion to the riddle behind Arab-Israeli co-existence with a possibility for a modicum of peace. Israel's requests and overtures for peace do not elicit a like Arab desire. The Muslim culture code is contemptuous of generosity or goodwill offered by a non-Muslim protagonist. A view from the *North China Herald* in 1867, at another place and in another time, conveys the correct categories of inter-cultural communication: "If politeness and ceremony be observed toward the Mohammedans, they imagine they are feared and become arrogant; but in showing severity and rudeness, they are impressed with fear and respect, and they are supple and manageable."

The belief that direct negotiations serve Israel well is further exposed as erroneous in considering Israelis' awkwardness in the diplomatic arena. We recall Yitzhak Rabin's uncomfortable handshake with Yassir Arafat in Washington in 1993 at the Oslo Agreement signing, and Ehud Barak's absurd jostling with Arafat at Camp David in 2000. Here were graceless body movements symbolic of misconstrued political behavior. Of substantive importance in the diplomatic theater of conflict resolution was the "ganging-up on Israel" scenario, characteristic of Carter cornering Menachem Begin at Camp David in 1978.

Coming into political contact with the nations of the world has been an opportunity, but a tortuous one, for the Jewish people in modern times. Betrayed by the British, abandoned by the United Nations, and embargoed by the United States, depicts the momentous period — full of grandeur and danger — accompanying Israel's founding in 1947 through to 1949. Since the 1967 war, the international community has sought to deny Israel the territorial fruits from a just war, while promoting the Palestine Liberation Organization as a legitimate national movement at Israel's expense. The Israelis, adept in war and military-related technologies, are more than somewhat out of their element at the tables of negotiations and in the halls of diplomacy. These are almost always unpleasant occasions, where Israel is snubbed, or bends in sycophancy, yet often straining laboriously to explain its situation and policy. Notorious was Kissinger's sneering attitude toward the Israeli troika of Rabin, Peres, and Allon, in the mid-70s. He did, after all, sense that negotiations aroused the sensation of a political guillotine being lowered on the confounded Israelis.

Panting for peace is not the correct emotional pose by which Israel can hope to arouse a serious Arab attitude of reconciliation and rapprochement. To avoid talk of peace and negotiations would highlight Israel's political maturity and national honor, by communicating that the core of the Zionist return is guided not by accommodation with the Arabs but self-fulfillment as a Jewish restoration in the ancient homeland.

This is nonetheless not to suggest that Israel refrain from all contact or dialogue with the Arab world. Relations should be promoted at all levels and in every feasible domain, commercial or otherwise, for the purpose of mutual advantage and acquiring familiarity with the various peoples in the region. Self-ostracism born of pique and policy is not a dignified approach, but nor is one that succumbs to Arab political ranting and accusations, deviousness and false pretences. While Israel should refuse signing any written agreements, Israelis should initiate any possible ties with the other side. Participating in the matrix of life in the Middle East, with a broad humanizing sweep of social openness, will reflect well on Israel's cultural acclimatization and political adaptation to the Oriental terrain of which it is an honorable part.

The Arab world does not want peace with Israel, rather a Middle East without Israel. However, if through peace Israel can be eradicated from the Middle East, then peace becomes an attractive and cunning opportunity. Negotiations become in this case a tried-and-tested method to restrict Israel's size and wither its national will, demoralize its people, and divide its political elites.

In conclusion, the path to peace does not travel through negotiating with the Arabs, but in refusing to negotiate with those who tempt Israel into concessions and sign agreements that become empty promises. While the Arabs are willing to sign accords, they do so while sharpening their swords and amassing weaponry for their next military adventure — if and when it comes. Arab strength is in dissecting the psychology of the enemy and not only in warring against the enemy. Broadcasting threats, planting traps, using political double-talk, while repeating their commitment to peace and negotiations is how the Arabs relentlessly hound their enemy and blame him for the failure of diplomacy. Consider Arafat the master liar, Sadat the expert of stratagems, and Hafez el-Asad the scheming tactician. At every meeting with the Arabs, Israelis believe that a political breakthrough is imminent. Israel's demeaning self-degradation is limitless, never-ending.

It clearly appeared incomprehensible to the Israelis that the Palestinians would be willing to pursue the war for an unlimited period of time. After all, since the intifada had erupted in October 2000, thousands of Palestinians had been killed by Israeli forces, thousands were detained by the Israeli army, and the Palestinian economy was in shambles. But a hundred years had passed since the beginning of this Jewish-Arab standoff, and the Palestinians showed no true sign of contrition or guilt, fatigue or peace-lovingness. This people is bound by bonds of tribal solidarity, and through its traditional culture considers death, like murder, as the acceptable and necessary price to pay for liberating all of Palestine from the Jews. Facing this reality, Israel should do nothing less than engage in expelling or eliminating the enemy from the country. Palestinians, ever arrogating the right to interfere in other countries and destabilizing and undermining them from within, were in fact expelled from Jordan in 1970 and Lebanon in 1982. Menaced and murdered by Palestinians who reject the Jewish state's right to exist, Israel could learn a lesson from the experience of her near-neighbors.

When Israel will finally reject negotiations with the Arabs, they will be denied the acrobatics of diplomacy so vital to them, and employed with such dext   Disarmed of their diplomatic machinations, the Arabs will then be exposed as politically unreliable. All of the agreements, understandings, and initiatives will be thrown to the wind. They will then realize they can no longer squeeze concessions from Israel under the impression of making peace. Just as the Arabs were forced to a certain recognition that they have come to a military dead end with Israel, so too will they be forced to recognize they have come to a political dead end in confronting Israel. Then a practical mode of peace between Israel and the Arabs will be feasible, but Israel will wisely refrain from putting that arrangement into writing. It would be careless to block the ray of light emerging from behind the shadows of darkness, as a new era of hope arises in the troubled Middle East.

This speech was first published as a policy paper by the Ariel Center of Policy Research, 2002, and appears here by the courtesy of the ACPR publishers.

ARIEH ZARITSKY, a professor at Ben-Gurion University of the Negev, was born in 1942 and raised as a Social Zionist, remaining so despite the fast leftward, anti-Zionist shift of the official movement he had belonged to. Since the Oslo process, he is active in public affairs, doing his best to reverse the suicidal course of events inflicted on us by the extreme Jewish left, aided by our worst enemies. Among other activities, he was an executive member of an organization called Professors for a Strong Israel from 1993–2001, and is the editor/moderator of EISH-L (Eretz ISrael SHelanu) e-mail list, with over 1,100 contacts worldwide.

Academia: Researching Truth or Breeding Hatred?

by Arieh Zaritsky

My first serious encounter abroad was soon after the Six Days War, when Israel was admired all around the world as a winning power. Those of us who are old enough still remember how people covered one eye to demonstrate sympathy with the heroic Israeli fighters symbolized by General Moshe Dayan, whether they had a common language with us or not.

What has happened since then, that contempt of Europeans toward Israel, Israelis, and Jews tops a new peak that is reminiscent of the black days of the 1930s? Let me try to analyze some of the causes of this dramatic change in such a short time; *at least one major reason is self-inflicted.*

Universities are sites of higher learning and research institutions meant to preserve and progress civilization. On the one hand, "truth" is a most important value and asset needed to advance knowledge; on the other, advancing knowledge requires preservation of previous culture. Europe's culture is soaked with Christianity's hatred toward Jews; haven't *we all* killed their trinity? This attribute is so deep-rooted in their history, literature, economy, psychology, and other aspects of life, that one does not grasp use of anti-Semitic expressions *as such*. It is the task of humanity and social sciences faculties to investigate these aspects in an attempt to expose them, thus influencing the communities that they are supposed to educate to *abandon evil!*

The 50 years following WWII were a window of opportunity due to the Holocaust that annihilated a third of the Jewish world population. According to the traditional Christian culture, we fulfilled the Jewish role to suffer but remain alive. Another tradition of theirs is to express sympathy with the underdogs, the role of which we certainly played during that "window" period. Thus, a sort of "dual cognitive dissonance" has developed among Europeans: they pitied the suffering Jews while not understanding our heroism, and admired us as winners after 1967, while hating Jews as killers of their God.

This dual discord was resolved, much to their relief, by the events that fruited and coincided in the 1990s: 50 years elapsed and the WWII generation, memories, and remorse faded away, Jews are not suffering any more, hence don't need sympathy. Moreover, we are despised as the apparent losers while hated for inflicting suffering to others. Don't we behave like them during WWII? Just as we used Christian kids' blood for Matza, we do now with Moslems. Their shame and guilt feelings were thus replaced by blaming us for supposedly similar evil. Here is a combination that can perhaps explain the marked change. Back to the black days of "bloodthirsty, God-killer Jews"!

This combination became lethal, however, with the so-called "Oslo Peace Process," and we are now consuming the "fruits of Oslo" stemming from the home-made deadly premise that Israel occupied in 1967 territories that belong to the so-called "Palestinian" nation. Everyone can judge the complete lack of truth in this premise. University investigators and teachers should have been the first to expose the lie. *They did not!* They rather *prostituted* their professions, be it history, ethics, archeology, geography, literature, logics, etc.

Unfortunately, we cannot simply criticize the faculty in the rest of the world: they did not themselves invent the newly made nation or emphasize the bad fortune of the poor Arabs under so-called "Jewish occupation" — they could simply cite some of their Israeli colleagues. It is with total amazement that we encounter a new breed of Israeli so-called "vanguard" that joins forces with the worst enemies of the Jewish nation, distorting the facts and blaming us for all maladies of the Moslem world, violence, hatred, illiteracy, xenophobia, and persecution of others.

Can we understand, for example, a yarmulke-wearing, "Peace Now" Israeli professor in politics, David Newman, who compares [in the *Jerusalem*

Post, 2002] the Jewish mothers' responsibility in exposing their kids to dangers by living peacefully in the "occupied territories" to that of Arab mothers who send theirs to become homicide bombers?

Can we imagine that the head of David Yellin Teachers College in Jerusalem, Dr. Itai Zimran, allowed Arab students there to observe a minute's silence in memory of the Palestinian *shaheeds* — martyrs for the cause — on Holocaust Memorial Day? Isn't this another way to breed hatred?

A typical example of hate-breeding is Ph.D.-less professor, the famous author Amos Oz, whose stories are translated into dozens of languages. He described the settlers and Gush Emmunim as "murderers, gangsters, sadists, pogromists." (*In the Name of Life and Peace*, published in Yedi'ot Acharonot, June 8, 1989.) Note this amazing paragraph by Amos Oz about the "Gush Emunim, an Orthodox Jewish Movement supporting the settlement:

> A fanatic cult, impervious and cruel, a bunch of armed gangsters, criminals against the humanity, sadists, pogromists and assassins that emerged out of a dark corner of Judaism . . . out of the cellars of bestiality and filth . . . in order to impose a blood-thirsty and lunatic ritual.

Some years later, the same "enlightened" professor claimed that he "would personally like to see Ariel Sharon and Yassir Arafat burning together in hell." (Published in *Ma'ariv*, August 11, 2002.) Then he is cheeky to tell us that (cited from his lecture "The Anatomy of Fanaticism," delivered at the 33rd Annual Ben-Gurion University's Board of Government Meeting, 2003) "the goal of all fanatics is conformity. They are not interested in transforming themselves; they are interested in transforming others — and placing them all in the same ideal world."

Doesn't he turn, again, the truth upside-down?

This process culminated recently in several senior faculty members at Israeli universities who signed the anti-Israel divestment petition at Harvard University. Worse still, more and other such hate-breeders have set off a petition to boycott the Israeli academia. Have we ever heard of such a mental disease, of people who boycott themselves? Why do they remain among the boycotted academia? On the other hand, have we ever heard of an organization who continues to feed those who boycott it?

Don't we recognize *hatred breeding* rather than *truth seeking* in the fortress of civilization?

The examples presented here are just the tip of the iceberg of what happens among Israeli academicians. Can we ease ourselves and blame Gentiles for hating us while we are breeding auto-anti-Semitism at home?

DR. DAVID BUKAY teaches in the Political Science Department at the University of Haifa. Among his fields of specialization, Dr. Bukay concentrates on Arab-Islamic political culture as a key source to understanding the Middle East and Arab politics, publishing a book on the subject in June 2003. In addition, he focuses on Islamic fundamentalism within the framework of international terrorism emphasizing bin-Laden and the New Islamic Fundamentalists. His book on Arafat titled *The Politics of the Mask* is scheduled to be published in the near future. Dr. Bukay is currently exploring the symbiosis between international terrorism and the media, and working on a new book titled *Jihad and Da'wah: Homicide Bombers against the Free World.*

Cultural Fallacies in Understanding Islamic Fanaticism and Palestinian Radicalism

by David Bukay

On September 11, 2001, the *New York Times* published an article by its senior commentator, Thomas Friedman, stationed in Israel, in which he described the fears of terror there. At about that time, the attack on the Twin Towers and the Pentagon took place. Two days later, Friedman wrote another article, stating that the world is facing a "Third World War."

Indeed, the world is witnessing a new kind of world war. But it did not start in September 2001. Its marks were clear years ago, but the United States, under the Clinton administration, did not want to sober up that the aggressiveness of the Islamic fanaticism is an existentially lethal phenomenon. The reason for this is mainly psychological: we do not want to look into the threatening reality. Rather, we prefer to live in a wishful-thinking world. The West was busy with what Francis Fukuyama has called "the end of history" and "the end of ideology," which means the march of victory of the West over communism politically, and over social-ism economically. The Islamic fundamentalism was washed away from memory and sight.

In July 1993, Prof. Samuel Huntington wrote his insightful article about the clash of civilizations, in which he showed very keenly that Is-lam is in total confrontation with all other civilizations. In his book from 1996, he wrote that the "borders of Arabia are borders of blood." For that, Huntington was condemned as a racist and anti-Islam. But was he? Or perhaps he forced us to look at something very deep, which we wanted very much to ignore? Was he racist, or were we all negligent, irresponsible hedonists?

Let's begin with the definition of the phenomenon. The most popular word is "fundamentalism." Yet, this word comes from the heart of the Christian religion. It means faith that goes by the word of the Bible. It does not mean murdering and butchering human beings; it does not mean practicing inhumane acts of terrorism; it does not mean trying to demol-ish other civilizations.

In Judaism and Christianity, one of the main ideas is that man was created in the image of God. So, you cannot massacre him in a hope for salvation. Yet, this is totally different in Islam. According to it, Islam was born with the idea that it should rule the world. Allah sent Muhammad with the true and complete religion, and this is the reason why Islamic religious leaders are almost in one voice: they abhor the Western way of life, and they wish to liquidate it.

The Middle East has the dubious honor of being the main location of states that support and sponsor international terrorism — in conformity with the American administration definition: five out of the seven states are Arab and Muslim: Iran, Iraq, Syria, Libya, and Sudan. Yet, an updated list would include four others: Saudi-Arabia, Afghanistan, Somalia, and the Palestinian Authority. Saudi-Arabia is the most important of all. It is the crucial factor in international terrorism, by sponsoring and financing Islamic terrorist groups all over the world: from the Balkans to Chechnya, from the Philippines to America, and of course the many Palestinian ter-rorist organizations.

Moreover, 22 of the 41 terrorist organizations on the terrorism list are Arab and Islamic from the Middle East. And this does not include yet the many Palestinian terrorist organizations, under the support and auspices of the Palestinian Authority, which is the main source of de-stabilization in the Middle East, and at the same time is a pure terrorist entity, as much as Hizbullah and al-Qaeda, and is the main location of executing total terrorism.

Terrorism is the meanest and most despised kind of warfare in the history of mankind. Yet, don't be misled. It is only a method. Brutal and inhumane, it is nonetheless a method. Our real enemy is Islamic fanaticism: this is totally different culture, from our Western political culture. It is merciless, cruel, and the embodiment of evil, in the name of Allah.

Indeed, the religious element is the dominant and most important one. Civilizations, wrote Prof. Samuel Huntington are observed by history, language, culture, tradition, and above all — religion. Out of deep ancient fear of retreating to the religious wars of the Medieval World, Western world leaders, policy-makers, especially intellectuals, refuse to define the clash of civilizations between Islam and the Free World as a total religious conflict. Yet, Bin-Laden, al-Qaeda, and all fanatic Islamic groups purposely use the word Crusaders when relating to the West. For them it is a holy war, of which religion is the essence of their struggle. This is why the Crusaders Wars are exactly the symbol, and Salah al-Din al-Ayyubi, who had driven them out, is the model.

Indeed, it is culture that matters. The Islamists start their politics of hatred and *jihadi* ideology from infancy. The children learn to hate before everything, even without knowing why: at home, in mosques, in *madrasses*, and in summer camps. They hate Jews and Americans, because they are what they are, and not because they know anything about American or Israeli foreign policy. The hatred is in their drink and in the air they breathe, and this is the fuel that directs and motivates the massacres, lynches, and murders. Above all, they are fully convinced that these are the demands of their religion.

He who tries to understand this cultural phenomenon is perplexed by the fact that the mosques are precisely the place of recruitment of suicide bombers, and the place of destination; that from the mosques come the call to use violence and cruelty against the enemies of Islam, which is the whole world; and that the mosques are the main place of socialization and indoctrination to terrorism. This fact reveals the deep gap in comparison to the Jewish synagogue and the Christian church, which preach love and compassion.

He who wishes to comprehend Islamic aggressiveness, fanaticism, and murderous acts, needs to listen to what they cry out enthusiastically with their eyes burning with hatred when they murder, butcher, and slaughter innocent people. They cry out *allahu-akbar*, which means Allah is the greatest. They cry for the sake of Allah when they kill, and they shout in the name of Allah when they murder. They are practicing any kind of cruelty and evil for the sake of religion. They do no not separate between their atrocious activities and their religion. From their vantage, their religion triumphs, because the Muslims love death, while their enemy loves life. Yet, not only are the Muslims willing to die, they have the passion to kill.

The argument that we are seeking to make is that there exists a wide gap between Western political culture and the Arab-Islamic political culture. These gaps are the basis for fallacies of thinking and distortion of perceptions that have culminated in national disasters.

We would like to elaborate two cultural factors: the first, "the mirror image," denotes the phenomenon where you look at your adversary and you see his conceptions and images as fitting yours. However, this is a profound fallacy, since what you see is your own reflection in the mirror. This is the most well-known march of folly of the West, and it is exemplified, unfortunately, in many ways in our day-to-day life.

One example stands clear: the Israeli wise men of Oslo view Arafat and the PLO leaders as wishing to reach peace accords as much as the Israelis, and imagine that Arafat and the PLO leaders define the peace terms as much as the Israelis. Unfortunately, the Israeli wise men of Oslo do not want to face that the Palestinians are totally different culturally — concerning the will, the definitions, and the terms of which to conclude peace, and that the Palestinian authority works relentlessly to demolish Israel in accordance with the "phased strategy."

The second factor is the politically correct approach, which defines direct speech as expressing exaggerated and one-sided positions. Yet the problem is obvious: if you adopt the politically correct approach to the political level, you lose the ability to call a spade a spade, and you cannot correctly understand the severe situation and cope with it.

One example may clarify our view. When the accusation is made that the Palestinian national movement is a Fascist group that sanctifies blood and death, that it is a Lynch society that sanctifies the suicide-bombers, the *shuhadaa*, the reaction is that it is an exaggerated and extreme allegation. But is it? The reality is that you will not find Palestinians that deny, let alone that act against, the horrible activities of the suicide bombers.

In Western political culture, it is neither perceived nor understood that the phenomenon of homicide bombers is Islamic in nature, that it is culturally deep-rooted in the hearts: from Pakistan to Chechnya, from Afghanistan to Lebanon, from the Balkans to the Palestinians. It is a social norm of behavior, a cultural reflection of society that sanctifies it as the most exalted form in the struggle against infidels, and it indicates, as they declare publicly, a "mentally healthy society."

Still, Western political culture refuses to comprehend that this is a much wider and deeper phenomenon than what we would like to believe.

This is not a matter of a few fanatics, and it is not a problem of a minority of extremists — it is supported with much enthusiasm and praised by the majority of Arabs and Muslims all around the world.

These cultural fallacies — the mirror image, and the politically correct approach — are exacerbated by the globalization era, which considers a unified political world, and imagines that if we all wear the same fashionable clothes, and we all speak English, then we all are the same culturally, and that our activities are aimed at the same political targets, and we all strive for the same political solutions, and we all have the same good intensions to end conflicts.

Yet, this is totally mistaken. We are not the same culturally, and we are not aimed at the same political targets and solutions. The situation in Iraq reveals the phenomenon of the deep cultural gaps, which is not understood in the West. While the United States tries so hard to bring democratization to the Iraqi people, all they want is Islamic rule. Yet, Islam and democracy are totally incompatible, and are mutually inconclusive. The same applies to modernity, which is perceived as a threat to Islamic civilization. Its permissiveness and materialism are disastrous, since it has placed man and the rule of reason at the center, instead of total submission and devotion to Allah.

Judeo-Christian culture internalizes the guilt. The Jewish version is "we have sinned, we have transgressed, we have committed crime," and all the time seek the moral stock-taking. The Christian version is "mea culpa." Western political culture argues that one side cannot be completely right while the other is completely wrong. It tries to investigate the inner soul, to understand the other side, and asks what is our responsibility?

In contrast, Arab Islamic political culture externalizes the guilt: Do I have a problem? You are guilty! The Arab-Muslims have no guilt remorse toward the outsiders; certainly not to share the guilt with them. They don't feel any shame toward the infidels. They don't blame themselves. They are always right.

One of the most well-known Western cultural fallacies is the view that education and prosperous economy promote democratization and prevent terrorism. Yet it is difficult to internalize that all 57 states that are defined Arab and Islamic are authoritarian regimes and their leaders are patrimonial. There is no democracy, no political liberalism, no civil rights, and no citizenship possessed by a sovereign "people."

The distorted perceptions in Western political culture claim that terrorism derives from economic distress and social despair. Removing poverty, hunger, and misery, and providing education, will lead to economic prosperity that will put an end to terrorism.

This is exactly the "mirror image" which reflects Western reality. Misery and poverty lead to crime, but never to terrorism. A fanatic ideology and religious zealotry are the causes and motivations for terrorism. The famous researcher De Tocqueville, in his books on French and American revolutions, proved that violence of political revolutions breaks out precisely when economic improvement arrives. When you are hungry, you have no time to fight for values.

The Palestinian suicide bombers are the proof. From September 2000 until May 2003, 197 suicide bombers were sent on suicide actions, among them 35 women. Of all the 115 successful murders, 65 percent had university education, and 50 percent came from al-Najah University. They were not hungry or miserable. They were in total repulsion of Jews and Zionism, and motivated by dehumanization of Israeli existence.

The Palestinian uprisings in 1936–1939, in 1987, and in 2000, were erupted precisely when the economy was prosperous, and the standard of living of the inhabitants was very good proportionally. If you compare the Palestinian economic and social situation to that in most Arab states, it is much higher and better. The year 2000 was the best in the Palestinian economic history. Yet, under these circumstances Arafat had moved on with his total inhuman terrorism.

The leaders of Islamic fundamentalist terrorist groups are members of the middle class and upper class. They have university education and many, with doctoral degrees, are physicians and engineers. They never declared that the reasons for their activity were poverty or ignorance. They speak of Western crusaderism, which they want to expel, and of Israeli aggression which they aspire to destroy. They have no programs for social progress, economic well being, improving health, or broadening education to the masses.

The 19 murderers in the September 11 terrorist attack lived in the West, in economic well being, and had higher education. They were not poor or wretched. The leadership of al-Qaeda prove this reality clearly. Bin-Laden is a multi-millionaire with an MA degree in public administration from the University of Jeddah. His deputy, Ayman al-Zawahiri, is a surgical physician, from the upper class in Egypt. The same applies to other leaders. What motivated them is a profound hatred for all that Western culture stands for.

This is the reason why it is totally mistaken and useless to fix a profile of the suicide bomber. Everyone can potentially be a suicide bomber: women, the elderly, and children. Even a peaceful Muslim person, born and living in the West, if required, will perform atrocious suicide acts in the name of Allah.

Western political culture needs to internalize how a peaceful Muslim community, even in the West, becomes politically fanatic and violent. All that is needed are three ingredients: a central active mosque among the Islamic community, the preaching of an influential charismatic religious leader, and monetary activity and religious volunteering for the Islamic case *(da`wah)* — and the community is stirred up with extremism and pathos.

Our suggested strategy of fighting Islamic fundamentalism and Palestinian terrorism is based on the biblical outlook: "Noah had built the ark before the deluge." That is, it is necessary to prepare and get ready before the crisis begins. The second conception is the approach of Jewish sages: "Think first before you act." This means planning and readiness as a basis for successfully coping with problems. The third conception is the Jewish approach in the *Mishnah*, which was adopted by all nations: "He who comes to kill you — kill him beforehand," which means you should act to eliminate your enemies before they execute their targets.

We need to internalize that fighting terrorism is a must. The terrorists have no basic human morality and no human values. They will not stop their atrocious deeds; they will not stop being terrorists. They are not soldiers, they are not freedom-fighters, and they do not deserve to be protected by the laws of nations. They should be eliminated. They deserve to be liquidated without hesitations, without concessions, and without provisions.

There are laws of war between states and nations, but Islamic and Palestinian terrorism, by its own definition and deeds, violates any basic human law and human morality. Therefore, fighting them can succeed only when it is executed by a strategy of initiation and not by a policy of retaliation. Moreover, negotiations, mediation, and appeasement are not only futile and useless, but encourage these deadly terrorists to continue with their evils deeds which threaten modern society.

Leaders and policy-makers in the West refuse to internalize what they clearly perceive: That the Islamic fundamentalism is a world-wide strategic threat, and that the battlefield we are facing is horrible. Any scenario is possible, even the most imaginative and the most unbelievable: biological, chemical, and atomic warfare is potentially at the hands of a few fanatics, which are determined to use it.

Leaders and policy-makers in the West refuse to comprehend that the struggle is between two polar cultural concepts: a society that aspires to modernity, liberalism, and human rights, against a society of religious extremism, totalitarianism of thought, and tribal values.

Until it is understood that this struggle is the war between the Son of Light and the sons of darkness, that they represent the invasion of the

Huns in order to destroy modern culture — the world will continue to face an existential ever-growing threat.

Leaders and policy-makers in the West must learn that the use of military power against these brutal and vicious Islamic and Palestinian terrorists is crucial. Western political culture is characterized by complacency and serenity. It tends to ignore threats and is oblivious of hazards. It wakes up only after disasters are here. But, if we will not sober up, if we will not fight for our modern democratic society by a strategy of initiation, with the cooperation of the free world — they will win, by bringing their past into the future of our humanity.

DR. AHARON YAFFE is currently senior researcher for the war against terror in the Interdisciplinary School of Hertzelia. He achieved his doctorate based on his work concerning American foreign policy in the Middle East, and has published numerous articles on the subjects of religious fundamentalist terror and national security which are respected both in Israel and worldwide.

Some Ways to Combat the Suicide Bombers' Terror

by Aharon Yaffe

One of the unpredicted furious surprises we all faced during the last Intifada is the intensive use of the suicide bomber's weapon. This weapon was soon turned from being a tactical weapon to a powerful operative weapon — one that changed the whole face of the military campaign including a painful damage to the national morale. The suicide bomber phenomenon accelerated during February–April 2002 to such a degree that it crippled the Israeli national economy and society's order. Some areas seriously suffered, such as tourism, the restaurant business, and retail commerce. This crisis brought the Israeli economy (coupled with the world economy crisis) to a grave state.

Although it was well known that suicide terror existed in some other cultures, such as the Tamils in Sri-Lanka, and the Chechnyans in Russia, the continuity of this phenomenon is very worrying. It is hard to decipher the motivation and characterize the type of person who is ready to volunteer for such a fatal mission. Such a disposition could give Israeli intelligence an instrument which could help identify a potential suicide bomber so he could be arrested just before he detonates.

Some of the religion researchers, including myself, pointed up religious fanaticism and devotion as the most persuasive factor in the suicide bomber's motivation. He will imagine what the Koran has promised in paradise for him and his family, as well. The terror organizations will need for their recruitment some selected zealous imams and preachers, together with some other envoys who use their religious authority for their mission. This phenomenon accumulated to its peak in spring 2002 during Netanya's Park Hotel bloody massacre. The bloody massacres' chain exposed a multitude of secular suicide bombers. The religious-oriented motivation was still left with not enough basis.

So, going back to the beginning of the research presumptions, trying to characterize the suicide bomber's personality and his motivation, what else can generate his action except religious feeling? Here we have to use some psychological and sociological skills and concepts. We also have to dig deep in the national concepts or in the social education indoctrination in order to look for the suicide bomber's motivation.

The Suicide Bomber as a Product of the Palestinian Society

Up until December 2003, we counted more than 300 suicide bombers. Only 8 of them were women. Another 20 or more women were captured before given their chance. The rate of accomplishing the mission among men was close to 50 percent. Investigations of their relatives, and specifically their recruiters, gave us a lot of valuable information.

One of the important missing parts is the fact that research couldn't characterize just one personal type of potential suicide bomber such as religious type, psychological type, or secular type. The researchers examined the Palestinian society in order to try and realize if there is one component that is responsible for assembling a potential suicide bomber. The research assumption was that a Palestinian bomber could be clearly characterized.

At this point, the researchers were successful. Palestinian society, since 2000, has been poverty-ridden. Such a condition provides a long line of suicide bombers backed by their family's support. We can realize, in that chaos, a clear activity of mobilizers responsible for enlisting some young, zealous, and fanatical volunteers, ready to do their horrible act. The mobilizers don't have to work hard. Young men and women even knock on their doors, and in some cases they have the luxury of selecting the most effective ones. Once the volunteer agrees, his family and his close society use a social pressure which they can't ignore and regret without jeopardizing their social status.

On the other hand, the volunteer's mobilization to this horrible duty will elevate him to a higher and better status. This elevation is very important to those new recruits who just moved on from the society's margins. Such elevation may secure them a place in paradise and a pardon for them and their families from sins they committed in the past. But still, the most important benefit is the economic retribution he will enjoy. According to some accounts, Saddam's Iraq regime paid the shahid's family over $15,000 in return for his horrible act.

A man will not volunteer to become a "human bomb," claims this thesis, without his "Mille" support. His expanded family's support may also save him some side duties, such as object selection and equipment collection.

So, most of the presumptions were wrong in trying to describe a suicide bomber profile. Instead, we have to draw a social profile of the Palestinian society, or at least parts of it.

We've heard certain claims that some Palestinian cities, such as Jenin or Nablus, are a birthplace for suicide bombers. I presume such a claim will almost be a pretension. Instead we will have to sharpen our observation and claim that the Jenin refugee camp or Nablus's Al-Najah University can serve as a good example for the suicide bomber's birthplace.

What Should We Now Do?

If we are correct, and the family "Mille" pressure is the main important component for the suicide bomber's motivation, we have to now look at the geo-social profile instead of the personal. We now have to try to change the social atmosphere in which the potential suicide bomber grows. Or, in other words, why kill the mosquitoes if we can dry up the swamp?

We know it is very hard to stop a single suicide bomber who has already started his bloody mission. Instead, it is possible to try and cure an infected society and lead her in a better direction. Looking for some examples? It is possible to maneuver this society's leadership to a *soulcha* (reconciliation), a compromise, or to *houdna* [cease-fire]. We can improve the society's economy situation. We can improve its education and offer it rapprochement alternatives. But if worst comes to worst, we can always hit the suicide bomber, his mobilizers, or his operational leadership, as well.

MOSHE SHARON is an internationally known expert who teaches Islamic history at the Hebrew University in Jerusalem. Sharon received his doctorate in Medieval Islamic History from the Hebrew University in Jerusalem. He has served as an advisor on Arab affairs to former Israeli Prime Minister Menachem Begin, as well as the Ministry of Defense. Professor Sharon is a former director of the World Zionist Organization branch in Johannesburg, South Africa.

The Agenda of Islam — A War between Civilizations

by Moshe Sharon

The war started a long time ago between two civilizations — between the civilization based on the Bible and the civilization based on the Koran. And this must be clear.

There is no fundamental Islam.

"Fundamentalism" is a word that came from the heart of the Christian religion. It means faith that goes by the word of the Bible. Fundamental Christianity, or going with the Bible, does not mean going around and killing people. There is no fundamental Islam. There is only Islam full stop. The question is how the Koran is interpreted.

All of a sudden, we see that the greatest interpreters of Islam are politicians in the Western world. They know better than all the speakers in the mosques, all those who deliver terrible sermons against anything that is either Christian or Jewish. These Western politicians know that there is good Islam and bad Islam. They know even how to differentiate between the two, except that none of them know how to read a word of Arabic.

The Language of Islam

You see, so much is covered by politically correct language that, in fact, the truth has been lost. For example, when we speak about Islam in the West, we try to use our own language and terminology. We speak about Islam in terms of democracy and fundamentalism, in terms of parliamentarianism and all kinds of terms, which we take from our own dictionary. One of my professors and one of the greatest Orientalists in the world says that doing this is like a cricket reporter describing a cricket game in baseball terms. We cannot use for one culture or civilization the language of another. For Islam, you've got to use the language of Islam.

Driving Principles of Islam

Let me explain the principles that are driving the religion of Islam. Of course, every Moslem has to acknowledge the fact that there is only one God.

But it's not enough to say that there is only one God. A Moslem has to acknowledge the fact that there is one God and Mohammed is His prophet. These are the fundamentals of the religion that without, one cannot be a Moslem.

Beyond that, Islam is a civilization. It is a religion that gave, first and foremost, a wide and unique legal system that engulfs the individual, society, and nations with rules of behavior. If you are Moslem, you have to behave according to the rules of Islam which are set down in the Koran and which are very different than the teachings of the Bible.

The Bible

Let me explain the difference.

The Bible is the creation of the spirit of a nation over a very, very long period, if we talk from the point of view of the scholar, and let me remain scholarly. But there is one thing that is important in the Bible. It leads to salvation. It leads to salvation in two ways.

In Judaism, it leads to national salvation — not just a nation that wants to have a state, but a nation that wants to serve God. That's the idea behind the Hebrew text of the Bible.

The New Testament that took the Hebrew Bible moves us toward personal salvation. So we have got these two kinds of salvation, which, from time to time, meet each other.

But the key word is salvation. Personal salvation means that each individual is looked after by God, himself, who leads a person through His word to salvation. This is the idea in the Bible, whether we are talking about the Old or the New Testament. All of the laws in the Bible, even to the most minute, are, in fact, directed toward this fact of salvation.

Secondly, there is another point in the Bible which is highly important. This is the idea that man was created in the image of God. Therefore, you don't just walk around and obliterate the image of God. Many people, of course, used biblical rules and turned them upside-down. History has seen a lot of massacres in the name of God and in the name of Jesus. But as religions, both Judaism and Christianity fundamentally speak about honoring the image of God and the hope of salvation. These are the two basic fundamentals.

The Essence of Islam

Now let's move to the essence of Islam. Islam was born with the idea that it should rule the world.

Let's look, then, at the difference between these three religions. Judaism speaks about national salvation — namely that at the end of the story, when the world becomes a better place, Israel will be in its own land, ruled by its own king, and serving God. Christianity speaks about the idea that every single person in the world can be saved from his sins, while Islam speaks about ruling the world. I can quote here in Arabic, but there is no point in quoting Arabic, so let me quote a verse in English. "Allah sent Mohammed with the true religion so that it should rule over all the religions."

The idea, then, is not that the whole world would become a Moslem world at this time, but that the whole world would be subdued under the rule of Islam.

When the Islamic empire was established in A.D. 634, within seven years — 640 — the core of the empire was created. The rules that were taken from the Koran and from the tradition that was ascribed to the prophet Mohammed were translated into a real legal system. Jews and Christians could live under Islam provided they paid poll tax and accepted Islamic superiority. Of course, they had to be humiliated. And Jews and Christians living under Islam are humiliated to this very day.

Mohammed Held That All the Biblical Prophets Were Moslems

Mohammed did accept the existence of all the biblical prophets before him. However, he also said that all these prophets were Moslems. Abraham was a Moslem. In fact, Adam himself was the first Moslem. Isaac and Jacob and David and Solomon and Moses and Jesus were all Moslems, and all of them had writings similar to the Koran. Therefore, world history is Islamic history because all the heroes of history were Moslems.

Furthermore, Moslems accept the fact that each of these prophets brought with him some kind of revelation. Moses brought the Taurat, which is the Torah, and Jesus brought the Ingeel, which is the Evangelion or Gospel — namely the New Testament.

The Bible vs. the Koran

Why then is the Bible not similar to the Koran? Mohammed explains that the Jews and Christians forged their books. Had they not been changed and forged, they would have been identical to the Koran. But because Christians and Jews do have some truth, Islam concedes that they cannot be completely destroyed by war [for now].

Nevertheless, the laws are very clear — Jews and Christians have no rights whatsoever to independent existence. They can live under Islamic rule, provided they keep to the rules that Islam promulgates for them.

Islamic Rule and Jihad

What happens if Jews and Christians don't want to live under the rules of Islam? Then Islam has to fight them and this fighting is called *jihad*. Jihad means war against those people who don't want to accept the Islamic superior rule. That's jihad. They may be Jews; they may be Christians; they may be polytheists. But since we don't have too many polytheists left, at least not in the Middle East, their war is against the Jews and Christians.

Recently, I received a pamphlet that was distributed in the world by Bin-Laden. He calls for jihad against America as the leader of the Christian world, not because America is the supporter of Israel, but because Americans are desecrating Arabia with their filthy feet. There are Americans in Arabia where no Christians should be. In this pamphlet there is not a single word about Israel. Only that Americans are desecrating the home of the prophet.

Two Houses

The Koran sees the world as divided into two — one part which has come under Islamic rule and one part which is supposed to come under Islamic rule in the future. There is a division of the world which is very clear. Every single person who starts studying Islam knows it. The world is described as Dar al-Islam (the house of Islam) — that's the place where Islam rules — and the other part which is called Dar al-Harb — the house of war. Not the "house of non-Muslims," but the "house of war." It is this house of war which has to be, at the end of time, conquered.

The world will continue to be in the house of war until it comes under Islamic rule.

This is the norm. Why? Because Allah says it's so in the Koran. God has sent Mohammed with the true religion in order that the truth will overcome all other religions.

Islamic Law

Within the Islamic vision of this world, there are rules that govern the lives of the Moslems themselves, and these rules are very strict. In fundamentals, there are no differences between schools of law.

However, there are four streams of factions within Islam with differences between them concerning the minutiae of the laws. All over the Islamic world, countries have favored one or another of these schools of laws.

The strictest school of law is called Hanbali, mainly coming out of Saudi Arabia. There are no games there, no playing around with the meanings of words. If the Koran speaks about war, then it's war.

There are various perspectives in Islam with different interpretations over the centuries. There were good people who were very enlightened in Islam who tried to understand things differently. They even brought traditions from the mouth of the prophet that women and children should not be killed in war. These more liberal streams do exist, but there is one thing that is very important for us to remember. The Hanbali school of law is extremely strict, and today this is the school that is behind most of the terrorist powers. Even if we talk about the existence of other schools of Islamic law, when we're talking about fighting against the Jews, or fighting against the Christian world led by America, it is the Hanbali school of law that is being followed.

Islam and Territory

This civilization created one very important, fundamental rule about territory. Any territory that comes under Islamic rule cannot be de-Islamized. Even if at one time or another, the [non-Moslem] enemy takes over the territory that was under Islamic rule, it is considered to be perpetually Islamic.

This is why whenever you hear about the Arab/Israeli conflict, you hear — territory, territory, territory. There are other aspects to the conflict, but territory is highly important.

The Christian civilization has not only been seen as a religious opponent, but as a dam stopping Islam from achieving its final goal for which it was created.

Islam was created to be the army of God, the army of Allah. Every single Moslem is a soldier in this army. Every single Moslem who dies in fighting for the spread of Islam is a *shaheed* (martyr) no matter how he dies, because — and this is very important — this is an eternal war between the two civilizations. It's not a war that stops. This war is there because it was created by Allah. Islam must be the ruler. This is a war that will not end.

Islam and Peace

Peace in Islam can exist only within the Islamic world; peace can only be between Moslem and Moslem.

With the non-Moslem world or non-Moslem opponents, there can be only one solution — a cease-fire until Moslems can gain more power. It is an eternal war until the end of days. Peace can only come if the Islamic side wins.

The two civilizations can only have periods of cease-fires. And this idea of cease-fire is based on a very important historical precedent, which, incidentally, Yassir Arafat referred to when he spoke in Johannesburg after he signed the Oslo agreement with Israel.

Let me remind you that the document speaks of peace — you wouldn't believe what you are reading! You would think that you were reading some science fiction piece. When you read it, you can't believe that this was signed by Israelis who are actually acquainted with Islamic policies and civilization.

A few weeks after the Oslo agreement was signed, Arafat went to Johannesburg, and in a mosque there he made a speech in which he apologized, saying, "Do you think I signed something with the Jews which is contrary to the rules of Islam?" (I have obtained a copy of Arafat's recorded speech so I heard it from his own mouth.) Arafat continued, "That's not so. I'm doing exactly what the prophet Mohammed did."

Whatever the prophet is supposed to have done becomes a precedent. What Arafat was saying was, "Remember the story of Hodaybiya." The prophet had made an agreement there with the tribe of Kuraish for ten years. But then he trained 10,000 soldiers and within two years marched on their city of Mecca. He, of course, found some kind of pretext.

Thus, in Islamic jurisdiction, it became a legal precedent which states that you are only allowed to make peace for a maximum of ten years.

Secondly, at the first instance that you are able, you must renew the jihad [thus breaking the "peace" agreement].

In Israel, it has taken over 50 years in this country for our people to understand that they cannot speak about [permanent] peace with Moslems.

It will take another 50 years for the Western world to understand that they have a state of war with the Islamic civilization that is virile and strong. This should be understood: when we talk about war and peace, we are not talking in Belgium, French, English, or German terms. We are talking about war and peace in Islamic terms.

Cease-fire as a Tactical Choice

What makes Islam accept cease-fire? Only one thing — when the enemy is too strong. It is a tactical choice.

Sometimes, he may have to agree to a cease-fire in the most humiliating conditions. It's allowed, because Mohammed accepted a cease-fire under humiliating conditions. That's what Arafat said to them in Johannesburg.

When Western policy-makers hear these things, they answer, "What are you talking about? You are in the Middle Ages. You don't understand the mechanisms of politics."

Which mechanisms of politics? There are no mechanisms of politics where power is. And I want to tell you one thing — we haven't seen the end of it, because the minute a radical Moslem power has atomic, chemical, or biological weapons, they will use them. I have no doubt about that.

Now, since we face war and we know that we cannot get more than an impermanent cease-fire, one has to ask himself, what is the major component of an Israeli/Arab cease-fire. It is that the Islamic side is weak and your side is strong. The relations between Israel and the Arab world in the last 50 years, since the establishment of our state, has been based only on this idea, the deterrent power.

Wherever You Have Islam, You Will Have War

The reason that we have what we have in Yugoslavia and other places is because Islam succeeded in entering these countries. Wherever you have Islam, you will have war. It grows out of the attitude of Islamic civilization.

Why are the poor people in the Philippines being killed? What's happening between Pakistan and India?

Islamic Infiltration

Furthermore, there is another fact that must be remembered. The Islamic world has not only the attitude of open war, but there's also war by infiltration.

One of the things to which the Western world is not paying enough attention is the tremendous growth of Islamic power in the Western world. What happened in America and the Twin Towers is not something that came from the outside. And if America doesn't wake up, one day the Americans will find themselves in a chemical war and most likely in an atomic war — inside the United States.

End of Days

It is highly important to understand how a civilization sees the end of days. In Christianity and in Judaism, we know exactly what is the vision of the end of days.

In Judaism, it is going to be as in Isaiah — peace between nations, not just one nation, but between all nations. People will not have any more need for weapons, and nature will be changed — a beautiful end of days and the kingdom of God on earth.

Christianity goes as far as Revelation to see a day that Satan himself is obliterated. There are no more powers of evil. That's the vision.

I'm speaking now as a historian. I try to understand how Islam sees the end of days. In the end of days, Islam sees a world that is totally Moslem, completely Moslem, under the rule of Islam. Complete and final victory.

Christians will not exist, because, according to many Islamic traditions, the Moslems who are in hell will have to be replaced by somebody and they'll be replaced by the Christians.

The Jews will no longer exist, because before the coming of the end of days, there is going to be a war against the Jews where all Jews should be killed. I'm quoting now from the heart of Islamic tradition, from the books that are read by every child in school. The Jews will all be killed. They'll be running away and they'll be hiding behind trees and rocks, and on that day Allah will give mouths to the rocks and trees and they will say, "Oh Moslem come here, there is a Jew behind me, kill him." Without this, the end of days cannot come. This is a fundamental of Islam.

Is There a Possibility to End This Dance of War?

The question which we in Israel are asking ourselves is what will happen to our country? Is there a possibility to end this dance of war?

The answer is, "No. Not in the foreseeable future." What we can do is reach a situation where for a few years we may have relative quiet.

But for Islam, the establishment of the state of Israel was a reverse of Islamic history. First, Islamic territory was taken away from Islam by Jews. You know by now that this can never be accepted, not even one meter. So everyone who thinks Tel Aviv is safe is making a grave mistake. Territory, which at one time was dominated by Islamic rule, now has become non-

Moslem. Non-Moslems are independent of Islamic rule; Jews have created their own independent state. It is anathema.

And (this is the worst) Israel, a non-Moslem state, is ruling over Moslems. It is unthinkable that non-Moslems should rule over Moslems.

I believe that Western civilization should hold together and support each other. Whether this will happen or not, I don't know. Israel finds itself on the front lines of this war. It needs the help of its sister civilization. It needs the help of America and Europe. It needs the help of the Christian world. One thing I am sure about, this help can be given by individual Christians who see this as the road to salvation.

This article was published in Nativ, *and appears here by the courtesy of the author and the Ariel Center of Policy Research publishers.*

DR. ATALIA BEN-MEIR is a researcher at the Ariel Center for Policy Research. She taught history and social sciences in Israel and lectured at Natal University, Durban. Her doctorate analyzed the evolution of the SA Jewish Board of Deputies' policy toward the National Party and apartheid. Dr. Ben-Meir has written extensively on the Israeli-Palestinian conflict, especially on the threat to the state of Israeli's integrity as a Jewish state. In this respect, she has written two Ariel Center for Policy Research papers on "The Palestinian Refugee Issue and the Demographic Aspect" and "The War Against Israel: Exploiting Democracy to Disenfranchise the Jewish Nation."

The War Against Israel:
Exploiting Democracy to
Disenfranchise the Jewish Nation

by Atalia Ben-Meir

For decades, Israeli leadership was convinced that Israeli-Arabs had undergone an Israelization process, characterized by intensified involvement with Israel and a diminishing Palestinian identity. Reality has upset their whole frame of reference. In the past decade, Israeli-Arab identification with Israel has undergone a steep decline, while their identification as Palestinians and the Palestinian Authority has soared. In tandem with this process, the demarcation between the realization of civil rights and the Palestinian national struggle has gradually blurred, manifesting in an agenda that imperils the continued existence of the state of Israel.

Another linchpin in Israeli-Arab policy is the concerted effort to abolish the Jewish-Zionist character of Israel and transform it into a "state of all its citizens," thus depriving Jews of their national rights, including the right for self-determination in a Jewish state. Concomitantly, they have conveyed their unequivocal demand to be recognized as a national minority with national rights, including autonomy. These demands create a zero sum game; capitulation would disenfranchise Jews and dismember Israel into a bi-national state.

The weapon of choice to achieve these goals is democracy. The strategy adopted and implemented by Israeli-Arabs is to demonize Israel as anti-democratic while they are the true democrats. Within the framework of this credo, support for terrorist organizations bent on slaughtering Jews is democratic; the advocacy of the overthrow of the Israeli government is subsumed under the exercise of free speech; dismembering Israel and disenfranchising Jews is the realization of the Palestinian's right for self-determination.

Standing at the forefront of the war against Israel's integrity are the Arab-Israeli members of Knesset. Abusing both Israel's democratic ethos and Israeli laws, they have alienated the Israeli-Arab population from Israel and from its Jewish population, aligning them with the Palestinian Authority and its insidious stratagem to destroy the state of Israel.

Clearly, the Arab-Palestinian conflict transcends territorial and equalization issues, but rather relates to the core existence of the state of Israel as a Jewish, Zionist, Western, and modern state in the heart of the Arab world.

Conclusions

To truly grasp the Israeli-Arab confrontation it must be perceived as a microcosm of a conflict that encapsulates issues that transcend Israel and have existential impact for the Western world. Analyzing the Israel-Arab conflict in isolation of its Islamic imperialistic underpinnings is to view the flow of events through tunnel vision. To ignore its ramifications for modern, democratic, Western and Eastern societies is to be grossly negligent.

Defining the Israeli-Palestinian conflict as a clash over borders is more than misleading; it is deceptive and dangerous as it leads to conclusions that not only do not resolve the conflict but also aggravate it and endanger the existence of the state of Israel. Trivializing the religious factors inherent in the Israeli-Palestinian conflict is an indication of ignorance and total absence of comprehension of what the real issues are surrounding the conflict. For Palestinians, the Israeli-Palestinian conflict is only the territorial aspect of an unbridgeable dichotomous relationship between Islam and Judaism. It is an existential battle that can never be resolved by territorial concessions but only by the destruction of the state of Israel.

From this perspective, the conflict raises issues that strike to the heart of democracy and the very existence of the state of Israel. Do Israeli-Arabs have the democratic right to support the goals and the strategies of the PLO? Does the inflammatory invective against Israel, its government, Jewish citizens, and the IDF constitute sedition, or merely the exercise of the right for free speech? Does support for terrorist organizations and for the murder of Jews constitute treason, or is it a democratic right? As things stand, Israeli-Arab MKs [Knesset members] assert that their support for the PLO terrorist regime and the devastating intifada unleashed upon Israel is democratic, while squashing their espousal of the PLO's goals is undemocratic. This paper argues that such a stance turns democracy on its head; rather than protecting human rights, it condones mass murder.

Israeli-Arab leadership couches their condemnation of Israel's policy in terms of oppression and a struggle for equality. However, in essence, the crux of the oppression imputed to the state of Israel is that its Jewish-Zionist character is undemocratic and discriminatory toward the Arab minority. Thus, underlying the Israeli-Arab categorical demand for equality is the aim to disenfranchise the Jewish population of Israel. By demanding the eradication of the Jewish character of Israel, Israeli-Arabs seek to abrogate the Jewish nation's right to self-determination in their own independent state. The culmination of all these processes would be the reversal of the Zionist movement's gains; Jews will once more be stateless, dependent, defenseless, and impotent, an easy target. Capitulation to these demands would create the conditions for the establishment of a Palestinian state from "sea to sea."

In sum, Israeli-Arab leadership, using and abusing democratic principles, is unrelentingly striving to achieve goals that jeopardize the very existence of the state of Israel.

Recommendations

Many of the problems examined in this policy paper are not only well known to the authorities, but they have the laws and the legal tools to deal effectively with phenomena that threaten the integrity of the state of Israel. The prevalence of infractions of the law in the Arab sector, and the proliferation of blatant anti-Israel activities are the direct result of the authorities' failure to enforce the law.

1. Israel as a Jewish-Zionist State

Israel's essence as a Jewish and Zionist state must be anchored in law. Any person, organization, or political party advocating the eradication of the Jewish and/or Zionist character of the state of Israel is to be declared illegal. Advocating the abolishment of Israel as a Jewish-Zionist state is to be deemed illegal and such groups or organizations shall be declared illegal.

Israel has the right to retain its identity, like any other state in the world. Jews have the democratic right for self-determination in their own state.

2. Incitement

It is recommended that all laws relating to incitement be enforced. It should be made clear that anti-Semitism is racism. Demonization of Jews, Judaism, and Israel is against the law, and the perpetrator will suffer the full weight of the law.

All laws relating to meetings with people and/or organizations that seek to destroy the state of Israel and/or endanger the existence of both the state and any of its citizens must be enforced. Leaders and members of all the various anti-Israel groups in the Palestinian Authority should not be allowed to enter Israel, let alone participate in anti-Israeli rallies.

Solidarity rallies with the enemies of Israel, who murder Israeli citizens and soldiers with impunity, must be outlawed and their organizers arrested. Support for the murder of Israelis and/or the destruction of Israel must be considered a crime and the perpetrator arrested and placed on trial. Statements in support of organizations that call for the murder of Israeli citizens and soldiers and/or call for the destruction of the state of Israel must be considered to be treasonous and the perpetrator arrested and put on trial, even if an elected official.

3. Governmental Monitoring and Control Over Political Movements and Groups That Threaten the Integrity of the State of Israel

A democratic government cannot tolerate the establishment of a "state within a state" over which it has no supervision or control. A democracy cannot abide groups that plot, or even aspire to, its destruction. It is the right and the obligation of a democracy to protect itself and its citizens. Arising from this, the authorities must monitor the activities of the Islamic movement, and any other political movement that endangers the state of Israel. The purpose of this is to ensure that they do not lead to aspirations of separation from the state of Israel, as well as to frustrate any attempts to create an affinity with groups or organizations that threaten the integrity of the state of Israel. Anti-Israel and anti-Jewish incitement is to be outlawed and the perpetrator placed on trial. Groups or organizations disseminating anti-Jewish or anti-Israel propaganda are to be deemed illegal.

This policy paper was published by the Ariel Center of Policy Research, 2002, and appears here by the courtesy of the ACPR publishers.

Rachel Ehrenfeld, Ph.D., is the director of the New York-based American Center for Democracy (ACD) (previously the Center for the Study of Corruption and the Rule of Law). She is an acknowledged expert on corruption, money laundering, transnational organized crime, international terrorism, drug trafficking, and substance abuse. She is the author of *Funding Evil; How Terrorism Is Financed — And How to Stop It.*

The United States v. Arafat: A Necessary Policy

by Rachel Ehrenfeld

If "failure is not an option" in the war on terror, and if we are determined to win this war "to make our kids and grandkids . . . and our nation safer," as Vice President Dick Cheney stated on "Face the Nation," then the United States should support Israel in her quest to remove Arafat. Now that President Bush has clearly declared that "Arafat failed as a leader," leaving him in place is dangerous and counterproductive to U.S. national-security interests, the war on terror, and the effort to stabilize the Middle East.

More than a year ago, the Bush administration called on the Palestinians to change their leadership. But now the United States has joined the U.N.'s warning to Israel not to remove Yassir Arafat. How does this correspond with President Bush's statement that "You can't negotiate with these [terrorist] people, you can't try to talk sense to these people. The only way to deal with them is to find them and bring them to justice"?

Yassir Arafat has been the terrorist prototype since the inception of the Palestinian Liberation Organization in the mid-1960s. Both he and the PLO served as a model and a precedent for other terrorist organizations. It is reasonable to assume that they inspired Osama Bin-Laden when he set out to create the infrastructure of al-Qaeda.

The PLO was the first and, until al-Qaeda established itself in Afghanistan, the only terrorist organization that had its own territory for a base of operation (first in Lebanon and later in the West Bank and Gaza). Even the use of "martyrdom" as a tool of terrorism was incorporated into the PLO agenda as early as 1978. And the PLO, like al-Qaeda later, enjoyed multi-state sponsorship.

Despite continuing terror attacks, the U.N. embraced the PLO in 1974 by granting it observer status. This legitimization — which was accompanied by financial backing — allowed the PLO not only to continue its terrorist and criminal activities with impunity, but also to fund a worldwide propaganda campaign, win great popularity, and increase its influence.

The PLO opened offices worldwide, obtained financial backing, and significantly increased its assets and income between 1974 and 1981. Two months after the Camp David agreement of September 1978, which ended the state of war between Egypt and Israel, ten Arab heads of state met in Baghdad and agreed to provide $3.5 billion annually to aid the PLO, and countries such as Syria, Lebanon, and Jordan; the money was meant to help fuel anti-Israel activities. Of a total of $250 million allocated annually to the PLO, $10 million was designated for the "families of the martyrs."

Like al-Qaeda, the PLO received financial and political support from many countries, not all in the Middle East. The money came from the Soviet Union and its satellites in Europe (until the collapse of the Soviet Union in 1991), Latin America, Africa, members of the Arab League, Third World countries, and the U.N.

In 1987, the United States finally declared the PLO a terrorist organization; a 1988 presidential waiver was issued that "permitted contact" with it. The PLO used this waiver to increase its influence, fundraising, and propaganda capabilities as well as their cooperation with other terrorist groups, international criminal organizations, drug cartels, and rogue states.

Nor did the PLO's transformation into the Palestinian Authority (PA) in 1993, as a result of the Oslo Accords, impede the organization's illegal activities. On the contrary, led by Arafat, it accelerated them. Now granted legitimacy by the entire world, the PA abused this status to expand its illegal activities and to rob the Palestinian people of their money and their lives.

For decades, the West turned not only a blind eye to the PLO's and PA's terror activities, fundraising endeavors, and hate propaganda, as they did with Osama Bin-Laden and al-Qaeda, but it continued to negotiate and fund them. Arafat even supported Saddam Hussein's invasion of Kuwait. The more concessions were made, the bolder their demands and their terror activities. The PLO/Arafat "martyrdom" strategy set the tone and became the leading weapon in their terror arsenal.

The Palestinian example did not escape al-Qaeda, Hezbollah, or Hamas as their new terror networks organized and strategized. Concessions and appeasement have only one interpretation for Middle East terrorists: weakness.

Arafat made his own roadmap clear in a June 6, 2001, interview on Radio Palestine: "War is a dream, peace is a nightmare," he said. Everything that Arafat did and continues to do proves that he meant what he said. Since September 2000, close to 900 Israelis and other — including Americans — have been killed by Palestinian terrorists and about 6,000 have been wounded. How many more dead Israelis and Americans will it take for the United States to understand that as long as Arafat and his henchmen control the West Bank and the Gaza Strip, he serves as inspiration to all other terrorists?

PART III

ANTI-ZIONISM: MORAL CANCER OF INTERNATIONAL POLITICS

REVEREND MALCOLM HEDDING was appointed the executive director of the International Christian Embassy Jerusalem (ICEJ) in November 2000. He has been an ordained minister of the Assemblies of God of South Africa for 25 years.

Anti-Semitism: The Basis
of Immorality

by Rev. Malcolm Hedding

Recently a university in England relieved Israel lecturers of their positions, or attempted to do so, only because they are Jews. In addition, the Red Cross still refuses to allow Magen David Adom to become a member of its organization, but the Red Crescent is and has been for years. We ask, therefore, the question: What drives this immoral position? The answer is anti-Semitism.

Anti-Semitism is the basis of immorality because, while it is many things, it is chiefly an expression of humankind's rebellion against God. The Jewish people remind the world of an ethical, moral requirement. In short, that the heart of humankind out of which springs all its attitudes and actions, is accountable and will be held accountable. The New Testament scholar Paul put it this way: "We know that whatever the law says, it says to those who are under the law, that every mouth may be stopped and all the world may become guilty before God" (Rom. 3:19).

In other words, destroy the Jew and you will destroy God. This is the power, not thinking, of anti-Semitism. Anti-Semitism, then, is evidence of a dark sinister reality that is called evil. This "thing" is more than an attitude or feeling. It is, in fact, perpetuated and injected into the human heart by a personality that the Bible calls Satan. When you look into the ovens of Auschwitz, you look at this personality! This is not to say "the devil made me do it." Rather, humankind, using its own moral judgments, decides to cooperate with evil.

Anti-Semitism is also a test. Genesis 12:1–3 declares that those who curse Israel will be cursed. Israel is the vehicle of moral light and redemption. To curse her is to curse the light; it is to work with powers of darkness. Every generation has to face up to this test. It is a human thing. It means being weighed in the balances, and surely the Book of Esther, that makes no reference to God, is a reminder of this test. This is not a small matter. Nations have fallen and have risen on the basis of this examination.

Note: It is true that Israel and the Jewish people have suffered because of their own disobedience to God, but there is a suffering in Israel's history, as we see mirrored in the Book of Esther, that is supernatural and demonic. This suffering found its fullest expression in the Holocaust. What conclusion do we draw from this? Mainly that all things Jewish or places Jewish, like the land of Israel and the great city of Jerusalem, will be dealt with by a prejudice that no other nation has to grapple with. Anti-Semitism births an immorality that is far more sinister than any other expression of this. It can therefore be considered the foundation of all immoral actions and attitudes.

The truth is, the wider world better wake up since this immoral evil first attacks Jews but it destroys nations. Jews have been attacked through the centuries, but nations have been totally removed from history and destroyed. The Nazis attacked the Jews for years before the Second World War but thereafter their anti-Semitic immorality consumed 50 million people.

Israel has been in the forefront of a contemporary struggle in this very same context. She has faced terrorism for years. A world afflicted with unholy prejudices constantly turned a blind eye and even legitimized it. Suicide bombers in any other part of the world are barbaric and evil, but in Israel they are considered "Freedom Fighters"!

However, all this is changing because this evil is now striking at the wider world and suddenly the moral response is that they are evil. Why the change? Because when it comes to Israel, an age-old hatred and prejudice afflicts the "collective mind." To be honest, I weep more for the world than for Israel because, in the end, Israel will "rise and shine" but the nations will fall into perpetual darkness (Isa. 60:1–3).

God will always judge His people; that is, His nation Israel, but He will not make an end of them. The nations, He declares, will come to a full end (Jer. 30:11).

ZALMAN SHOVAL has served two tenures as Israel's ambassador to the United States. During these periods he was a participant in many peace efforts between Israel and its neighbors, including Camp David (1978), the Madrid Conference (1991), and the Wye River Conference (1998), and was a member of the Israeli negotiating team with the Jordanians and Palestinians. Ambassador Shoval is a member of the board of trustees of the Dayan Center for Middle Eastern Studies and the Interdisciplinary Center in Herzylia. Among his many business achievements are the founding of the Bank of Jerusalem (1964) and INVENTECH venture capital fund.

Is It the Beginning of a New, More Frightening Chapter in History?

by Zalman Shoval

Over a century ago, Bismarck, the great German statesman, said, "We live in a wondrous time in which the strong is weak because of his moral scruples — and the weak grows strong because of his shameless-ness." The message is clear and it is appropriate — now more than ever before — and not only in the case of Israel.

The left — led by a self-anointed cultural elite in Europe, and partly in America — has become mired in anti-Americanism and anti-Semitism *disguised* as anti-Zionism or anti-Israelism. And many of our own self-styled intellectuals will always look for some attenuating circumstances where Palestinian terror is concerned, will always blame the Israeli govern-ment or the Israeli people as a whole, never the Palestinians. But, as I said, this is not exclusively an Israeli experience.

Gore Vidal, the American writer, in addition to never missing an op-portunity to attack Israel or the Jews, has opposed every American admin-istration after Kennedy — and, as someone has written, "never fails to find the keen ears of the European Liberal Left." Among his special "pearls" of hatred was comparing the "Bush-Cheney *Junta*" to Saddam Hussein! And one remembers the German minister who compared Bush to Hitler. Then there was the intellectual fraud and falsifier of history, including his own, Edward Said — no longer with us, alas — who duped many well-meaning people to believe that he was a man of peace and tolerance rather than what he really was, namely someone who wanted to destroy Israel.

Not to be outdone by anyone, there is the Anglo-Pakistani writer Tariq Ali, darling of the left, who in the British Guardian wrote about the brutal "re-colonization" of Iraq by the United States and its blood-shot British adjutant" — which may perhaps be deemed fairly mild for him, if one compares it to what he wrote two years ago in the *Washington Post*, namely "that though for most of its history Islam" had supposedly "enjoyed cordial relations with Judaism" — which, by the way, factually is wrong — the breach "appeared only in the mid-20th century with the imposition of a Jewish "settler-state," Israel, on and at the expense of the local Arab population. . . . The Palestinians were to be punished for a European Judeocide."

This is another twist and falsification of history — which, by the way, the former German Socialist Chancellor Helmut Schmidt was one of the first to perpetrate — namely that as a consequence of the Holocaust the world owed a debt not to the Jews, but to the Arabs, because of the creation of Israel. That Zionism had preceded the Holocaust, that though the Holocaust had deprived Zionism of most of its natural human reserves — the return of the Jewish people to its homeland and the re-establishment of its state was not *because* of the Holocaust but *despite* the Holocaust — is ignored by the re-writers of history. For the Arabs, by the way, this presents a certain dilemma: while they prefer to deny the Holocaust altogether — they also want to blame the Christian world for bringing it about — and for "planting this settler-state in their midst."

By the way, having mentioned the *Guardian* before, in one of its own editorials, that same paper wrote that though the world hadn't really behaved well during the Holocaust — "the establishment of the state of Israel may have been too high a price to pay for that. . . ."

Israel is perceived as the "cat's paw," as Ian Buruma in the *Financial Times* of September 13, 2003, put it, "of U.S. imperialism in the Middle East, and the colonial enemy of Palestinian nationalism." All this, of course, is a way for many Europeans to cleanse themselves of their own colonial guilt. The fact that Israel and the Zionist movement were in the very forefront of rising up against colonial rule after World War II is conveniently ignored by the left. And the writer adds, "The contemporary anti-Zionists of the left sound just like the crusty old Arabists of the old foreign office school" and one might add "foreign offices" in plural; "the fact that Jews can now safely be compared to Nazis is an added sop to European guilt about another horrible blot on their collective conscience." In Britain today you can have an apparently well-known writer of children's books — I repeat, children's books — a lady called Laird, writing an anti-Israel, pro-Palestinian book about "poor" Arafat in Ramallah — and get the BBC to devote a fairly lengthy program to it.

Zionism is not just a political movement, not only an ideology and an ideal — it is perhaps the most significant victory of the human spirit over the forces of evil that modern history has known. But in addition, it is also one of the few ideologies in modern times which has been by and large successful — surely against greater odds than most other ideologies or national movements. But could this not be the very reason for the envy-based hatred against Israel — just as the success of America is one of the reasons for the antagonism against it in many parts of the world, especially in Europe? And there is, of course, another factor, not always sufficiently recognized: the corrupt, nepotist, politically bankrupt regimes in most of the Arab world are scared to death that their own societies might be contaminated by the Israeli ideas of democracy, rule of law, women's rights, and all the rest.

America itself is not immune to self-hatred and/or Israel hatred either, though this is on a much smaller scale compared to Europe. But even in New York, though not yet fashionable, it's become permissible to stage anti-Israel plays or to make anti-Jewish movies. France, of course, is a special case — it always is. So we had a well-known writer and pundit, Jean Baudrillard, writing in the leftist *Le Monde*, just a few weeks after 9/11, that what had happened on that day was "how we have dreamt of this event — how all the world without exception dreamt of this event — for no one can avoid dreaming of the destruction of a power that has become hegemonic — *it is they who acted, but we who wanted the deed.*"

Another troubling recent manifestation in the same spirit of anti-Israelism and anti-Americanism has been the so-called "human shield" — which in an article in the *Washington Times* I have called "Human Shields for Human Fiends." You may remember the young man, Tom Hurndall, a self-styled British "peace-activist" who was critically wounded in Gaza while trying to impede Israeli army actions. Before arriving in Israel, he had been volunteering as a "human shield" in Saddam Hussein's Iraq, "intending to protect Iraqis against U.S. attack." Earlier, another "human shield," Rachel Corrie, was accidentally killed in the Gaza strip — an area where Israeli soldiers (no older than Hurndall and Corrie) were daily risking their lives fighting terrorism. Corrie had also been photographed burning an American flag. Not to be outdone, other "human shields," mostly from France, but also from other countries, including Israel, have made a habit of positioning themselves around Yassir Arafat's bunker in Ramallah.

Hurndall and Corrie belonged to what I consider a terrorist front organization calling itself ISM, short for "International Solidarity Movement," which last March was suspected of giving shelter in Jenin to a senior commander of "Islamic Jihad." More recently, the two suicide bombers involved in the attack on a Tel Aviv pub near the American Embassy on April 30, had spent time meeting with ISM functionaries in the Gaza strip. Perhaps some of the volunteers who have joined ISM honestly believe that they are doing something for peace and humanity — just as in the more distant past, not all of those joining the various communist front organizations, e.g., the World Student Movement, Professors for Peace, etc., realized that they were being used by one of history's most vicious and murderous regimes. The same probably applies to the present-day activists who do not realize (or refuse to accept) that they are being used by Hamas, Islamic Jihad, and other brutal terror groups.

What makes an apparently normal human being want to become a "human shield"? Perhaps only professional psychologists will be able to explain why there are people who have an almost pathological urge to identify especially with the bad guys — the dictators, the terrorists, the human fiends. But in the present situation there is also another side to it; less than 60 years after the Holocaust, the world is again faced with a rising wave of anti-Semitism, disguised as anti-Israelism or anti-Zionism, joining neo-Nazis with parts of the old and the new left, Holocaust deniers, and other assorted ill weeds — all bound together by their common admiration for Palestinian terrorists ("freedom fighters") on the one hand — and hatred of Israel, and often its very right to exist, on the other hand.

Suicide killings have become a culture among many Muslims, including some of those who do not even belong to fundamentalist or Islamist terror organizations; we have had suicide bombers also from Fatah. It isn't just a means to an end — but a cultural phenomenon which is closely related to the tradition of at least parts of Islam as a whole.

As our friend Max Singer noted, "It is clear that there was no general Muslim revulsion" against 9/11, "no broad community reaction that would rule out further attacks." Samuel Huntington actually had it wrong. It isn't a war between the West and all other civilizations, it is a war between fundamentalist Islam plus those in the West who willingly or unwittingly aid and abet it, on the one side, and all the rest — the West, democratic India, the Far East and moderate Islam or what's left of it — on the other side.

But no less than Huntington, Fukuyama also got it wrong: it wasn't the end of history at all — it was the beginning of a new, perhaps even more frightening, chapter in history.

As long ago as the twenties of the last century, Winston Churchill wrote about the fundamentalist Wahhabis of what was later to become Saudi Arabia, that they intended to kill anyone who didn't adopt their beliefs.

As Robert Kaplan wrote in the *New York Times* book review, reviewing Bernard Henri-Levy's very important book about the brutal murder of *Wall Street Journal* correspondent Daniel Pearl: "Those who can so gruesomely destroy an innocent individual, may well be capable of destroying millions." Therefore, just as Nazism tried to destroy all those above-mentioned human values, and, therefore, had to be destroyed, not assuaged, the scourge of Islamist terror has to be destroyed, not assuaged.

And just as the war against Nazism, and one could say communism too, this war of ideas will probably have to be backed by force, or at least by a credible threat of force — and America and Israel have shown the way in this respect. None of us is enamored with this reality, but ignoring it won't make the threats facing us go away.

Otherwise, one day we shall say to ourselves, "Why did we repeat the mistakes of the free world in the 1930s when Hitler could still have been stopped — and wasn't?" This war must be won. There is no alternative.

MIKE EVANS is a journalist and minister who has, for the last three decades, covered most major events surrounding Israel and the Middle East. He has appeared on Fox News Channel, CNN, MSNBC, and other major radio and television networks. Mr. Evans is the recipient of the Ambassador Award from the state of Israel. In addition, he is the founder of America's largest pro-Israel Christian coalition, the Jerusalem Prayer Team, which comprises over 300 national leaders, representing over 30 million Americans. He is also chairman of the board of the Corrie ten Boom Foundation in Haarlem, Holland, and chairman of the Evangelical Israel Broadcasting Network.

It's about Islam, Stupid!

by Mike Evans

In a mere 45 minutes on Monday, October 2, suicide bombers drove carloads of explosives into five buildings around the capital of Iraq. Four police stations and the International Red Cross building were destroyed. More than 200 were wounded, and 45 died in the attacks. These terrorist attacks followed the overnight killing of three American soldiers, and came just a day after a rocket attack on the Rashid Hotel where Deputy Defense Secretary Paul Wolfowitz was staying.

Yet while people die, the charade continues. Liberals, lunatics, and liars are still attempting to sell an American public, still in shock over 9/11, that Islam is a peaceful religion.

If that is true, then Islamic states need to prove it by their actions. Peacefulness does not come to mind when 68 Islamic heads of state gave a standing ovation to the prime minister of Malaysia at the Islamic World Summit when he said, "The Europeans killed 6 million Jews out of 12 million, but today the Jews rule the world by proxy." One of those applauding loudly was Crown Prince Abdullah of Saudi Arabia.

When he visited President Bush in Crawford, Texas, three members of his entourage were confined to the plane. Why? They were known terrorists wanted by the FBI in connection with terrorist activities. The U.S. State Department turned a blind eye, and allowed them to lounge in safety aboard the Saudi royal jet.

Islamic fundamentalists are attempting to recruit as many Moslems as possible by appealing that it is the obligation of every Moslem to fight a holy war in Iraq. The reason for the acceleration of attacks is because Islamic fundamentalists teach that America is the "Great Satan." To attack the "Great Satan" on Ramadan and succeed, in their minds, is to prove that Satan is chained, and that the door to hell (America's ability to retaliate) is closed. This creates linkage between the faith of Islam and Islamic fundamentalism.

This new 21st century terrorism now is a direct confrontation against the "Great Satan — America," who, in the eyes of the Bin-Ladens of the world, is desecrating the cradle of Islam. Is it a coincidence that the bombers struck on the first day of Ramadan? Absolutely not!

Organized crime is about greed. Terrorism is about glory — the glory of humiliating the "Great Satan — America" — the glory of believing that all of the terrorists' family members are guaranteed a place in heaven because of their acts, and that, as young men, they will be greeted in heaven with a room full of voluptuous virgins.

The terrorist crosshairs are on the "Great Satan — America." They see the United States as a pig polluting the world with her prosperity, power, and pornography, and infecting the Islamic vision with her moral and religious perversion. Terrorists don't hate the West because of Israel; they hate Israel because of the West.

Sheikh Omar Abdel Rahman, spiritual leader of the World Trade Center bombers in 1993, said, "The obligation of Allah is upon us to wage jihad for the sake of Allah. We have to thoroughly demoralize the enemies of God by blowing up their towers that constitute the pillars of their civilization . . . the high buildings of which they are so proud."

On the morning of February 26, 1993, Yigal Carmon, then counter-terrorism adviser to Prime Minister Yitzhak Rabin, warned the Pentagon that radical Islam was an imminent threat to America. At the end of his briefing, smirking critics told him that they did not consider a religion to be a threat to national security.

Later that morning, Carmon flew on to New York City, where, while having lunch, a huge explosion took place nearby: Islamic terrorists had attempted to blow up the World Trade Center, killing 6 people and wounding 1,000. When the FBI arrested Sheik Omar Abdel-Rahman, who was involved, they wrote on the boxes confiscated from his apartment, "irrelevant religious stuff."

The popular concept of trying to convince the American people that Islam is a religion of peace — as if this will shut down the engine of terror — is the theater of the absurd and a festival of hypocrisy. It will do just the opposite; in time, it could open the floodgates for glassy-eyed, demon-possessed human bombs (H-bombers) to roam the streets of America waiting for the most opportune moment to hit the detonator.

Simply put, the H-bomb is a time-tested weapon that works. It causes panic and reduces the will and power of resistance so as to advance political goals — no matter how unrealistic. The H-bomb forced the United States and Israel out of Lebanon; Islamic fundamentalists are attempting to achieve the same goal in Iraq. They must not succeed! If they do, there is a 100 percent chance that they will bring their war to the streets of America.

The truth is, this is a battle between two books (the Bible and the Quran) and two kingdoms, democracy and theocracy (Islam). Islamic fundamentalists believe that the Great Satan defeated the USSR with their Judeo/Christian invention — democracy — and are attempting to do the same in the Middle East.

I had a conversation with Prince Khalid in Dhahran, Saudi Arabia. He said, "Don't exaggerate! No more than 10 percent of the Moslem population are fundamentalists." Well, call me a taxi! That means there are only 100 million Islamics who want to kill Americans instead of one billion. I don't find that very comforting.

ELYAKIM HA'ETZNI is a resident of Kiryat Arba, and a member of the steering committee of the "Council of Jewish Towns and Settlements in Judea, Samaria, and Gaza." Ha'etnzi, an attorney, was a member of the Knesset for the Tehiya Party from 1990 to 1992. He writes widely on the issue of the "peace process" and has a regular weekly column in Israel's largest-selling newspaper, *Yediot Aharonot*. Ha'etzni lectures frequently and contributes to the bi-monthly journal, *Nativ: A Journal of Politics*.

What Is the Place of Morals in the International Arena?

by Elyakim Ha'etzni

What is the place of morals in the international arena, where interests, first and foremost, are the name of the game? What, for instance, is the moral distinction between the Palestinian lack of statehood which troubles the "conscience" of the world and the systematic denial of statehood to the Kurdish nation, a real nation, with a long history, a language, etc.?

There are extreme cases where immorality between nations cries out to the heavens. The best example is, of course, the betrayal of Czechoslovakia by France and Britain in 1938, which went down in history as the "infamy of Munich."

Equally immoral and in breach of international obligations is the blatant non-compliance by Great Britain of its obligations toward the "Jewish people" as laid down in the "Mandate for Palestine" (7-24-1922), by which the League of Nations entrusted Britain with the administration of Palestine:

Article 2: "The Mandatory shall be responsible for the placing of the country under such political, administrative, and economic conditions as will secure the establishment of the Jewish national home. . . ."

Article 6: "The Administration of Palestine . . . shall facilitate Jewish immigration . . . and shall encourage, in co-operation with the Jewish Agency . . . close settlement by Jews on the lands, including state lands and waste lands not required for public purposes."

[The moral justification for the preference given here to the "Jewish people" is clearly set out in the preamble to the Mandate, as follows: ". . . recognition has thereby been given to the historical connection of the Jewish people with Palestine and to the grounds for reconstituting their national home in that country. . . ." The full moral and universal import of this international instrument was well understood by personalities of the time.]

Lord Balfour: Why Palestine? The answer is that the situation of the Jews is unique: . . . a correlation between race, religion, and land without par in any other religion or country on earth. . . .

Lord Snell (Labour): "The most important international undertaking ever entrusted in the hands of one nation. . . ."

Lord Robert Cecil (on the Balfour Declaration, which is embodied in the Mandate): "The rejuvenation of a nation . . . will have a far-reaching influence on world history and inestimable consequences on the history of mankind in the future."

Let me add to this two more quotes, also taken from Barbara Tuchman's book, *Bible and Sword*, showing how deeply rooted among the nations was the concept of Jews "reconstituting" their ancient homeland in "Palestine" — as an act of international justice:

Napoleon's Proclamation — The Jews: "The legal heirs of Palestine"

"Arise, children of Israel, arise exiles! Hurry, this is the moment . . . to demand for yourself a political existence as a nation among nations. . . ." Napoleon promised "guarantee and support" of the French nation for the return of their patrimony to "remain its masters and hold on to it against any foe and enemy" (1799).

Lord Palmerstone (foreign minister, then prime minister) to his ambassador in Constantinople:
". . . at this time a strong idea lives among the Jews in Europe, that the time is approaching for their nation to return to Palestine . . . it is important for the sultan to encourage the Jews to return and settle in Palestine . . . it is my duty to order your Excellency to recommend strongly to give the European Jews any just encouragement to return to Palestine" (11-8-1840).

All this is to demonstrate the prominence of idealistic ultra-political motives, beside — no doubt — sober, practical interests in all political action involved with the return of the Jews.

But we meet with the same phenomenon on the other side. The opponents and enemies of the Zionist idea also were — and are — not motivated only by interests and practical considerations, such as oil and Arab power, but by a mixture of ideology and sentiment, by a racial, historical, and religious prejudice known as anti-Semitism.

A glance at the early years reveals a surprisingly fresh and relevant actuality. Our star witness to this will be Colonel R. Meinertzhagen, one of the heads of British army intelligence in WWI, thereafter member of the British delegation to the Peace Conference in Paris and then chief political officer of the British Military government in Palestine (1918–1920). In his *Middle East Diary* we find these notes:

12-31-1919
I'm not sure whether the world isn't too selfish yet, to esteem rightly the virtues of the Zionist goals.
It is certain that the world is too anti-Semitic too much suspicious of the mind and money of the Jews.
. . . At any rate, I am here alone among "Goyim" in my support of Zionism. . . . [Meinertzhagen was not a Jew. E.H.]
It seems to me that the best in Zionism is an ideal worth to fight for, which ultimately will necessarily materialize and win.

In Pessach 1920, riots broke out in Palestine — according to Meinertzhagen, instigated by Colonel Waters-Taylor, the chief secretary of the military government in Palestine.

On 4-14-1920 — Meinertzhagen wrote to Lord Curzon, the British Foreign Minister, "All military government officers almost without exception are anti-Zionist and encourage the Arabs."

Waters-Taylor to Chaj Ammin before Easter: "In Easter you have a big chance to show the world that the Pal. Arabs won't tolerate Jewish rule . . . if violent enough riots will take place, then General Bols [military governor of Palestine] and General Allenby will abandon the National Home. Bols explained that liberty can be gained only by force."

Later, after Meinertzhagen had been transferred to the Ministry of Colonies, he wrote:

6-21-1921
The atmosphere in the Ministry for Colonies is saturated with explicit Jew-hatred . . . anti-Semitism, abhorrence of Zionism and Jews.

Meinertzhagen's remark after a meeting with the South African General Smuts in Capetown (1-29-1949) could have been written today: "I pointed out to Smuts the decline of many nations after persecuting the Jews. Egypt . . . Spain . . . which never returned to become a great nation as before. Before WWI, France and Russia persecuted the Jew and were ruined. We befriended the Jews in the 18th and 19th centuries and we were strong and successful. Our deterioration came with . . . the sabotage of Zionism. There was retribution for the persecutions of the Jews. America was friendly to the Jews and she is now the greatest power in the world. It is not possible that all this is a mere coincidence."

The British anti-Jewish–anti-Zionist policy in Palestine lingered like a chronic disease through all the years of the Mandate (1920–1948), culminating in the infamous 1939 "White Paper," which virtually annulled all "Zionist" clauses of the Mandate, closing the gate to their "National Home" before the Jewish people in its darkest hour. From 1939 to 1941 (the Wannsee "Final Solution" decision) occupied Europe's gates were still wide open for the Jews, and millions could have saved themselves. The "White Paper" occurred only one year after Munich, and they rival in infamy. The crowning anti-Semitic deed of the dying British rule in Palestine was the brutal deportation of tens of thousands of Holocaust survivors, some of them to camps in . . . Germany.

PART IV

PUSHING FOR ARMAGEDDON: RAMIFICATIONS OF A PALESTINIAN STATE

ITAMAR MARCUS is the director of the Palestinian Media Watch. Mr. Marcus was appointed by the Israel government as the Israeli representative (communications specialist) to the Trilateral [Israeli-Palestinian-American] Anti-Incitement Committee established under the Wye Accords. From 1998–2000, Mr. Marcus served as director of research for the Center for Monitoring the Impact of Peace, and composed reports on PA, Syrian, and Jordanian schoolbooks. Mr. Marcus testified before the Senate Appropriations Committee, Subcommittee on Labor, Health and Human Services and Education, chaired by Senator Arlen Specter.

The Indoctrination of Palestinian Children to Kill the Jews and Seek Death

by Itamar Marcus

There is significant evidence documenting Palestinian Authority (PA) incitement of its children to hatred, violence, and death for Allah — the *shahada*. This incitement is advanced by the PA through the entire social-educational structure, including sporting events and summer camps, the media including music videos for children and schoolbooks. Jews and Judaism are presented as inherently evil, Israel's existence as a state is de-legitimized and denied, and fighting Jews and Judaism is presented as justified and heroic.

The PA Ministries of Education and Sport have turned the most abhorrent murderers of Jews into role models and heroes for Palestinian youth. A soccer tournament for 11-year-old boys was named for Abd Al-Baset Odeh — the terrorist who murdered 30 in the Passover Seder suicide bombing [sports section, *Al Hayat Al Jadida*, January 21, 2003]. This past summer, during the period of the U.S.-sponsored "Road Map," numerous summer camps were named for suicide bombers, including a camp for teenagers named after a teenage suicide bomber, a 17-year-old girl, Ayyat Al Akhras.

Another camp for girls was named after Wafa Idris, the first woman suicide bomber. Many schools, cultural events, educational programs, and trophies, are named after terrorist murderers and suicide bombers. There can be no greater incitement to hatred and violence than the recurring portrayal of Palestinian terrorists as role models for children. As recently as September of this year, PA Chairman Arafat and 13 PA leaders jointly sponsored a soccer tournament honoring arch terrorists. The PA leaders included Saeb Erikat; Jibril Rajoub; the minister of sport, Abdul Fatach Hamal; the mufti of the PA, Ikrama Sabri; and 10 other senior PA officials. Each of the 24 soccer teams was named for a terrorist or other *shahids* [martyrs] including some of the most infamous murderers like Yechya Ayash, the first Hamas bomb engineer, who initiated the suicide bombings, and Dalal Mughrabi, a terrorist woman who hijacked a bus killing 36, including American Gail Ruben in 1978 [*Al Ayyam*, September 21, 2003]. At the completion of this tournament, Saeb Erikat distributed the trophies.

It is important to note that the PA is making use of foreign funding to promote this hatred among its children. Summer camps named for suicide bombers this summer were funded by UNICEF [*Al-Hayat Al-Jadida*, July 22, 2003; *Al-Ayyam*, July 18, 2003; *Al-Quds*, July 23, 2003]. Renovation of a school named for Dalal Maghrabi was funded by USAID [*Al-Hayat Al-Jadida*, July 30 2002]. And whereas the PA announced two days later that they had changed the name, in order to receive the USAID funding, PA press reports indicated that the name was still being used [*Al-Hayat Al-Jadida*, August 16, 2002].

Clearly, children are being incited to hatred, violence, and shahada, not merely by fringe elements in the PA, but by the entire mainstream of PA leadership and society. This incitement to hatred and violence penetrates the minds of the PA children and, after terrorism itself, is the single greatest long-term obstacle to peace.

Under the Oslo Accords and subsequently under the Wye Accords, the PA obligated itself to cease this incitement, but has ignored its own laws. In the interest of achieving a lasting peace, pressure must be brought on the PA, through all available means, including temporary political isolation and the temporary freezing of financial support, in order to impress upon the Palestinians the importance of peace education.

The following concrete steps should be taken by the PA immediately:

1. Music videos promoting hatred, violence, and shahada must never again be broadcast on PA TV.

2. The practice of naming schools, cultural events, educational programs, sport events, and trophies after terrorists and suicide bombers must cease. Educational institutions and cultural frameworks currently named for terrorists must be changed.

3. PA children must be taught that Israel is a legitimate country with a right to exist.

4. There is no greater incitement against Israel's legitimacy as a state, than to mark the word "Palestine" or "occupied Palestine" in place of Israel on all maps in the PA. These maps must be removed from Palestinian schools, schoolbooks, and TV broadcasting and be replaced by maps that show Israel by name in Arabic. This will be the most important act of recognition of Israel by the PA, more important than the signing of the Oslo Accords. To continue the current practice makes the statements of recognition of Israel at Oslo irrelevant and sends a clear message to the population that it was not said with integrity.

5. The hatred and anti-Semitism in the PA schoolbooks must be removed. The PA argument that many of the books are copies of Jordanian books is not relevant to the issues at hand, which is the educational damage being done to the children. A child being taught that Jews are evil is not going to be less influenced because of the identity of the publisher. In addition, even the new PA-produced schoolbooks educate to de-legitimize Israel, and include anti-Semitic themes. The PA schoolbooks must be reprinted without the hatred before the start of the next school year.

If these steps are not taken, all efforts toward peace in the political realm will ultimately be futile.

YOSSEF BODANSKY is the director of the Congressional Task Force on Terrorism and Unconventional Warfare of the U.S. House of Representatives. He is also the director of research at the International Strategic Studies Association, as well as a senior editor for the Defense & Foreign Affairs group of publications. Additionally, he is a member of the Prague Society for International Cooperation.

Ramifications of a Palestinian State

by Yossef Bodansky

Since I still work for the Congress, I have to include a disclaimer that what I am going to say is my personal opinion and does not necessarily represent the opinion of the House of Representatives or any other branch of the U.S. government.

The threat of a Palestinian state goes way above and beyond being a source of x number of would-be suicide bombers. There is a profound change in the nature of the Palestinian state or a Palestinian entity, and I think the word *entity* is far more important here than *state*, because the PA already functions as one. The Palestinian entity plays a tremendous role that is changing right now, profoundly changing. Rather more important than whatever agreement, initiatives, and political activities that happen here, or for that matter in Washington in suggesting Roadmaps and other wonderful ideas, are the activities that ultimately determine the belligerency, the militancy, the level of terrorist activities of the entity.

The reason for this is the impact of the war in Iraq on the Muslim world. And don't get me wrong, I think that if one need criticize President

Bush on anything vis-à-vis Iraq, it is the time that it took between the consolidation of intelligence data that it was imperative to go and remove Saddam Hussein before he blew up the region and the time that the first American forces crossed the Kuwaiti border. It had to be done, and had to be done, I think, a few months earlier than it was done.

Until the war in Iraq, Arab governments insisted that the Palestinian conflict was the core of the Islamist-inspired political instability in the region. The claim was that it is because of the "threats to Al-Aksa" and the misery of the Palestinians that the population would be incited and threaten the stability in the region. As a result, these governments have been putting tremendous pressure on Washington to solve the Palestinian problem before they — the regimes of the oil-providing countries of the Middle East — are toppled by the Bin-Ladens of the world.

It was wrong in the sense that most of these governments are being challenged by the Islamists because of their own corruption and un-Islamic ways rather than the plight of the Palestinians.

If we look at the documentation — the transcript of the consultation with Abdul Rachman — that led to the assassination of Sadat in 1981, for example, Sadat was assassinated because of his modernizing way, because he became a Westernized leader and changed the internal situation in Egypt — not because he made peace with Israel. So that's one point of extreme, but the same thing applies to other Arab leaders as well.

However, it was extremely easy for both Washington and the Arab countries to avoid dealing with the stability of the oil regimes, their relationship with their own people, the absence of legitimacy, etc., and just come up with a scapegoat; just have the Jews withdraw from that chunk of real estate, and everything will be wonderful. That can no longer be done today because the Arab world is reacting to the changes in the entire region — profoundly to the challenge of the U.S. presence, and changes that are ongoing in Iraq today.

Although Arab governments still come and complain (the Saudis do it repeatedly) that the Palestinian problem is the number one problem that affects stability in the region, this is no longer the case. When one follows the day-to-day activities in the Arab world, the sermons, etc., one finds that the Arab governments are far more preoccupied with the situation in Iraq than with the Palestinian problem, and therefore, to a great extent, sensitive to the issue that I want to elaborate on.

For the United States, the war in Iraq is very simple — Saddam Hussein has been a megalomaniac dictator, had regional aspirations, accumulated weapons of mass destruction, supported terrorists in order to be able to realize his manifest destiny. The time was ripe to cut him down, and so it was done.

In the Arab world, we find a completely different war. It is the replay of the invasion of Baghdad by Hulagu Khan, the grandson of Genghis Khan. Back in 1258, Hulagu's armies were closing in on Baghdad when one of the generals of the caliphate betrayed the city to the invading forces. They came in, ransacked the city, and committed one of the greatest massacres and bloodsheds in the history of Baghdad. They continued westward in the direction of what today would be Syria and Palestine, or Israel. Two years later, Egyptian armies climbed up into Israel, not far from Nazareth today, and were soundly defeated by the Mongol armies, the forces of which were predominantly Turkic forces — a very important distinction. It took protracted guerilla warfare by Arabs from Syria, part of Israel, and from Iraq to defeat the Mongols.

At that point, something profound happened. The vast majority of the Turkic forces converted to Islam and started the mass defection that brought the collapse of the Mongol forces. It was the first new strategic defeat of the Mongol army since they embraced conquest and started on their way westward.

From that, there began the greatest geographic and population spread of Islam in history. Islam spread to Turkey, and then to Central Asia, all the way to the East through Indonesia and the Philippines. The greatest accumulation of manpower, the conversion to Islam, started from this catharsis, the crisis that happened in 1260. Furthermore, several preachers rose up over the next century or so to concentrate, stress, and highlight this victory of jihad as the source of salvation of Islam. Most important of these is a guy named Ibn Taimiyah, who grew up in Damascus and ended up in jail. The important thing is that one guy, Osama Bin-Laden, considers himself the reincarnation of Ibn Taimiyah today. He has been doing that since the early 1990s, and continues to do so, thus bringing a continuity to the preoccupation with that period.

If one reads the sermons about the religious written description of the war in Baghdad or the war in Iraq, throughout the Muslim world, from the preachers of Abu Sayaf in the Philippines all the way to the three border areas in Argentina or to the preachers in San Diego and Los Angeles, for that matter, they are all talking about one Hulagu — Bush who has invaded Baghdad. For them it is the repeat of the same crisis. Yes, they've only undergone the first phase.

Baghdad has been betrayed with something that Saddam Hussein is complaining about and the CIA is bragging about, but this is the first phase. There has been a curse on Baghdad, just like in 1258. Now is the time to mobilize the jihadist forces and fight the next war and start the next spread of Islam, the next explosion of Islam, just like in 1260.

The PA is positioning itself as the bastion from which the forces would spring, from where the new armies are going to come. And this is the profound change that is happening in the Israeli-Palestinian conflict. This is no longer a fight of Israel versus Palestine, a Muslim state from the sea to the river or whatever it is. Now it is the bastion from which the historic victory of Islam, they believe, is going to be delivered again. This is the catalyst from which Islam will be able to surge again and attain its long overdue global glory, as preached by Bin-Laden and all others.

Arafat, being an old Muslim brother, is adamant about having a central role in this game. And no matter the negotiations in Geneva, Washington, Jerusalem, or wherever else — he is not going to deprive himself of his chance to be a central part of this global historical drama that is unfolding in front of his eyes. This is what we need to understand when we look at the Intifada on a day-to-day basis. Now there is a direct connection.

In other words, the Palestinian jihad of the Intifada is no longer only for destruction of Israel and the liberation of Al-Quds. Don't get me wrong, they haven't given up on that objective — but it is now the precursor of the new historic struggle.

The role of Arafat's state, or the Palestinian entity, now is the catalyst for global explosion that will steal the thunder from Osama Bin-Laden. The Palestinians will deliver the goods, something that Osama Bin-Laden had not been able to do. Arafat believes that he can do it. Well, actually to be precise, the guy sitting next to him is convinced that he can do it, and there is a profound difference in the attitude to destabilizing the Arab world.

Bin-Laden is reaching out to the grassroots, and he's reaching out with tremendous amounts of effectiveness and quality. He is by far the most popular, articulate, eloquent spokesman for the plight of the average Muslim today. If you want proof of that, the French, who sometimes do the most wonderful research about the most outrageously irrelevant subjects, did a study on names given to children in the Muslim world, and a few years ago, before September 11, number one was Muhammad, and number two, very close, was Osama.

So Bin-Laden's doctrine is to have the masses overthrow or pressure the Arab regimes into participating in the global jihad, etc. Arafat is going to subvert the governments and provoke them into joining the jihad, and in the process he will gain popularity and acceptability of all Muslims. He is moving much faster than Osama Bin-Laden, and that gets him tremendous booty over here, because the Hamas, the Islamic Jihad, the Al-Aksa

Brigade, and the like cannot challenge him. He is doing the jihad, the global jihad.

The other thing emerging that is extremely important is that just as it was the case in Afghanistan in the 1980s, there is a blurring of the ideological organizational distinction of those who either pull the trigger or blow themselves up. We're now seeing this trend definitely in Iraq, and we're seeing it in contemporary Afghanistan, not the Afghanistan of the1980s. We see it again in the three border areas in Argentina, in the Philippines, etc. There is merging of groups, of people who may belong on a day-to-day basis to this organization, that organization, or follow this preacher, that preacher. When it comes to an operational challenge, they work together.

That phenomenon is reaching out to the territories, and therefore you have a blurring in the emergence of localized groups that are far more difficult to identify because they don't maintain lines of communication with a central committee, but they do listen to the bosses, they do depend on supplies and training from the other side.

The other thing that is extremely important to understand is the rise of the sponsoring state. Both Iran and Syria see themselves in mortal threat by the emergence of the U.S.-dominated Iraq. Both regimes know that they will be stifled to death if the United States is capable of sustaining a pro-Western democracy in Baghdad, with a U.S. military presence in Iraq. Therefore, they are adamant on escalating, sponsoring, and supporting the guerrilla warfare against the United States in Iraq because their own survival depends on it.

For the same reason, they are adamant on escalating the Islamist struggle against Israel, because it polarizes and spreads the conflict beyond one front. Again — Arafat is eager and ready to support all that because, at the end of the day, it escalates his jihad against Israel, and one had to expect an escalation in the Intifada because of that.

DEBORAH BODLANDER just completed over 20 years on Capitol Hill, most recently as a senior advisor on Middle East policy to Representative Benjamin Gilman. Bodlander supervised congressionally mandated oversight of the Middle East peace process, multi-billion dollar foreign aid programs to the Middle East, bilateral relations, regional terrorism concerns, and other strategic issues of importance to Congress and the United States. Currently, Bodlander is a consultant to the Gilman Group and enthusiastically avails herself of opportunities to speak about the role Congress plays in the formulation of foreign policy in the Middle East.

The Economic, Social, and Strategic Implications of a Palestinian State

by Deborah Bodlander

One of the things that I found, working on Capitol Hill, is that regardless of which administration is in power, U.S. policy toward the Middle East remains fairly constant. U.S. policy in the Middle East has three primary goals. The first goal is to ensure the free flow of oil at reasonable prices. The second goal is to resolve the Arab-Israeli conflict, and the third goal is to sell U.S. products abroad. That has been the policy of every single administration for as far back as I can remember.

In 1993, which in retrospect, of course, opened a Pandora's box, we entered a process by which the United States government was more than willing to help remove item number two from its agenda, and that led me ultimately to believe that the United States will do whatever needs to be done to resolve the Arab-Israeli conflict. That doesn't mean that what is going to be agreed to is necessarily going to be in Israel's interest; it's going to be whatever it will take to get the issue off the table, and the United States will be willing to fund it.

As an example, let's remember that U.S. troops on the Golan Heights was quite an issue a number of years back. We did not even say whether we were going to be willing or not to put U.S. boots on the ground, and yet there was a letter that basically promised it all, in the event that the two parties came up with a resolution. We didn't even rule it out. There were no meetings, no discussions about what U.S. interests were, whether or not we were going to put soldiers there, the decision was made: if the parties come up with a decision, we were going to abide by it, so you have the exact same situation here. Whatever the two parties agreed to was what the United States was going to agree to. I think that is something that we are going to have to bear in mind as we follow every single step of the way.

Within that construct, I have to say, however, that I think the assumption of the United States is that any Palestinian state that comes about is going to be secular, and that democracy and the rule of law are going to *somehow* come about. Now, back in 1993, after Oslo, we had a senior government official whose initials are DR, who came up to Capitol Hill and talked to us, assuring us that assistance for the Palestinians would only require three years of foreign aid, because the economic situation was going to be so revitalized, and there was going to be so much business and investment, that we weren't going to have to give them any assistance after three years.

We discussed the issues of corruption and lack of rule of law, and I said: "D, what are you going to do about it? We've got a situation here, there's corruption. I mean, Arafat's not exactly the cleanest guy in the world. What are we going to do?"

"Well, we're going to put money into programs that are going to promote the rule of law and promote democracy, and hope that these things take hold." And I said, "Oh, you mean that's going to trickle up, rather than trickle down," and he said, "Yes!" I said, "Okay. Now I understand. This is what we've got to deal with.

We've got to deal with trickle-up, we've got to deal with an assessment that there's only going to be three years of aid, and you've got the assumption that this is going to be a secular Palestinian state." Well, we also have an assumption that before the agreement, there's going to be a Palestinian crackdown on the terrorist groups, which, as we have seen, has not happened.

Asking, at the time, what was going to happen with the weapons that were in the territories, a prominent Palestinian member of PLO, who has been discussed as a cabinet minister, told me that they were going to keep an eye on everybody, and that they knew where everyone had the weapons, but that they were certainly going to act, if and when the time came. We've seen the time has not come.

Now, the other belief that the United States government had overlooked is the belief that Arafat would *somehow* sideline the Islamists. In the end, Hamas has a lot of popular support, because Hamas frankly poured a lot of money into the social programs. So they have a lot of grassroots support, and one cannot assume that just because they themselves are not totally ultra-religious, that they are not going to support Hamas.

One of the reasons we have the problem that we have is because Arafat and the PA won't crack down on Hamas. We believe that perhaps Hamas is going to be a part of a national unity government, or that Hamas may go the way of Hizbollah in Lebanon, where it's going to become a political party, at which point, if there's a Palestinian state — watch out. I think you've got a whole new set of issues that people have not yet sufficiently considered.

The other thing I would talk about is the ongoing lack of U.S. willingness in the last ten years to penalize Arafat, and it's only been recently that he has been penalized. But, even so, the United States and Israel together have not been able to dismiss him totally, and, in fact, he's such a crafty guy that he manages to come back stronger and stronger and stronger. Frankly — he's the one who controls the money, he's the one who controls the people. He is the Palestinian George Washington, for better or for worse, and there is no one else, as you can see, not Abu Mazen, not Abu Allah, not Abu anybody, who really has the kind of power that Arafat has among the Palestinian population.

Now, as for strategic concerns, strategic implications of statehood, if he were to have a Palestinian state, I would say that the growth of Hamas would probably go unchecked. You would have more and more contacts between members of Hamas and individuals, for instance in Iran. They would be able to come and go, and travel, without anybody checking, without anybody seeing who's meeting with whom, and we already know how much Iran funds Hamas, and how much Syria provides assistance, and this would be allowed to flourish. This would get much worse than it is now.

PART V

THE RIGHT COURSE OF ACTION

YORAM ETTINGER is a consultant on U.S.-Israeli relations as well as the Chairman of Special Projects at the Ariel Center for Policy Research. Formerly the Minister for Congressional Affairs to Israel's embassy in Washington, DC, Ettinger also served as Consul General of Israel to the southwestern United States. He is a former editor of *Contemporary Mid-east Backgrounder*, and is the author of the Jerusalem Cloakroom series of reports which is featured on the ACPR website.

A Palestinian State and National Interests of the United States — A 3-D Vision of Peace

by Yoram Ettinger

I. THE STRATEGIC GOAL

The post-9/11 world has highlighted the fact that the primary feature of anti-U.S. Islamic terrorism is state sponsorship (in the Middle East and beyond), rather than merely a law enforcement challenge (in the United States). The strategic goal of the United States and Israel is to defeat terrorism and stabilize the Middle East, which is inconsistent with the establishment of a new terror-supporting regime on the shores of the Mediterranean.

II. THE ROOT CAUSE OF ANTI-U.S. AND MIDEAST TERRORISM

The establishment of a Palestinian state will not bring down Middle East terrorism in general, and anti-U.S. terrorism in particular. The issue of a Palestinian state has not been the root cause of the Arab-Israeli conflict. Regardless of the Palestinian issue, of Israel's policy and Israel's existence, the following factors should be considered concerning anti-U.S. Islamic terrorism:

- Throughout history, inter-Muslim and inter-Arab politics have been a combination of terrorism, political violence, violation of agreements, dictatorships, and suppression of human rights. Those who resort to terrorism against domestic rivals are expected to employ terrorism against foreign ones.

- Iran, Iraq, and Syria consider the United States to be the chief obstacle on the way of realizing their megalomaniac ambitions: control of the Persian Gulf, takeover of Saudi Arabia and Kuwait oil fields, occupation of territories in Turkey and Jordan, acquiring nuclear, chemical, and biological capabilities, etc.

- The United States represents the bastion of ideas that threaten the dictatorships of the Middle East: free market, freedom of religion, freedom of expression, etc.

- Anti-U.S. Muslim forces have targeted Israel as a Jewish state, as well as the "Little Satan" that serves as the outpost of the "Big Satan," advancing U.S. interests and values in the Middle East and deterring radical regimes in the Middle East. In fact, an Israel-like outpost in the Persian Gulf would eliminate the need to deploy hundreds of thousands of American GIs and spend billions of dollars in order to protect U.S. interests.

- Islamic terrorism has targeted the United States, regardless of Israeli concessions and independent of U.S. pressure on Israel (1993 — Twin Towers, 1995/96 — Saudi Arabia, 1998 — Kenya and Tanzania, 2000 — Aden).

- Islamic terrorism has targeted the United States in spite of the fact that six times in the last decade the United States has gone in harm's way in defense of Muslims in Kuwait, Northern Iraq (Kurds), Somalia, Bosnia, and Kosovo.

III. THE PALESTINIAN ISSUE IS <u>NOT</u> THE ROOT CAUSE OF THE ARAB-ISRAELI CONFLICT AND MIDDLE EAST VIOLENCE

The 1948 war was launched by the Palestinians, and then joined by Arab countries due to Arab ambitions and at the expense of Palestinian interests. The 1956, 1967, and 1973 wars were launched irrespective of the Palestinian issue. The 1982 Israel war on PLO terrorism in Lebanon, the 1987–92 intifada and the current 1993–2004 war between Israel and Palestinian terrorism have not evolved into Arab-Israeli wars, because Arabs do not shed blood — or significant financial resources — for Palestinians; Arabs shower Palestinians with rhetoric.

The Middle East has been characterized — since the seventh century — by inter-Arab and inter-Muslim conflicts, unrelated to Israel's existence, to Israel's policies, or to the Arab-Israeli and Palestinian-Israeli conflicts. The Sunni-Shi'a, religious-secular, have-have not, Iraq-Iran, Syria-Iraq, and the Saudi-Yemen conflicts, and internal strifes in Iran, Egypt, Jordan, and other Arab countries, have produced much more violence, instability, and damage to U.S. interests, than the Arab-Israeli and Palestinian-Israeli conflicts.

IV. THE PALESTINIAN AUTHORITY (PA) INTENSIFIES TERROR

The Palestinian Authority was established in 1993 by Palestinian terrorists headquartered until then in Tunisia and terrorist camps in Yemen, Iraq, Lebanon, Syria, Jordan, and Sudan. The establishment of the Palestinian Authority was perceived by terrorists as a reward to a systematic campaign of terrorism and intimidation against Israel, the role-model of counter-terrorism. Thus, the Palestinian Authority has bolstered the forces of regional and global terrorism.

Palestinian terrorists murdered 254 Israelis in the 15 years PRIOR to the establishment of the Palestinian Authority; 1,400 Israelis were murdered by Palestinian terrorists in the 10 years SINCE the establishment of the Palestinian Authority. Proportionally, the number of Israelis murdered since the establishment of the Palestinian Authority, would be equal to 70,000 Americans (23 World Trade Centers).

The Palestinian Authority has become the largest and most (diplomatically) protected anti-U.S. terrorist base. The Palestinian Authority was established in 1993 by the Oslo Accord and perpetuated through the Wye Accord and the Roadmap. The most intense wave of anti-U.S. terrorism has been conducted since 1993, culminating on 9/11.

Never has a political process (from Oslo Process to the Roadmap) produced as much terrorism, bringing the participants closer to war and further from peace, as has the process centering on the establishment of the Palestinian Authority and aiming at the establishment of a Palestinian state.

Recent history (since 1968) suggests that the broader the authority of the PLO/PA, the more intense is terrorism. International terrorism intensified during the 1968–70 PLO autonomy/independence in Jordan, and plummeted upon PLO's expulsion from Jordan. Terrorism subsided in 1991–92 when the PLO was increasingly constrained in Tunisia, but was exacerbated without precedent upon the establishment of the Palestinian Authority in 1993. The upgrading of the Palestinian Authority to the status of a state would drastically escalate terrorism.

V. THE PA UNDERMINES U.S. INTERESTS AND VALUES

Since the demise of the USSR, the United States has faced the following threats stemming from the Middle East: Islamic terrorism: ballistic missiles and non-conventional military systems, Iran, Iraq (until the destruction of Saddam's regime), and other rogue regimes such as Syria.

The Palestinian Authority — and its source of power, the PLO — have been traditional strategic allies of Bin-Laden, Saddam, Khomeini and his successors, and other rogue regimes in the Middle East and beyond. The ideological mentors of the PA were the allies of the Nazis (Haj Amin Al Husseini) and the Communist regimes of the USSR and East Europe.

Three U.S. attachés were murdered in 2003 upon entering the Gaza Strip, by PA-harbored Palestinian terrorists, as were other U.S. citizens residing in Israel, and as were the U.S. ambassador to Sudan and his deputy by Arafat's terrorists in 1972.

The PA has harbored — and has led — the largest terrorist base in the world. Every territory conceded by Israel has become a safe haven for terrorists. The PA has become a breeding ground and a test site for "modern-day terrorism," such as suicide bombing and car bombing, which has been exported to other arenas in the Middle East and beyond. Modern-day hijacking was introduced by the PLO in the late 1960s, and then was employed by other terror organizations.

Official PA education, media, and clergy systems have promoted anti-U.S. hate education, heralding Bin-Laden and Saddam and encouraging anti-U.S. terrorism.

The PA has become a role model of suppression of (Palestinian) human rights.

The PA regime has caused an unprecedented flight of the Arab Christian community in Bethlehem, Beit Jallah, and Ramallah.

VI. THE TRACK RECORD OF THE PLO/PA

The PLO has been the role model of inter-Arab terrorism, treachery, and murderous violation of agreements.

In the late 1950s, Arafat, Abu Mazen, Abu Ala', and other leaders of Fatah fled Egypt due to subversive activities.

In 1966, they fled Syria — which provided Fatah with logistic infrastructure — after executing a number of Syrian intelligence officers.

In 1970, the PLO attempted to topple the Hashemite regime, which had provided them with a safe haven since 1968.

In 1975, the PLO tried to topple Lebanon's government, and in the process initiated a multi-year civil war.

In 1990 (when the Bush/Baker team was brutally pressuring Israel), the PLO participated in Iraq's invasion of Kuwait, which had accorded the PLO and Fatah diplomatic, financial, and terrorist safe haven since the late 1950s.

As a result of PLO's track record, no Arab regime allows PLO personnel to bear arms on its soil, for fear of subversion.

The PA/PLO track record since 1993 has been consistent with PLO's inter-Arab track record, and true to the axiom: Leopards don't change spots; they change tactics.

VII. A PALESTINIAN STATE WOULD UNDERMINE U.S. INTERESTS AND VALUES

Based on the aforementioned PLO/PA track record, one can expect that the proposed Palestinian state would aggravate the damage caused by the PA to U.S. interests and values:

- A Palestinian state would intensify international terrorism.

- A Palestinian state would destroy the Hashemite [Jordan] regime — a U.S. ally — which would expand the territory and bolster the radical clout of the Palestinian state.

- A Palestinian state would provide Iran with another ally.

- A Palestinian state would provide the pro-Saddam (or other radical) elements in Iraq with another ally in the unpredictable and volatile Mideast.

- A Palestinian state would export terrorism into the Persian Gulf, threatening the survival of Saudi Arabia, Kuwait, Oman, Qatar, Bahrain, etc.

- A Palestinian state would become an outpost for anti-U.S. regimes in the Middle East and beyond.

- A Palestinian state would have prevented Israel from forcing Syria *upon U.S. request* into a withdrawal from Jordan in 1970 (while the United States was bogged down in Vietnam, Cambodia, and Laos).

- A Palestinian state would have provided Khomeini, in 1980, with another springboard for the exportation of his revolutionary anti-U.S. ideology.

- A Palestinian state would have complicated the forming of the 1991 anti-Iraq coalition.

- A Palestinian state would have transformed Israel from a power-projecting strategic ally of the United States into an assistance-requiring strategic liability.

VIII. STOPPING PALESTINIAN TERRORISM

The last ten years — since the establishment of the Palestinian Authority — have been proliferated with agreements signed and violated by the PA. They have demonstrated that there is no political solution with the PA. The only effective solution to terrorism is military, as has been demonstrated by the United States (vs. Iraq and Afghanistan), Turkey (PKK), Germany (Baader Meinhoff), Italy (Red Brigades), France (Action Direct), Egypt (Muslim Brotherhood), etc.

Israel should follow the U.S. leadership in the global war on terrorism, adopting U.S. tactics in its wars against the Taliban and Saddam regimes:

- The prime responsibility of a leader is to the security of his own people, rather than to the prestige of the U.N., West Europe, or other parts of the globe. A nation does not subcontract defense against terrorists to a third party (let alone to a terrorist authority), does not complain about terrorism, but rather launches an offensive against terrorism. Would the United States consider entrusting anti-terrorist activities to Saddam or to the Taliban?!

- Moral clarity suggests that terrorists are not partners to negotiation, but rather enemies to be crushed. Members of the Saddam regime were not "president," "prime minister," "national security advisor," or "legislator." They were "terrorists," "liars," and "cancerous elements."

- War on terrorism solves, rather than creates, problems.

- No negotiation with a regime that has systematically and violently violated every agreement.

- The aim shouldn't be a compromise or a cease-fire, but rather the destruction of the infrastructure, which feeds the fire of terrorism.

- No defensive, deterrence, retaliatory or containment tactics, but rather offense, pre-emption, and prevention on the enemy's own ground.

- No low-intensity war, but rather a swift, comprehensive, and traumatic military campaign.

The political, ideological, and financial echelons constitute the key terrorist elements to be eliminated. Thus, the initial bombing in the 2003 war on Iraq targeted the political leaders of Saddam's regime.

General MacArthur barred all Japanese connected to the Hirohito regime from participation in Japan's political, educational, and business systems, locally and nationally. Paul Bremer followed in McArthur's footsteps, excluding Ba'ath Party members from participation in the rebuilding of New Iraq.

Israel should adopt the same attitude toward the Palestinian rogue terrorist regime, the Palestinian Authority. The problem has never been a personal one (Arafat); it has always been organizational and systemic (the PA).

IX. THE THREE-STAGE SOLUTION

The track record of the PLO/PA demonstrates that no Palestinian state should be established west of the Jordan River.

The nature of the Middle East, the most violent region in the world (no inter-Arab comprehensive peace during the last 13 centuries!), the nature of regional topography and geography (Israel's vulnerable narrow waistline and the threatening topography of Judea and Samaria mountain ridges), the track record of the last ten years (since the signing of the Oslo

Accord), and the resulting security requirements, determine that Israel's control of the area from the Jordan River to the Mediterranean (40 miles) is a prerequisite for Israel's survival.

Israel is facing a unique enemy (the PA), idolizing suicide bombing through its formal education, media, and clergy systems. Anti-Jewish, anti-Israel, and anti-U.S. hate (K-12) education has been perpetrated by the PA since 1994. It has corrupted the minds of Palestinians, especially the youth for the next one or two generations.

Stage 1: Removing the Terror Regime of PA

Co-existence between Israelis and Palestinians requires the dismantling of the morally illegitimate PA. The effective dismantling of the PA requires the destruction — via war on terrorism — of the infrastructure established by the 60,000 terrorists, imported since Oslo from Tunisia, Iraq, Yemen, Lebanon, Sudan, Syria, and Jordan.

The removal of the PA's despotic regime would enable moderate Palestinians to assert themselves. The dismantling of the PA is a precondition for the democratization and pacification of the Palestinian society, following ten years of damage caused by the PA, and in defiance of the non-democratic and non-pacified Arab Middle East (with scores of inter-Arab conflicts and not a single democratic regime).

The democratization and the pacification of the Middle East can be secured primarily by deterrence. The bolstering of Israel's posture of deterrence — which requires Israel's military control of the 40-mile stretch between the Mediterranean and the Jordan River — is a prerequisite for stability, for the defeat of Palestinian terrorism, and for the prevention of the establishment of a Palestinian terrorist state.

Stage 2: Transition to Democracy and Co-existence

Palestinian human rights and democracy are preconditioned upon the removal of the terrorist, tyrannical, and corrupt PA regime, whose primary victims have been ordinary Palestinians.

Democratization and pacification are not attained via rhetoric and declaration of intent. The transformation of a rogue society into a democratic and peace-loving society is reflected through an intense overhaul of the education, legal, political, media, civil service, business, and clergy systems. The transformation process must feature a drastic change of personnel, excluding the members of the rogue regime (at all levels). The transformation must be proven over a long period of time, overcoming ideological, political, and physical challenges from within and from without. The transformed political institutions, education system, the courts, the civil service and financial system, and other institutions, must demonstrate their departure from the jihadist norms of the PA and their adaptation of democratic norms.

Following the removal of the PA, day-to-day activities of Palestinian Arabs will be managed by regional autonomous councils. The regional councils will be assisted by Israel, as well as by outside entities, such as the United States, Jordan, and other member countries and organizations of the International Coordination Body (ICB).

Local Palestinians, with the assistance of Israel and members of the ICB, will elect representatives to the regional councils. No candidate shall be elected who was directly or indirectly involved in the PA's activities, which directed, financed, incited, organized, or carried out acts of terrorism.

Israel shall invite representatives of the ICB to observe — and facilitate — free democratic elections to the regional councils; preservation, upgrading, and democratization of civil institutions; restoration and preservation of Palestinian human rights: women's rights, children's rights; and eradication of torture and corruption.

Stage 3: Final Status Settlement

All plans for partitioning the area between the Mediterranean and the Jordan River (from the 1937 Peal Commission, through Oslo, the 2000 Camp David, and the Roadmap), have radicalized Arab and Palestinian anti-Israel policies, destabilizing the region, producing unprecedented terrorism and bloodshed, undermining U.S. interests, and distancing Jews and Arabs from peace.

Additional attempts to partition the area would amount to another costly victory of wishful thinking over experience. As the old saw says, "Fool me once — shame on you; fool me twice — shame on me!"

The area between the Mediterranean and the Jordan River accounts for less than 1 percent of the land possessed by Arab countries, to a mere 25 percent of British Mandate Palestine, while constituting the cradle of Jewish history. Israel has sacrificed 75 percent of historic Palestine, designated to become the Jewish National Home, in order to have peace with its Arab neighbors. The largest Palestinian community resides in Jordan, constituting 65 percent of the population, commerce, and banking, and at least 50 percent of Jordan's government and military, thus making it population- and territory-wise a true Palestinian state. Is there a need for an additional state for the Palestinians? A two-states-for-one-people solution?

Once the long-term democratization and pacification stage is attained, then the road is clear to a political solution between Israel and the Palestinian Arab residents of Judea, Samaria, and Gaza.

Each party will have the right to introduce its own proposed solution. The Palestinians would be able to propose an independent state, while Israel would be able to propose annexation, regional and an administrative autonomy for the Palestinians, or any other solution.

Proposed solutions should consider the lessons of the past ten years, the unpredictable and violent nature of the Middle East, the threatening topography of the mountain ridges of Judea and Samaria, and the vulnerability of Israel's narrow waistline (which is comparable to the length of the Dallas-Ft. Worth airport).

While the Palestinian residents of Judea, Samaria, and Gaza will administer their own local affairs (legal, financial, municipal, law-enforcement, issuing ID cards, etc.) Israel shall retain all security and external relations authority, lest it repeat the grave terror-producing errors of Oslo.

Palestinian residents of Judea and Samaria, most of whom possess (or used to possess, until 1988) Jordanian citizenship, will be allowed to participate in the Jordanian electoral process, in addition to their own regional elections. They will be citizens of Jordan and residents of the regional administrative autonomy.

Democratization and pacification would enable Israel to remove road blocks, to obtain closure, to open the labor market (for Palestinians), and to expand, significantly, the transportation, communications, and utilities infrastructure in Judea, Samaria, and Gaza for the benefit of Palestinians and Jews residing there.

The Palestinian/Jewish Refugees Resettlement Regional Cooperation Project will be launched by members of the International Cooperation Board, with active involvement by Jordan, Egypt, Syria, and Lebanon. The project will follow in the footsteps of similar projects, which have resettled almost 100 million refugees, throughout the globe, since 1945. It will commit itself to a factual account of Jewish and Palestinian Arab refugees, of the origin and the number of Palestinian refugees, and of the circumstances which produced their misery. The project will involve a multi-billion dollar investment in Jordan, Egypt (especially in Sinai, which is contiguous to Gaza), Syria, and Lebanon, in order to resettle the refugees.

RAPHAEL ISRAELI is a professor of Islamic, Middle Eastern, and Chinese history at the Hebrew University of Jerusalem. He spent several sabbatical years in Boston, Toronto, Pittsburgh, Canberra, Japan, and Belgium. Professor Israeli is the author of 15 books and some 80 scholarly articles in those domains. In addition, he is a member of the Truman Institute. Professor Israeli's works have frequently appeared in Hebrew, French, and English in leading international publications, including *Nativ*.

Principles for a Just Peace in the Middle East

by Raphael Israeli

All solutions proposed to date regarding the Palestinian problem have been predicated upon the slicing of Palestine into three different and separate territories: the West Bank and Gaza, Israel proper, and Transjordan; and upon the differentiation of the Palestinian people into Palestinians (those in the West Bank, Gaza, the refugee camps, and the various Diasporas in the West — about 3 million in all, or 40 percent of the total), the Israeli Arabs (1 million, or 15 percent of the total), and the Jordanians (again 3 million, or 40 percent of the total).

These artificial divisions have run counter to the proposed solutions, inasmuch as the Palestinians have refused to accept as a permanent settlement any arrangement that would not encompass the majority of the territory of Palestine or of the Palestinian population. At the present stage, even if everything else should go right, and the Palestinians would make possible by their cooperative conduct a total withdrawal of Israel from the entire West Bank and Gaza, a Palestinian entity there would not resolve more than a third of the problem in terms of both territory and population.

It is therefore suggested here that a novel solution be negotiated which would rest on the three following principles:

1. That there should be a mutual recognition between the Israeli Jews and the Palestinian Arabs not only of their mutual right for nationhood, but also for their respective movements of national liberation: Zionism versus the PLO;

2. That the entire land of historical Palestine (the West Bank and Gaza, Israel proper, and Trans-Jordan) is on the negotiation table for partition between its legal owners: the Israelis and the Palestinians;

3. That after the boundaries are agreed between the two neighboring entities, each will continue to harbor as foreign residents the nationals of the other party under special reciprocal arrangements which will be part of the peace accords.

And so, rather than allowing the Palestinians to claim a state in Jordan, where they already constitute the majority; another in the West Bank and Gaza currently under negotiation and implementation under the "Peace Process"; and one-half of Israel by the Israeli Arabs, who refute the Jewish nature of their country and regard it as a bi-national state, they will end up with one large and strong state, encompassing most Palestinians, which will live in peace and harmony.

The Israeli-Jordan Peace Agreement: A Missed Opportunity

According to conventional wisdom in Israel and the rest of the world, the peace between Israel and Jordan was a positive step in the peace process in the Middle East. This assumption rests on the premise that with King Hussein being moderate and pro-Western, it was necessary to accommodate him and reinforce his rule by binding him more closely with the West via Israel.

This paper shows that not only was Hussein neither moderate nor pro-Western per-se, but that he lacked legitimacy for his throne in the eyes of the Palestinian majority in his country. And so, instead of supporting democracy and the rule of the Palestinian majority in Jordan, the West and

Israel found themselves approving of an autocratic king, thus exacerbating, not resolving, the Palestinian issue.

The paper also makes the point that the Palestinian problem, which needs to be addressed and resolved if there is to be peace in the Middle East, cannot even begin to taper off if we exclude Jordan, the main demographic and territorial basis of the Palestinians, from the settlement equation.

However, addressing the Palestinian problem in all its components, territorial and demographic (in Israel, the territories and Jordan), does not necessarily have to mean the removal of the king, if he consents to rename his realm the "Hashemite Kingdom of Palestine," turns his rule into a constitutional monarchy, and delivers the power to the Palestinian majority. Once in government, that majority, under Arafat or otherwise, will negotiate with Israel the permanent settlement in the West Bank and Gaza, these being a small part of the much larger Palestino-Jordanian entity. Under these circumstances, solutions will not only be easier but they could ultimately accommodate the Palestinian aspiration for statehood and in-gathering of the refugees, Hashemite survival as a royal house, and Israeli security concerns.

Great cries of exhilaration were heard in Israel, from the left and the right, blurring the boundaries between government and opposition, when the late Prime Minister Rabin announced to an overjoyed Israeli public the conclusion of a peace treaty with Jordan in 1994. Finally, it was said and felt, the long-standing "friendly" and "intimate" relationship with the "moderate" and "pro-Western" monarch was formalized and institutionalized, thus eliminating, once and for all, the abiding threat of the eastern front.

The wall-to-wall rare consensus among the Israeli public toward this dramatic event overshadowed the deep divisions between the "peace camp" and the "hard-liners," and threw to the sidelines their radically different, even diametrically opposed, motives for supporting this peace arrangement. Rabin and his group thought that the isolated Palestinians would more easily come to terms once King Hussein openly allied with Israel; the Likud and its allies hoped that by resolving the Palestinian problem within Jordan, which is home to half the Palestinian people (3.5 out of 7 million), they could avoid addressing the thorny question of Palestinian nationhood in the territories.

Both ends of the Israeli political continuum behaved as if Jordan were the main source of Israeli concerns, and they rushed to settle with it, as if such a settlement would put an end to those concerns. Both were wrong on both premises.

The Essentials of the Israel-Jordan Peace Agreement (1994)

The Madrid Process, which opened in the wake of the Second Gulf War (1991), resulted in a series of bilateral meetings in Washington between Israel and its neighbors during 1992, which were geared to produce bilateral peace treaties. At first, at Israel's insistence and with American connivance, the Israeli delegation negotiated with a joint Jordanian-Palestinian counterpart in search for a solution to the Palestinian issue that was to meet the terms of the Camp David Accords (1978) which had recognized the "legitimate rights" of the Palestinian people, in contrast with the 242 Security Council Resolution which had only mentioned the need to resolve the refugee problem.

The talks soon stalled, due to the Palestinian need to lend the PLO stamp of legitimacy to the Palestinian contingent in the negotiations, something that Israel rejected out of hand. But when the change of government took place in Israel in June 1992, the new administration decided to short-circuit the ongoing Washington talks, established a parallel channel to the PLO in Oslo, and concluded an agreement with the Palestinians behind the backs of the American facilitators of the official channel of negotiations. Newly elected President Clinton seized the occasion, aligned with the Rabin government's volte-face, and sponsored the signing ceremony of the accords on the lawn of the White House (September 1993).

Once the Israeli government acknowledged the separate existence of a Palestinian entity, it was only a matter of time before King Hussein jumped on the bandwagon. His motives were obvious: if he could get a separate legitimacy from Israel for his rule in Jordan over half the Palestinian people, which constituted two-thirds of the population of his kingdom, the entire Palestinian problem would be handed over to Israel to resolve. He had washed his hands clean of the Palestinian "headache" back in 1988, at the height of the Intifadah, when he renounced his claim to the West Bank which had been his fief between 1948 and 1967, and the retrieval of which he had been pursuing thereafter. He was delighted to pass on to Israel the Palestinian hot potato and to entrench himself as the legitimate ruler of Jordan who has recognized interests in the Islamic holy shrines in Jerusalem.

The accords which he negotiated and rapidly concluded with Israel covered six different areas, all of which worked in Jordan's favor:

1. Border Adjustments — Three areas on the border between Jordan and Israel necessitated Israeli withdrawals as follows:

a. Out of *236.75 square miles* claimed by Jordan south of the Dead Sea since 1949, Israel agreed to hand over almost 190.

b. In the Naharayim area on the border between Israel and Jordan, at the convergence of the Jordan and Yarmuk Rivers, Jordan got part of the 5 km² under dispute and turned them into the "Island of Peace," where meetings between the populations of the parties were to be facilitated.

c. In the southern Arava Desert 30 km² which had been reclaimed and fertilized by Israeli kibbutzim over the years, were formally returned to Jordanian sovereignty although they remained practically under lease in the hands of their Israeli users.

2. Water Distribution — Under the accords, Jordan was to receive more water from the Yarmuk River than its original share, and Israel undertook to raise the necessary funds to finance the dams that were to ameliorate the storing capacity of the river. Beyond those agreements, thirsty Jordan never desisted from demanding more water from Israel's own shrinking supplies, to an extent which has necessitated dipping into the Kinnaret [See of Galilee] national reservoir, itself under a severe process of depletion after many years of drought and changing climatic patterns.

3. Palestinians living in Jordan were put on the agenda as candidates for repatriation to West Palestine. This 60 percent majority component of the Jordanian population, which is potentially inimical to King Hussein, was further increased by 10 percent following the escape during the Gulf War of some 350,000 Palestinian refugees from Kuwait to Jordan. The rise of their ratio from 60 to 70 percent, with the attending socioeconomic problems of unemployment, crime, political unrest, and Islamic inroads into the social fabric, meant that the regime had to do anything it could to negotiate them away to anyone ready to take them. Some 800,000 of them, dubbed by Jordan and the PLO as the "1967 refugees," were forced onto the agenda of negotiations and were considered as candidates for immediate repatriation to the West Bank and Gaza, while hundreds of thousands more were to be discussed in the

context of the permanent settlement between Israel and the Palestinians. Worse, Israel agreed to discuss the question of these refugees in a quadripartite forum (with Egypt, Jordan, and the PLO) where she would be outnumbered, isolated, and accused by the Arabs of obstructing the solution.

4. The Islamic holy places in Jerusalem were recognized, according to the Washington Statement of July 25, 1994, as pertaining to Jordan's "unique historic role" in the city. That meant that subsequent to Jordan's illegal occupation of East Jerusalem for 29 years, and its removal by force from there in 1967, and after Hussein had waived his claim to the West Bank (including Jerusalem) in 1988, the Hashemites were now introduced once again through the back door and given a role in the city, to the detriment of Israel who claims it as her "eternal capital" and of the Palestinians who succeeded in forcing it onto the Oslo agenda. By playing Jordanians against Palestinians in the city, Israel runs the risk of losing to both and of seeing its own authority eroded.

5. Security and normalization are the key concepts which have induced the Israelis into the accords with Jordan. Israeli national psyche has a hard time expecting, as a matter of course, that Jewish independence and recognition of Israeli security needs are to go hand in hand with any peace arrangement between Israel and its neighbors. Indeed, Israel's almost pathological need to seek acceptance and recognition from any quarter the world over, and at almost any price, and to rejoice beyond measure when this seems to be achieved, lay behind the great and unjustified concessions she had to make to Jordan to get these accords. Thus, in getting legitimacy from an autocratic king, himself in search of legitimacy, and in obtaining permission for the besieged Israelis to walk the alleys of Petra, Irbid, and Karak, Israel found its aspirations fulfilled. But Israel is also unmindful that, judging from the Egyptian precedent, the peace with Jordan is not fool-proof and King Hussein or his successors are likely to join anti-Israeli coalitions in the future as they did in 1967, and once again during the Gulf War in 1991.

6. Economic cooperation — a euphemism for a one-sided Israeli line of credit, technical assistance, fund-raising, and lobbying

in the West for grants to the kingdom, as well as aid in land conservation, agro-technology, water supply, industrial parks, etc. The only reward Israel got in return were warnings of the impending economic imperialism of Israel. Tangible gains in selling Israeli products are difficult to envisage due to the inability of the Arab markets in general to purchase Israeli high-tech and other expensive products.

When the Peace Accords Become a Trap

Israel's concessions to Jordan in land and water, and allowances in terms of fund-raising and lip service to the Hashemite house, in return for practically nothing, in themselves will not make or break the Jewish state. The problem is with the premises underlying Israel's policy which led to that agreement regardless of whether or not it was initiated by the government or backed by the opposition. And at the end of the process, due to the expectations we helped raise across the world, Israel will be punished, pay all the prices, and get nothing in return like in the famous Jewish story whose lessons we have refused to heed.

As indicated above, the calculus of the Israeli government has been to shift the center of gravity from unreliable and unpredictable Arafat to "moderate" and pro-Western Hussein, in order to dwarf the Palestinian issue, while the right wing opposition has sustained Hussein in order to eliminate Arafat. Both were wrong, and the king outsmarted both. He understood his problem of legitimacy in the eyes of his Palestinian majority which remembers him as the descendant of the Hashemite house whose roots are in Hijaz, Saudi Arabia. Hussein, like his grandfather Abdullah, had been taking great pain to cultivate the new Jordanian identity in eastern Palestine, whose population consists of either veteran Palestinian Bedouins or newcomers from the West Bank and elsewhere either before 1948, or during the wars that ensued, or as a result thereof.

But when the Israeli government lent to Hussein the legitimacy he needed for his rule, it fell into the trap of recognizing it as "Jordan," as if Hussein and his house were a people or a country and not merely a disposable regime, an autocratic one at that, probably against the will of his people which are basically Palestinian and identify themselves as such. Had Israel insisted on the Palestinian nature of Jordan, a proposition repeatedly hailed by Hussein himself ("Jordan is Palestine and Palestine is Jordan"), a proposition supported by history, geography, and demography, and demanded that the right of self-determination be accorded to the entire Palestinian people, including those in Jordan and in Israel, then

Jordan, being part of Palestine and home to half the Palestinian people, should have become part of the solution of the Palestinian problem.

Under these circumstances, a "Hashemite Kingdom of Palestine" could have been declared, with the royal house at its helm as a constitutional monarchy as long as the people there wanted it, but with the actual power in the hands of the Palestinian majority.

Since this did not happen, the entire Palestinian burden now rests squarely on Israel's shoulders out of her own choice; and since Israel cannot alone resolve this problem it becomes insoluble for the following reasons:

1. If the PLO continues to claim that it represents the entire Palestinian people, including the 3.5 million in Jordan and the million in Israel, the dream of self-determination cannot be fulfilled as long as the Palestinians are divided between Jordan, the West Bank and Gaza, Israel (what is erroneously called the "Israeli Arabs"), and the Diaspora (refugee camps in Syria and Lebanon and Syria and Palestinian communities in the West).

2. The right of return, which is hailed by the Palestinians as one of their basic demands for a settlement, cannot be achieved in the territory west of the Jordan River which is already over-populated and whose permanent status is still disputed with Israel.

3. Even if Israel and the Palestinians were to come to a full agreement on the extent of the Palestinian autonomy/state in the present parameters of the negotiation, this would encompass only one-third of the Palestinian people, while the other two-thirds would continue to vie for independence and to knock on Israel's door, violently or otherwise, in search of a solution.

4. A Palestinian entity west of the Jordan would insist on all paraphernalia of statehood such as a full-fledged army, which Israel cannot allow. This in itself would give rise to unrest and friction due to the difficulty of policing the unpredictable transition from police to military.

5. A state of irridenta would subsist in the Palestinian entity both toward Israel and the Jordanian state, due to the continuum of Palestinian population in all three.

6. This no-win situation would further deteriorate due to the mounting activity of the Muslim brothers in Jordan and west of the River (Hamas), who are committed to rejecting partial agreements between the Palestinians and Israel, and demand the application of Shari'a law over the entire territory of historical Palestine as a first step toward the re-creation of the universal Caliphate.

The problematic legitimacy of the Jordanian as well as of the PLO rule in East and West Palestine respectively, while the brothers are waiting in the aisles in both places and accumulating popularity, leaves open the question of whether Israel can conclude any permanent settlement with the governments in place on both sides of the Jordan River. The lesson of Western support to the military government in Algeria and to other autocrats in Egypt, Jordan, Morocco, etc., while legitimacy was shown to belong to the Islamists there, and the ensuing killings and chaos, ought to deter any wise administration from following the same road.

The Palestinians would not care to raise these concerns in public because they are mindful of the fact that if their problem were to be settled in such a way as to include Jordan too, and their official rule were recognized there, the pressure would be taken off Israel to accord them self-determination and statehood. Jordan is theirs, as a matter of course, and it is only a matter of time before their overwhelming majority will displace the Hashemites, at worse, or co-opt them in Hashemite Palestine at best. Therefore, they focus all their effort, military and diplomatic, on obtaining their independence from Israel so as to ensure its retreat from the West Bank, as a first step to demanding more and cashing in the rest which will fall into their lap like a ripe fig.

Squaring the Triangle

The Palestinian triangle (in Jordan, Israel, and the territories) cannot be squared unless all three parts are taken together in the context of one large territorial unit called Palestine/the land of Israel in which Palestinian Arabs and Israeli Jews have equal part and equal right. In this perspective, Jordan, which is part of Palestine, is not only part of the Palestinian problem, but also a vital part of its solution. Concluding a separate peace with Jordan constituted, therefore, from the Israeli point of view, a foreclosure of options for the solution of the core issue of Palestine. But going back to square one, even today, is not impossible.

In Oslo, a tragic mistake was done of assigning 80 percent of Palestine and 50 percent of the Palestinians to King Hussein as Jordanians, but this did not resolve the question of Palestinian nationhood. Quite the contrary, by excluding from the settlement the very components that could facilitate it, it was made impossible. There is no escape from the conclusion, therefore, that two paradoxical premises have to be adopted by both parties:

1. Only if the two parties, Israelis and Palestinians, who inhabit, have relations with and own Palestine/the land of Israel, openly advance maximalistic claims to the land in its entirety, i.e., on both sides of the Jordan, can they also make concessions to the other party: Israel in the East Bank and the Palestinians in the West Bank; only then do they have something to give up without precipitating an irreversible damage to their very existence.

2. Only if each party recognizes the rights of the other can it also expect its demands to be heeded. Each party wants the other to be "realistic" and accept to withdraw and make concessions, but unless each party also recognizes the symmetry and reciprocity built into the mutual system or recognition of rights, no one will move to make the necessary sacrifices. Thus, rather than list a series of "no's" to the partners in negotiations, namely spelling out the non-starters which become preconditions before any discussion is started, it is better to state the equal and parallel rights of both parties and discuss what each party is prepared to concede in order to reach a settlement. In other words, only if the Israelis and Palestinians accept the premise that each one of them owns all of historical Palestine, that is Israel, the territories, and Jordan, but so does the other, too, can the negotiations begin.

Once these principles are accepted, the issue becomes one of boundaries. This vast land can be divided north/south or east/west so as to accommodate both peoples and at the same time respond to their basic needs. If the Palestinians want to keep the Hashemite house and be loyal to it, it is their affair; if the king wants to test his long-standing claim that he is beloved of his subjects and is popular with them, they would certainly consent to turn the state into the Hashemite Kingdom of Palestine, and their king into a constitutional monarch, while the Palestinian overwhelming majority retains the actual reins of power.

This would be the government, whatever its composition, that Israel would have to deal with on the implementation of the permanent peace plan. The negotiations will be protracted, difficult, and tortuous before the final boundaries are agreed upon, but when they are, everyone would understand that the lot has been drawn, the land has been divided, and an acceptable peace settlement by the two peoples has been established. Because, under those circumstances, the debate between the parties would be a quantitative one, about territories and assets that can be agreed upon in the process of give-and-take as a means and a compromise to an end. It would no longer be a qualitative conflict where Israel denies the rise of a Palestinian state and Palestinians refute the idea of a Jewish state in part of Palestine, something that they did not fully accept yet in spite of Oslo.

Such a Palestinian state would not be, by nature, any stronger or more ill-willed than the present Jordanian state. Because if "moderate" Jordan could attack Israel in 1967, and associate with Israel's enemies in 1973 and during the Gulf War of 1991, there is no reason for Israel to fear that a Palestinian state in the same territory and with the same demographic composition would do any worse. The fate of the territories west of the Jordan, now ruled by Israel, would then be discussed with a self-confident Palestinian government, based east of the river, for whom the West Bank and Gaza, or parts thereof, would be no more than part of Palestine, and therefore more amenable to territorial compromise to satisfy Israeli security needs. In this regard, the Egyptian model could be enlightening: the Egyptians agreed in the Camp David process to demilitarize Sinai only because they could still maintain their armies along the Suez Canal and in the Egyptian hinterland.

After the partition of all Palestine between Israeli Jews and Palestinian Arabs, both populations who wish to continue to reside in the state that is not their own will be able to do so and will acquire the right of permanent residence. They will have to obey the local laws and submit to the local administrative system, but will owe their political loyalty, including citizenship, absentee vote, and military service, to their own state. Thus, regardless of the exact borders between the two states, the demographic realities would matter little. In Israel, the Palestinians/Jordanians, including Israeli Arabs who wish to reside there but maintain their national Arab identity, will continue to hold their alien passports while residing in Israel. Conversely, Israelis now residing in settlements that may revert to the new Palestinian/Jordanian entity would act likewise. But once the borders are drawn between the two parties, each one of them would devise and control its own immigration and citizenship policy to suit its particular needs within its own sovereign territory.

There are, however, two other concurrent (not substitute) possibilities to settle the nationality versus territory contradiction. First, people on both sides could, of their own will, decide to leave their place of residence, sell their property and move to the state with which they can identify and in which they can feel part of the ruling majority. This voluntary population transfer might take generations before the demographic balance settles at a permanent level. If the two states agree upon such a procedure during their negotiations, they can jointly declare their encouragement of voluntary population exchange as part of the general settlement between them. Alternatively, the alien residents could apply for citizenship in their country of residence and thereby cast their lot with their country of choice, partake of its economic, political, and cultural life, serve in its armed forces, be educated in their language, and identify with its aspirations.

The Question of Jerusalem

The question of Jerusalem may also be addressed within this framework, in the context of the new Jordanian-Palestinian state. Jerusalem had been the seat of the Palestinian grand mufti in the 1930s and 1940s, but was later relegated by the Hashemites to the status of a backwater provincial city. It reentered the world stage as a result of its reunification in 1967 under Israeli rule and the international attention it has attracted ever since. In the Israeli-Jordanian peace accords of 1994, Jordan was again given a say in Jerusalem, due to Hussein's insistence to regain part of the aura of the curator of the holy places in Jerusalem which he had lost in 1967 and which was part of his problematic political legitimacy in the first place.

The growing centrality of Jerusalem in the Muslim world, not least of all because it is currently not ruled by a Muslim power, makes it a major stumbling block on the road to peace between Israel and the Arabs/Muslims. It serves no purpose to invoke the sanctity of the city for the Jews or the Muslims and its centrality in their respective histories, cultures, politics, and religions, for such contentions, irrefutable as they may be, could immediately be countered by parallel claims from all parties concerned. No one has invented an instrument to gauge the intensity of religious feeling or the extent of political commitment. In history, and even more so in political behavior, it is perceptions that count, it is beliefs that are operationally important, it is convictions that are valid — not what we would like to see as the "objective truth" or "hard fact." Therefore, the harder one attempts to prove his point in this debate, the more the other feels constrained to emphasize his own heritage and to conjure up the entire length and breadth of history to plead his case.

Putting Jerusalem on the negotiation table, whatever be the mode of the permanent settlement, not only would meet the criterion that everything is negotiable, but it could also dramatically alter the ambiance of the talks and prod the Palestinians-Jordanians to adopt the principle of sharing when the two parties are irretrievably locked in a system of mutual exclusion. The model to follow is that of Hebron, where during all the centuries of Islamic rule that preceded 1967, the Jews never had access beyond the seventh step to the Tombs of the Patriarchs which the Muslims called the Ibrahimi Mosque. When Israel took over in 1967, and against the widespread expectation that it would act likewise and exclude the Muslims henceforth, it announced that since the shrine was holy to both Judaism and Islam, the days of worship would be equally divided between the parties. The Muslims never accepted that arrangement and continued to claim their exclusive right to the place, but had no choice but to reconcile to reality.

Similarly, the Muslims who had built their Aqsa Mosque and Dome of the Rock on the ruins of the ancient Jewish temples, claim exclusivity for the place, claiming, among other things, that Islam had displaced both Christianity and Judaism as the one revealed religion, and therefore no one else other than them had the right to the place. Israel, rather than inflaming the moods of Muslims across the world, decided to give in and not insist on sharing. This, in turn, has not only reinforced the Muslim claim of exclusivity, but has also induced them to expand their hold on the site by building a lower level dubbed the Marwani Mosque. If this could be reversed and the Muslims made to realize that they cannot monopolize a holy shrine which is claimed by others too, regardless of who rules the city, it would have gone a long way toward acceptance of the other and coexistence in Jerusalem that could facilitate other practical arrangements. As elsewhere, no one can get everything, but everyone will get something.

In the search for such a miraculous solution, many ideas have been proposed: from the internationalization of the city to the sovereignty of the monotheistic religions over their religious sites; from a condominium of the city by Israel and some Arab/Muslim entity such as Palestine, Jordan, or Saudi Arabia; to autonomous boroughs under one united municipal umbrella. Because nothing could be agreed upon, due to the lack of a universally accepted definition of sovereignty, autonomy, what is whose, etc., the problem was relegated to the end of the peace process. But the peace process does not seem to be served by this evasion, for the tensions are mounting and the parties are positioning themselves with fait accompli's to prepare for the ultimate showdown. Here, too, the shifting of the Palestinian center of gravity eastward would by necessity lessen the pressure on Jerusalem and promote other creative solutions for a Palestinian-Jordanian capital, while the Islamic sites could get recognition and autonomy on a basis of sharing as outlined above.

Balance of Gains and Drawbacks

Life in general, and diplomatic demarches in particular, is a process of choice. It would be too easy if the choice were between good and bad, cheap and expensive, beneficial and harmful. Very often the preferred choice bears a price tag which makes its worth questionable. Therefore, one has to analyze the proposed solution in light of the vital interests of the parties, and only if the projected benefits are not exceeded by the perceived drawbacks does the plan stand any chance of implementation.

Israel would have to pay with territory for any benefits she might draw from such a settlement. What territory, and to what extent, will remain a subject of negotiation between Israelis and Jordano-Palestinians. But it is clear that, having no other major tangible asset to yield, the Israelis must pay mainly in terms of land. Paying with territory, however, does not necessarily mean the complete Israeli withdrawal from the West Bank, for the Israelis could very well advance the argument that since they claim the right over all historical Palestine-Jordan, as do the Palestino-Jordanians, their readiness to yield the East Bank and retain parts of the rest is a territorial concession of major proportions. This argument, which would certainly be rejected by the Jordano-Palestinians, who could claim a right to the same, would also allow them to advance their counter-claims and posit their own territorial demands.

Protracted negotiations might ensue, which might lead to the brink of crisis, but ultimately an accommodation will be found, for territory is a quantitative issue amenable to concession, compromise, and negotiation. In return for Israel's admittedly high payment in territory, it would stand to gain much. She could claim and retain much of the territory of the West Bank necessary for her security, and after that agreement is attained, she will remain not as an occupying power but as of right; the Palestinian Arabs remaining under Israeli rule, once they are assured of nationhood, statehood, and freedom of choice as to their future, would calm down and desist from violence; the problem of Israeli Arabs, who are now torn between their country and their people, would be resolved and each individual would become the master of his own fate. Israel could then regain the image of a peace-loving and generous country, once its crucial contribution to the freedom of the Jordano-Palestinians is recognized. Under this plan, Israel would be able to remain Jewish and democratic, free from the demographic menace, within boundaries finally recognized by her neighbors and the international community. Israel's improved image and secure borders would render it an attractive place for Western Jews to settle in, and most of the present Israeli settlements in the territories would not only be maintained but could even be reinforced and expanded when Israel's sovereignty over them is assured. The Zionist nature of Israel would become clearer and more unshakable, and her nearly homogeneous citizenry would be able, under conditions of peace and prosperity, to revive its pioneering spirit.

The Palestino-Jordanians too must pay a heavy price: renouncing the removal of Israel from their midst; settling for the East side of Palestine as their main base, with incremental gains form the West Bank and Gaza; giving up the "right of return" and the PLO Charter. The Hashemites will have to yield their autocratic rule in favor of a democratically elected government where the Palestinians would have the determining voice. Certainly, no ruler has ever relinquished power out of his own will, but this would be a much smaller sacrifice than the territorial and ideological concessions that both the Palestinians and the Israelis would be called upon to make.

In return, the Palestino-Jordanians would get more than three-quarters of historical Palestine, where plenty of territory is available to resettle refugees who have been languishing in tepid camps for the past 50 years. Already in the context of the Oslo Accords, they have been raising their voice against the Palestinian Authority which has left them outside the settlement, due to its inability to absorb them in its confined territory, and they will inevitably continue to knock on Israel's door for a solution. Unless, that is, their problem is seen to be resolved in the vast land of Palestine across the Jordan River. The Palestinians would finally have a state of their own where they can implement their aspirations and gain recognition and support from Israel as a peaceful neighbor whose vital national interests would have been fulfilled, too. They would then control the fate of most Palestinians, not merely the one-third of them presently dwelling in the West Bank and Gaza, either through direct rule or by absentee citizenship for those remaining in Israel and elsewhere.

Under these conditions, the Palestinians would at last be able to channel their talent, energies, manpower, and creativity to developing their country, resettling their refugees, and cultivating their heritage and culture. They would also have a large and strong army posted east of the Jordan while their West Bank possessions will remain demilitarized so as not to pose a threat to Israel.

If the Palestinian majority decides to retain the king at its head, as a constitutional monarch in the Hashemite Kingdom of Palestine, he would regain parts of his lost territories and double the numbers of his subjects with the inflow of Palestinians to settle, or of their absentee citizenship in Israel, Syria, Lebanon, and the Diaspora. The king would then enjoy legitimacy as the head of Hashemite Palestine where popularity will have granted him the monarchy. He would then enjoy security and stability for his crown and would be able to devote his energies, not to foil attempts against his rule, but to benevolent government, to economic and cultural pursuits as a reigning but not ruling head of state. He could even retain some authority as supreme commander of his armed forces; he could dissolve the parliament, nominate the government, and the like. If he is so sure about his popularity among his subjects, he could even abdicate his throne and run for election as the head of the state or the executive authority thereof.

In this fashion, the vital interests of the parties would be fulfilled and safeguarded, and the new framework of peace would create the necessary ambiance for advancing far beyond the proposed plan once its feasibility and workability is tested and proven. Then imagination and goodwill may produce more advanced regional federations and confederations, common markets and security pacts, to respond to emerging needs. This can happen only after the Palestinians experience freedom and independence in conjunction with their Jordanian alliance and gain enough self-confidence to relinquish some of their sovereignty to the benefit of larger units. Then reality and its needs can perhaps carry the peoples of the Middle East further than anyone has imagined. Reality is not limited by imagination.

Stages of Implementation

It is evident that parts of this plan will be attacked by the parties and other interested powers, in accordance with their purposes and perceived interests. Israel would be reluctant to discuss the abandonment of more territory and the rise of a large and strong Palestinian state independent of her. Jordan will be loath to transfer much of the monarch's power to the Palestinians at the expense of the painstakingly cultivated Jordanian identity. The PLO will reject the plan because it undercuts its claimed leadership over all Palestinians, which under the present circumstances still maintains its hope for two and a half Palestinian states (the existing one in Jordan, the one it is claiming from Israel in the territories, and the autonomy of Palestinians living in Israel). The United States and other Western powers might view the weakening of Hussein [Abdullah] and Jordan as a blow to their interests in the Middle East, especially as there is no telling what kind of anti-Western government might come to power should the Palestinians have their way there.

However, if all parties are made to comprehend the alternatives to this proposed solution — the continued threat to Middle Eastern stability and the menace of war inherent in it — they may conclude that the proposed solution is bad, but the alternatives are worse. Statesmanship consists of seizing the bad before it becomes worse, when one takes into account that seldom does the easy choice between bad and good present itself to decision-makers. Since 1967, all the other alternatives have been based on the Oslo process and the ensuing peace between Israel and Jordan has become a realistic and universally agreed upon basis for a settlement. Most of those "solutions" have skirted the issue of the indivisibility of the Palestinian people in all three countries where they dwell, the problem of Jordan as part of Palestine, and the equal rights of Palestinians and Israelis over all of historical Palestine.

The key nations for the implementation of this plan are the United States and Saudi Arabia, which, if convinced of its feasibility, could prevail upon King Hussein to accept it. The king and his country depend very heavily for economic and military survival. If told that the choice is either his consent to share power or endure turmoil that might bring about his downfall, Hussein might be amenable to accommodation, knowing that otherwise he stands to lose support on which he depends. Then, of course, the Israelis would have to be persuaded of the benefits to them of such a plan whereby they would retain enough territory to ensure their security and keep their state Jewish and democratic.

There are, of course, double-edged considerations as to who should initiate the talks on this plan: if Israel did, it would immediately be rejected by all Arabs; if the United States did, some Arabs might reject it while others might consent to it as a renewed basis for negotiations after the waning of Oslo. If Arabs, say Egypt or Saudi Arabia, should announce the plan, it might stand a better chance. On the other hand, this plan, which is conceived as one package, has inherent in it steps that Israel might like to take unilaterally in order to promote its implementation without, or prior to, other parties' consent. If Israel publicly announced the principles underlying the plan, it would have accomplished a public relations tour de force, by pronouncing itself in favor of the elements the world has been expecting and breathing a new life into the dwindling peace process: yes to Palestinian statehood, yes to a permanent solution of the bulk of the Palestinian people, including the settlement of the sore refugee problem, and yes to peace on Israel's eastern border. The Arabs would then have either to accept the terms, or at least accept to negotiate on all or some of them, or to reject them. If they accept, the renewed negotiations will create a positive ambiance favoring a permanent peace settlement; if they refuse, Israel would have uttered her position in conciliatory terms and could then feel free to proceed on several fronts:

1. Israel could launch a worldwide diplomatic and information campaign explaining the benefits of this plan to all parties, bearing in mind that if Israel spelled out the principle of Palestinian statehood in the context of Jordan, and the details of its own version thereof, the discussion on the world stage would shift from blaming Israel for its negativism to debate on the merits of the plan. Then, everyone would be put to the test: Israel for its will to pacify its eastern border and negotiate for a large Palestinian state; the Jordanians for their readiness to accommodate their own people; the Palestinians for their desire to reach a permanent solution with Israel; the Israeli Arabs for their eagerness to resolve their national problem and make their own free choice as individuals. Statements by all these parties and their reverberations across the world will indicate the degree to which each is ready to compromise, and would allow Israel to separate between signals and noises in pursuit of the plan.

2. Israel can, at the same time, address the more than one million Palestinians under her rule and elicit their opinions as to their future relations with Israel and/or with the future Palestinian state. Those who feel that they can identify with the Jewish-Zionist state and opt to integrate themselves fully into the Israeli system will be naturalized without delay, begin to exercise their rights and fulfill their duties, and weave their lives into the national fabric. The others, probably the majority, who would rather join the Palestino-Jordanian state after it is established, or be its nationals while continuing to reside in Israel, would have to wait until this issue is resolved by negotiation.

   Once established, that Palestino-Jordanian government will negotiate with Israel the question of Palestinian nationality for the Palestinians remaining in Israel, the issue of the final disposition of the territories, and all the issues relating to water, the Israeli settlements outside Israeli sovereignty, common borders and the contents, and safeguards and modalities of the implementation of the bilateral peace between Israel and Palestino-Jordan. Arrangements will also be made regarding shared economic interests, labor markets, technical cooperation, open borders, and the like.

3. Until Jordano-Palestinian sovereignty is established in territories that might be evacuated by Israel, and unless other arrangements are agreed upon by the parties, Israel would maintain, even increase, the pace of settlement there. The rationale is two-pronged: to press the Jordano-Palestinians to come to terms with Israel at the earliest in order to bring to a halt the Israeli settlements within what they claim as their territory, but at the same time signal to them that by settling more Israelis in those territories, Israel is exercising its claim on that land until an agreement to the contrary is reached. By so doing, Israel would be approaching parity with the Palestinian settlement in Israel proper, now amounting to over one million (in contrast to the 250,000 Israelis in the territories, including the satellite towns around Jerusalem claimed by the Palestinians as their own). When a peace agreement is reached between Israel and Jordano-Palestine, Israelis whose settlements would fall within Arab territory would face the same choices as Palestinians in Israel: remain as resident aliens in the Jordano-Palestinian state, sell their property and return home, or apply for full-fledged Arab citizenship.

   In this respect, the Israeli settlements in the West Bank and Gaza can play a decisive role, just as the Israeli settlements in Sinai were a major incentive (not an obstacle) to peace between Israel and Egypt. It has become evident that one of the major factors behind Sadat's peace initiative in 1977 was his realization that the city of Yamit and the score of agricultural settlements in the peninsula were taking root and expanding, and there would be no way to dismantle them unless he hurried and arrested that process. In fact, his first demand before his trip to Jerusalem was that the settlements be removed. Only when he was assured of that, did he begin to negotiate. Similarly, only if the Palestino-Jordanians are assured of a plan that would test their readiness to consider this plan in exchange for Israeli concessions, would they begin to negotiate seriously. A fear of more losses if they waited might bring them around more quickly, even though they realize that many demographic and territorial changes have become irreversible.

4. Oslo and its aftermath has taught all parties that there is no gain to be made from "constructive ambiguities," because the desire to satisfy everyone by wording which is interpreted

differently by the parties collapses on the day of reckoning when implementation forces the signatories to the "agreement" into a head-on collision. But clear commitments and obligations, with a clear timetable and a series of tests along the way to ensure compliance, would not suffice. It is necessary to agree on the permanent settlement, no matter how protracted and frustrating the negotiations, and from it derive the steps of the gradual implementation. To sign interim steps which lead nowhere becomes a recipe for mutual accusations and a rapid erosion of the agreement, as we have seen since Oslo.

In Oslo, the parties embarked on the wrong train, which does not lead to any desirable destination and by now runs out of control and requires an immediate stop. If the parties want to get anywhere, they must go back to square one, put all the pieces of the puzzle on the table and begin to reconstruct the jigsaw from scratch. When they attain a compromise about the ultimate solution, all the rest would be details.

This speech was first published as a policy paper by the Ariel Center of Policy Research, and appears here by the courtesy of the author and the ACPR publishers.

DR. MARTIN SHERMAN lectures in political science at Tel Aviv University, and is a Research Fellow at the International Policy Institute for Counter-Terrorism (ICT) at the Interdisciplinary Center, Herzliya. He holds degrees in physics and geology (B.Sc.), business administration (MBA) and political science (Ph.D.). Dr. Sherman served for seven years in operational capacities in the Israeli Intelligence Services. From 1990–91 he held the post of senior advisor to the minister of agriculture.

Palestinian Statehood:
A Disaster Foretold

by Dr. Martin Sherman

Advocates of a Palestinian state habitually recite a long list of social and economic benefits that would purportedly accompany the establishment of such a state. On the economic plane, they promise, among other things, rapid growth, burgeoning prosperity, the reduction of the defense burden, and commensurately lower taxes. In the social sphere, they talk of greater national cohesion and unity of purpose, reduction of tensions in daily life, the alleviation of the demographic problem, and so on.

In reality however, it is extremely unlikely that any of these envisaged socio-economic benefits would actually materialize. Indeed, it is far more probable that most (if not all) of the problems that would allegedly be *eased* by the establishment of a Palestinian state, would in fact be *aggravated* by it.

Both past experience and reasoned analysis indicate that the scenario most likely to arise would entail:

- spiraling defense expenditure required to patrol and protect an excessively long and contorted frontier, snaking along the very fringes of major Israeli population centers;

- an increasingly inclement investment environment due to a deteriorating security situation;

- constant threats of disruption of vital infrastructure systems such as water and transportation;

- irresistible pressure from Palestinians seeking to find employment inside Israel as a result of failing economic conditions in their nascent state;

- growing alienation, frictions, and recriminations between various segments in Israeli society, fueled by a shrinking economy and mounting day-to-day hardships;

- adverse changes in the demographic balance due to a combination of illegal employment-motivated infiltration and political pressures to avoid harsh deportation policies, coupled with the specter of higher Jewish emigration.

Accordingly, the establishment of a Palestinian state would hardly be a recipe for ameliorating the socio-economic conditions in Israel, but rather a formula for making them far more onerous.

Remarkably enough, the perils inherent in the emergence of Palestinian statehood could have been — and indeed, were — foreseen, not only by the *opponents* of such statehood, by its current *proponents*. The following excerpt illustrates the point — with extraordinary foresight. Written a quarter of a century before the instigation of the Oslo process, it presages, with chilling accuracy, the realities that would accompany the creation of a Palestinian state:

> The establishment of such [a Palestinian] state means the inflow of combat-ready Palestinian forces (more than 25,000 men under arms) into Judea and Samaria; this force, together with the local youth, will double itself in a short time.
>
> It will not be short of weapons or other [military] equipment, and in a short space of time, an infrastructure for waging war will be set up in Judea, Samaria, and the Gaza Strip. Israel will have problems in preserving day-to-day security, which may drive the country into war, or undermine the morale of its citizens.

In time of war, the frontiers of the Palestinian state will constitute an excellent staging point for mobile forces to mount attacks on infrastructure installations vital for Israel's existence, to impede the freedom of action of the Israeli air force in the skies over Israel, and to cause bloodshed among the population . . . in areas adjacent to the frontier-line. . . .[1]

However, perhaps even more astonishing than the far-sighted precision of this prophecy — which in fact predicted almost exactly how post-Oslo events would unfold — is the identity of the prophet. For it was none other than . . . Shimon Peres. Indeed, it was the arch-architect of the Oslo process himself who, in the past, warned so vehemently against the very policy he later adopted with such unequivocal enthusiasm — and equally disastrous consequences.

However, Peres was not alone among present-day Oslophiles in vigorously repudiating the notion of a Palestinian state. Indeed, Professor Amnon Rubinstein, who later served as minister of education on behalf of the far-left Meretz faction, was perhaps among the most outspoken in his rejection of the notion of a Palestinian state. In an article entitled "Palestinian Lies," published in *Ha'aretz* some time prior to the Peres pronouncement, he declared:

> Of all the Palestinian lies there is no lie greater or more crushing than that which calls for the establishment of a separate Palestinian state in the West Bank. . . .
>
> Not since the time of Dr. Goebbels [head of the Nazi propaganda machine] has there ever been a case in which continual repetition of a lie has born such great fruits. . . .[2]

Rubinstein seems to have been keenly aware of the perils that a Palestinian state would imply, for a week later he published a follow-up article in the same newspaper under the title of "The Pitfalls of a Third State." In it he argued:

> [The proponents of a Palestinian state] claim if they [the Arabs] threaten us with artillery from Kalkilya,[3] we will threaten Kalkilya with our artillery.
>
> However, the answer to this is very simple. The Arab world can exist, prosper, and develop not only if our artillery threatens Kalkilya, but even if it hits it. Israel, small and exposed, will neither be able to exist nor to prosper if its urban centers, its vulnerable airport, and its narrow winding roads, are shelled.

This is the fundamental difference between them and us, this is the terrible danger involved in the establishment of a third independent sovereign state between us and the Jordan River. . . . A third state is liable to be an arrowhead directed at the very heart of Israel with all the force of the Arab world behind it.[4]

Peres also adroitly described how a policy of the Oslovian ilk would adversely affect not only vital aspects of security but also how it would undermine the economy, society, and education. He pointed out that:

> The resources available to a country are finite. In the absence of a strategic border, the investment in security that a country requires, comes at the expense of other needs.
>
> This difference in the level of investment in security creates in certain cases a qualitative change in the general level of a nation — in terms of its economy, its society, and education. . . . A country that has the advantage of a strategic frontier can invest less . . . in fortifications, maintenance of battle ready forces, armaments. . . .[5]

He went on to warn, in the most ominous tones, of the perils entailed in withdrawing to the lines he today so ardently advocates, especially in the era of modern weaponry:

> In 1948, it may have been possible to defend the "thin waist" of Israel's most densely populated area, when the most formidable weapon used by both sides was the canon of limited mobility and limited fire-power . . . [However], with the development of the rapid mobility of armies, the defensive importance of territorial expanse has increased. . . .
>
> Without a border which affords security, a country is doomed to destruction in war.[6]

But military dangers are not the only threats that Israel would have to contend with if a permanent Palestinian state were to be established in Judea and Samaria. Perhaps one of the least understood, and most overlooked aspects, is the hydrological and hydrostrategic one. This was aptly articulated in the well-known American weekly *US News & World Report* in the following fashion:

> Wells within Israel proper were tapping this water long before the Six-Day War.

But as the population and water demand on both sides of the Green Line have grown, the control of the western slopes has attained a new and vital importance for Israel.

It is the rain falling on the West Bank that recharges the aquifer; any new wells drilled between the recharge area and the Israeli taps could cut off supply and, by lowering the water tables in the part of the aquifer that extends to the west of the Green Line, allow saline water from greater depths to seep in, permanently ruining what is left.[7]

Interestingly enough, Israeli decision-makers at that time were well aware of the gravity of this matter. Oddly, this did nothing to induce them to oppose the Oslo initiative, which clearly implied Israel relinquishing control of these vital water resources to the Palestinians — with all the attendant hazards this is likely to entail. For example, Labor party Minister of Agriculture Avraham Katz-Oz submitted a resolution to the Shamir government on May 14, 1989, under the heading of "Water Security for Israel Now and In the Future" in which he requested that the government or the Cabinet take steps "to prevent the increase of pumping from present and future sources in Judea, Samaria, and Gaza" and initiate measures "to prepare the legal and political basis to ensure Israeli control and management of the water sources in Judea and Samaria in any conceivable political situation in the future." However, some five years later, during the negotiations on the water issue with the Palestinians, Katz Oz seemed totally oblivious of his previous concerns, nonchalantly agreeing to recognize "Palestinian water rights in the West Bank,"[8] thereby severely undermining any possibility of implementing his previous demand "to ensure Israeli control and management of the water sources in Judea and Samaria in any conceivable political situation in the future."

It is thus clear that there are glaring contradictions between the past and present positions of many the proponents of the Oslo Accords with their unequivocal and undisguised endorsement of Palestinian statehood. This is a totally unacceptable situation in Israeli public affairs! For these inconsistencies — with all their far-reaching ramifications for the future of the nation — appear unexplainable and have certainly been left unexplained.

Regrettably, right wing politicians have been unacceptably remiss in pressing this point home. In so doing (or rather, not doing), they have been inexcusably derelict in their duty to the Israeli electorate. In their impotence and incompetence, they cannot avoid shouldering part of the blame for the tragic events that befell the nation since 1993 when the Oslo process was initiated. Erstwhile opponents-turned-proponents of Palestinian statehood must be forced to account to the dramatic transformation of their political positions — especially in light of the disastrous failure of policy that arose from this transformation. They must be made to spell out why they chose so recklessly to disregard all the dangers which they themselves underscored. They must be compelled either to provide a convincing and plausible account for the extraordinary metamorphosis in their political convictions — or bear the brand of betrayal. For while it might be arguably understandable that an individual could change his opinion from "right" to "left," it is far more difficult to comprehend — and to forgive — a change of opinion from one that proved to be "right" to one that is manifestly and demonstrably "wrong."

Endnotes

1. Shimon Peres, *Tomorrow is Now* (Jerusalem: Keter, 1978), p. 232.

2. Amnon Rubinstein, "Palestinian Lies," *Ha'aretz* 7-30-1976.

3. A Palestinian town just across the 1967 "Green Line," almost adjacent to the Israeli city of Kfar Saba.

4. Amnon Rubinstein, "The Pitfalls of a Third State," *Ha'artez*, 8-6-1976.

5. Peres, *Tomorrow is Now,* p. 235.

6. Ibid., p. 235, 254.

7. *US News & World Report,* 12-16-1991.

8. The Israeli-Palestinian Interim Agreement on the West Bank and the Gaza Strip, Annex III, Article II, Appendix 1, Article 40 (1).

DR. CHRISTOPHER BARDER gained a foundation scholarship in history at Pembroke College, Cambridge, and has for some years been both head of history and politics at an Oxford tutorial college, as well as a tutor for the University of Bath. His work has been published in a number of politics periodicals. He is on the international advisory panel of the Freeman Center for Strategic Studies in Houston, Texas, and on the International Committee for Holocaust Truth. For some years, Barder has specialized in various aspects of Israel's strategic vulnerability and her position in international relations. He has written widely on the Middle East for, among others the *Bulletin of the Jerusalem Institute for Western Defence*, the *Maccabean, Outpost, B'Tzedek*, and *Nativ*.

Israel's Plight When Peace Is Used against Truth: A Brief Analysis and Some Pointers Toward a Solution

by Dr. Christopher Barder

The situation, to borrow a term well-known in Israel, is dangerously parallel to that of the appeasement years before World War II. The world requires peace and will make human sacrifices to that false god under the banner of "risks for peace." Arieh Stav has drawn our attention to the very real parallels between Czechoslovakia in 1938 and Israel now, in an illuminating historical comparison. He has also shown how nearly Islam mirrors nazism. However, the mindset of the appeasers then and the world community and media now force us to try to understand the mentality of those acting as the enemies of Israel today, yet supposed supporters of world peace, if we are to counter their evil and destructive influence successfully.

Neville Chamberlain did not recognize, or if he did, never chose to act upon, the serious nature of Hitler's speeches, programs, or writings. As Professor Robbins has put it, "He did not grasp the dynamics of Hitler's regime and did not display a deep understanding of the aims, beliefs and practices of National Socialism."

Chamberlain chose to regard Hitler as reasonable, someone with whom negotiation might be fruitful. In parallel, perhaps in the blaze of peace hopes, the speeches and media messages in Arabic of Arafat and the senior PA elite became inaudible in similar fashion, both to the Israel left and to the international supporters of the Oslo process (which meant virtually every government in the world). Shimon Peres even tried to rationalize by urging that words be ignored and actions taken into account — which are by now more than obvious, and are plainly and explicitly evil, just as Hitler's were.

Czechoslovakia was, Chamberlain asserted, in Germany's back yard and a country which he famously described, as "far off" and a place of which the British knew nearly nothing. Israel seems to appear like that to many: far off and of little significance. All past League of Nations and other legal obligations to its people are null and void. They are necessary sacrifices and, like the Czechs, apparently lack the essential dignity to be allowed to offer serious resistance because this would disrupt some moral power game with a higher ethical purpose than the safety of human lives. Like the Czechs, they are "obstacles to peace" and must be sacrificed in this higher cause. Such is the prevalent outlook we have to countenance and counteract.

Dr. David Bukay has put it well, and in so doing showed us that much of our task is to penetrate deep enough into western academia and into its educational curricula, and onto the streets, to disabuse all who are open to understanding it, of the error here described:

> Western decision-makers do not understand that the Islamic fundamentalist groups and the Arab fanatics do not play by the rules. They do not play by the democratic rules of the game; they do not play by the Western cultural rules of the game; they do not play by the rules of Judeo-Christian morality; and above all, they are different culturally and are totally devoted to forcing the fanatic Muslim religion on the Western infidels. They truly prove God's prediction about Ishmael: "His hand shall be against all men." Indeed, aggression against others has characterized Islam and the Arabs for most of their history.

The problem is why and how such decision-makers have failed to grasp the truth. For them, it is inconvenient to face reality; deep spiritual and cultural forces work this blindness in them. Anti-Semitism and deals with the Arabs prohibit an alternative view of reality and make truth anathema.

As Bat Ye'or has explained:

> After the Yom Kippur War and the Arab oil blackmail in 1973, the then-European Community (EC) created a structure of cooperation and dialogue with the Arab League. The Euro-Arab Dialogue (EAD) began as a French initiative composed of representatives from the EC and Arab League countries. From the outset the EAD was considered as a vast transaction: The EC agreed to support the Arab anti-Israeli policy in exchange for wide commercial agreements. The EAD had a supplementary function: the shifting of Europe into the Arab-Islamic sphere of influence, thus breaking the traditional trans-Atlantic solidarity.
>
> The EAD operated at the highest political level, with foreign ministers on both sides, and the presidents of the EC — later the European Union (EU) — with the secretary general of the Arab League. The central body of the Dialogue, the General Commission, was responsible for planning its objectives in the political, cultural, social, economic, and technological domains; it met in private, without summary records, a common practice for European meetings.

This goes far to explain the anti-Israel and anti-American stance of the Europeans as well as their Venice Declaration of 1981 and their pro-Palestinian position. The method of calculating foreign policy is very different and the means of dealing with the Islamic threat equally so. Israel is not, to many Europeans, more than a nuisance. It is neither something akin to the Cold War battleship, nor the bastion against militant Islam, which carries an essential, valuable burden. Europeans and Americans see the Middle East and other areas of the world quite differently. The Europeans, lacking in military power, refuse to view with longer-term concern, but only with short-term self-interest.

We all know that anti-Semitism is resurgent. That longest hatred has in no sense been expunged by liberal education or anti-racism legislation. It is altogether deeper than that in Western culture. We should not be surprised if, whether consciously or not, contemporary writers and politicians were affected by anti-Semitism today, because the great mass of published and official statements makes it clear that Israel does not have a case.

Suffice it to say here that the literature on the forsaking of the Jews in World War II is large and compelling; that the Allies could and should have tried to stop the trains; that Anthony Eden knew full well what Nazi policies intended for the Jewish people and early on, not late, but chose

278 • *The Jerusalem Alternative*

foreign office silence on the matter. The same was true of the State Department. Throughout Europe, willing hands were available to assist the Nazis in rounding up Jews. The mindset of the British and French politicians on the Right, Whitehall, and the Quai D'Orsay was that fascism was less to be feared than communism. No one wanted the Jews and in no sense can it be said that they do now, especially if we consider that anti-Zionism is very often really a form of anti-Semitism.

The simplest, most dramatic illustration of this drowning out of the Israeli voice and argument is reflected in the disgusting treatment of it in the U.N. and its discriminatory exclusion of Israel from the Security Council and elsewhere. Enforced dhimmitude is not classified as racism, but Zionism is still proclaimed to be so. Equally, November 29 is the "United Nations Day of International Solidarity with the Palestinian People." No other people has a U.N. Day of Solidarity. Israel is the only state to which a special investigator with "an open-ended mandate to inspect its human rights record" is assigned by the U.N. Since, notoriously, the lie often enough repeated becomes the orthodoxy of truth, Israel is portrayed, albeit incredibly, as mighty, aggressive, ambitious, a threat to stability in the Middle East, and in need of constant restraint. It is as if this caricature came straight from an Assad or Arafat, not the Western press and politicians!

Yet, in reality, no other people has such a determination to make its armed forces moral. "Purity of arms" doctrine, self-endangerment to avoid killing of RPG* boys in Lebanon, the refusal to bomb but rather to expose the IDF to booby traps and fire in Jenin — the list could go on and on. But none of this cuts any ice.

The standard talk from political platform to newspaper stand is that Lebanon was brutalized by Israel and that Sabra and Shatilla epitomized its ethos (and not that of the Lebanese working as an agent for Syria who really perpetrated the crime) while on Jenin, Terre Rod Larsen's absurd and ignorant description is the one which carries weight.

Recently, former Knesset speaker Avraham Burg himself declared that the "Greater Israel" idea had to go. "What is good for Israel is to give up the dream of the greater land of Israel, to dismantle the settlements, leave the territories, and live in peace alongside a Palestinian state. . . ."

In the sense in which it remains a complete misnomer, this is absurd. In the sense that what he also has voiced evinces no idea of the

---

* The RPG is an anti-tank missile which is Russian designed. It is simple and cheap — nothing but a launcher tube and a few rockets shaped like two ice cream cones glued together. More and more guerilla armies are making the RPG their basic infantry weapon. — Editor

real intentions of the Arabs toward Israel, he has echoed the mindset of Europe and the State Department, as well as President Bush, so suggesting a consensus of blind folly.

There are many pieces of evidence centered on the Jewish historical and biblical heartland, Judea and Samaria, which demonstrate the kind of near universal language with which Israel is denounced. Just three must suffice for a glut.

Yesha, and of course Jerusalem, are fulcrums in the clash between the chancelleries and forums of the world, and Islam, on the one hand, and Israel and its friends on the other. Indeed, the point I am making here is a profound one and a very important one for understanding and combating "Peace against Truth." We have to challenge this prevalent and powerful mindset which promotes this error on several different levels: the academic, the diplomatic, the spiritual, and the popular. The process involves using international law and a range of arguments and platforms on a scale which has not even been intimated since Menachem Begin commenced the use of Shmuel Katz as an information expert with cabinet rank.

Russia Calls Upon Israel to Stop "Settlements"

Russia issued a statement urging Israel to reconsider its policies concerning "settlements," referring to Jewish communities located throughout Judea, Samaria, and Gaza.

This followed an Israeli announcement pertaining to plans to annex the city of Maale Adumim to Jerusalem, extending the community some 3.8 square miles (10 square km). The announcement was met with sharp protests by the PLO Authority (PA), followed by similar objections from the Clinton administration.

The Russian Foreign Ministry declared that the annexation "may gravely jeopardize the prospects for breaking the deadlock and for making headway in the Palestinian-Israeli settlement."

"These illegitimate steps," the press release stated, "are disturbing the Palestinians very much, because Eastern Jerusalem is being isolated, in fact, from the remaining part of the West Bank territory. Elimination of this obstacle will help give a confident start to the Mideast talks right after the formation of a new government, from which constructive steps are being awaited in the region."

Russia was unceremoniously shunted out of its traditional diplomatic place in the Balkans but was allowed an inappropriate one in the Middle East. Furthermore, disturbing the Palestinians who have failed to deliver peace is really important but Israeli use of the land contravenes its surrender, which is mandatory to earn what every other country has a right to — to live in peace.

Statement by the Presidency on Behalf of the European Union

(UK) Foreign Office Minister Derek Fatchett said:

> We are disturbed by today's reports of further Israeli settlement building in the West Bank. This development is particularly damaging at a time when the United States, the EU, and the international community are intensifying their efforts to achieve a breakthrough in the peace process.
>
> The EU position is clear: settlements are both illegal under international law and damaging to the peace process. At the European Council in December, European leaders reiterated their view that, if we are to see progress in the negotiations, both sides must avoid counter-productive unilateral actions of this kind.
>
> This is a point which I will be making strongly to the Israeli government when I visit the region next week.

Implicitly there is the suggestion that the United States, the EU, and the international community want peace but apparently Israel does not.

Please compare these attitudes with those of C. Miloon Kothari, the housing expert of the U.N. Commission on Human Rights. Israel's policy of building settlements in Palestinian territories and destroying Arab homes and farmland is a war crime, this official has declared. "Israel has used the current crisis to consolidate its occupation" of Palestinian areas, said Kothari, an Indian architect who visited Israel and Palestinian territories earlier this year. He told reporters, "The serial and deliberate destruction of homes and property constitutes a war crime under international law." The building of new Jewish settlements is "incendiary and provocative" and settlers are "free to indulge in violence and confiscate land," he said.

Israel stands nearly alone, and almost all countries accept the Palestinians' arguments. They seem determined that appeasement of the violence may help create peace, despite evidence etched in Jewish blood over the last 10 or 55 years to the contrary. Oil speaks. So do arms sales. So does mentality. The violent tenor of the Palestinian media and their abuse of women and children make no difference.

Another hinge-point is the treatment of Yassir Arafat. Everyone seems to want him to benefit from his crimes, and Israel to ignore Professor Beres's international law dictum *nullum crimen sine poena* – "no crime without punishment." They care not at all about this injustice nor about the collapse of the rule of law inherent in letting criminals out of prison before sentence is served.

The degree to which Arafat's cruelty, criminality, and kleptomania have been ignored has been put superbly (as well as consistently) by Dr. Ehrenfeld:

> On the eve of the famous "hand shake" on the White House lawn which rewarded Rabin and Arafat with the Nobel Prize for Peace, the PLO made Britain's most dangerous terrorist/criminal organizations list. The British National Criminal Intelligence Service (NCIS) also reported that the PLO had worldwide assets approaching $10 billion and an additional annual income of about $1.5 to 2 billion, generated from illegal activities.
>
> Surprisingly, the report was not picked up by the media. Instead, it was Arafat's claim that the PLO was broke, in need of massive financial aid, that made the headlines. . . . The PLO has a long, sordid, and continuing involvement in narcoterrorism. . . . The traffic in arms and drugs has been assisted by airport investments. . . .
>
> The international media, organizations, and donor governments all seem to have been struck by "willful blindness." The silence around it appears to emanate from some irrational anxiety that cleaning house will signify the end of the PA and Arafat's leadership, which in turn will cause a breakdown in the "peace talks" in the Middle East. Instead of helping the Palestinian people to build democratic institutions and develop a free market system, the West continues to promote Arafat's kleptomania which continuously extorts money and violates agreements.
>
> Thus, the world has continued to shower Arafat and his corrupt leadership with money to the detriment of his people (at least a billion dollars out of a projected $2.4 billion have already been donated) and so the question that looms large is: why does it do so, despite the condemning evidence?

This is the key question: why do the governments and intelligence services willfully overlook the truth? Why is peace set against truth?

There are a number of reasons why this is so. We have cited so far, in relation to officialdom, mentality, anti-Semitism, oil and arms trading, and should mention with regard to the complicity of the press and its formation of public opinion, the list put forward by the Jerusalem Newswire.

The following account by Ehud Ya'ari in the *Jerusalem Report* cited by the Jerusalem Newswire writers, describes circumstances which need to be addressed seriously and changed.

> . . . over 95% of the TV pictures going out on satellite every evening to the various foreign and Israeli channels are supplied by Palestinian film crews. The two principal agencies in the video news market, APTN and Reuters TV, run a whole network of Palestinian stringers, freelancers, and fixers all over the territories [Judea, Samaria, and Gaza] to provide instant footage of the events.
>
> These crews obviously identify emotionally and politically with the intifada and, in the "best" case, they simply don't dare film anything that could embarrass the Palestinian Authority. So the cameras are angled to show a tainted view of the Israeli army's actions, never focus on the Palestinian gunmen, and diligently produce a very specific kind of close-up of the situation on the ground.

All this helps to explain the attitudes of the BBC and CNN, among many, although not why, almost exclusive to this theater, there is so little debate and range of opinions voiced. The single outlook is in contravention of the liberal and open ethos supposed to permeate Western intellectual debate and tradition. Instead, there is an almost totalitarian singleness of viewpoint, a veritable tyranny over the mind.

The journalists of the Jerusalem Newswire also characterize the means most usefully. This state of affairs is a challenge to all who write on Israel affairs.

- Imbalanced reporting
- Lack of proper context and background information
- Misleading definitions and terminology
- Opinion disguised as objective coverage
- Selective omission of facts and events
- Distortion of facts
- Drawing false conclusions

With regard to the Israeli public, Arieh Stav comments, "One of today's most worrisome aspects is the apathy of the public, which is ready to sacrifice everything for the sake of 'peace.' This apathy is largely the result of media brain-washing and ceaseless international pressure." These two elements must be challenged with all the resources possible.

The Israeli left-wing media bias is well attested and the Israel bashing by important organs like the *New York Times* and the *Economist* equally so. We have already seen the congruence of the EU, Russia, and indeed the U.N., in their thinking. There are many historical examples of the way the USA manipulates, such as currently over the positioning of the so-called security fence in relation to Ariel, and in the case of James Baker III over the loan guarantees with Yitzhak Shamir, in the recent past.

We should also add the following to the series of areas to be targeted for causing the abandonment of truth. The training of officials in the corridors of power and the work of Middle East studies departments and their various failures to understand Islam, as outlined by Dr. Kramer in his analysis of the ivory towers and in Dr. Kaplan's book on the Arabists. Long ago, Shmuel Katz drew our attention to the "Laurentian Arabism" in the British Foreign Office. In each of these cases, peace appetite at the expense of truth has warped the sense of reality. These causes and effects have to be countered, realistically, and on every level possible.

The Nub

The main issue is that Israel is not allowed to defend itself like any other state. The so-called war against terror is partial and selective: the PLO and its factions are never targeted by even the USA and Britain, verbally or otherwise. Israel responds with cosmetic actions designed for the domestic electorate, hitting buildings already emptied and garage workshops. The statistics are truly terrible. In the ten years before Oslo, a total of 211 Israelis were killed by Palestinian terror. In the ten years since the agreement, the number murdered has risen to 1,110, an increase of over 426 percent.

The high casualty numbers over the past three years are the result of 18,876 "successful" Palestinian attacks. This works out to an average of 17.6 attacks per day, and 5,878 people have been wounded. Since the outbreak of what the Arabs cunningly call the "Al Aqsa Intifada," 867 Israelis have been killed in acts of Palestinian terrorism (to the beginning of October 2003, so the figure has since grown hideously), carried out by forces the Palestinian Authority pledged to disarm and dismantle. (Multiply by 50 for the U.S. equivalents, by 10 for the Italian.) There are no "acceptable" casualty rates. No state in the world, as Britain has shown in Northern Ireland amidst speculation of a "shoot to kill" policy, and the USA demonstrates frequently, should tolerate such treatment. Even the Charter of the U.N. demonstrates the right of countries to defend themselves, but Israel is denied such a right. Over Entebbe and Osirak, as over the 1967 War, Israel has stood condemned. This is nonsense — far more than a double standard.

At the time of the 1ˢᵗ Summit, **AVIGDOR LIBERMAN** served as the minister of transportation for the state of Israel. In addition, he is the chairman of the Ha'Ichud Ha'Leumi party (a member of the current government). Liberman's long list of public activities includes secretary of the National Worker's Union (Jerusalem); chairman, board of directors of Information Industries; founder of the "Zionist Forum" and member of the board of directors of Economic Cooperation of Jerusalem. Liberman founded the Yisrael Beitenu party and was elected to the Knesset in 1999.

Creating Necessary Conditions for Political Settlement of Israeli-Palestinian Conflict

by Avigdor Liberman

The events of the recent weeks once again brought into focus an urgent need of a clear-cut solution to the Israel-Palestinian conflict. We have to realize that there is no easy way out here. No ethno-religious conflict in world history has ever had a simple and easy solution. Even in a Western country like Northern Ireland, where the conflict was not ethnic but confined to different streams of one religion, it has been going on for centuries, and, despite the efforts of Great Britain and the entire world community, it is far from over.

In our case we are dealing with a double conflict — both a religious and ethnic one — which suggests that easy or piecemeal solutions are doomed to fail. Any such solution can be expected to end in more violence and bloodshed. We must act like surgeons: first, diagnose the problem correctly, and then perform a serious surgery — painful but necessary.

This is the only way to correct the situation, save both sides years of suffering, and, moreover, save the entire region, and, perhaps, the world, from the further inflammation of the conflict and the situation getting out of control.

It is absolutely clear that the conflict is caused not by Jewish settlements in Judea, Samaria, and Gaza, but, rather, by the ethnic and religious confrontation of the two nations inhabiting the same territory. Most Israelis agree with this diagnosis, but politicians are afraid of mentioning it in public.

We propose a plan of resolving the Israel-Palestinian conflict that is based on the separation of the two nations and is similar to the Cyprus model implemented in 1974, when, following a long-standing confrontation, the Greek and the Turkish communities were settled in the different parts of the island. The two parts were separated with a border, complete with minefields and barbed wire. I will note that peace in Cyprus has still not been achieved, but the separation of the two peoples allowed them to gain security, stability, and economic prosperity — all the things our country aspires to.

I wish to emphasize that *we are not proposing a transfer, but an exchange of territories and populations: Jews go one way, Arabs go the other way.* This separation must be complete and, besides the Arabs of Judea, Samaria, and Gaza, include the Arabs who live within the 1967 borders. We consider the problem of Israeli Arabs to be the most serious for our country — perhaps more serious than that of Palestinian Arabs. Therefore, in my opinion, any attempt to solve the Palestinian problem that sidesteps the problem of Israeli Arabs is devoid of sense. We must call things by their proper names.

Our proposal deliberately avoids pinning down the exact location of the future border or the whole political map of our region. The main thing is to gain the approval of the society of the principle of separation as the only true and honest resolution of the conflict. Only then, in accordance with the plan outlined below, would we move on to intensive negotiations that will develop specific details.

Once the principle of territorial and population exchange, including the resettlement of individual Jewish settlements and Arab villages, is adopted, the issue of borders will become secondary and relatively easy to serve.

In order for the government to implement the separation principle, we should first hold a nationwide referendum, as it is done in democratic countries. For example, Canada held a referendum on the separation of Quebec, and Cyprus on the reunification of the two parts of the island.

According to current public opinion polls, 70 percent of Israelis support separation. Of the 30 percent against, 20 percent are Arabs, and 10 percent are those of the extreme left — Meretz and Communist Party. It is interesting that 95 percent of Labor and Shinui supporters back the separation principle. Without a doubt, this is the widest consensus reached in Israel in recent years.

Secondly, implementing the separation principle requires rallying support from at least two of the four international political entities, comprised of the United States, Russia, the U.N., and the European Union.

I have recently been to Washington on an official visit and held numerous consultations with members of Congress and highly placed members of the administration. The results make me fully convinced that Israel will gain approval of the separation principle from the absolute majority of the U.S. Senate and Congress.

I am also sure that Israel will be able to persuade at least one more member of the "quartet" — Russia, for example.

Defeating Terror

Political negotiations always start only after one side wins and the other side loses.

Only after Israel's victory in the Yom Kippur War did it become possible to sign a peace treaty with Egypt. Only after the successful military operation in the Falklands did Britain normalize its relations with Argentina. At the same time, in the areas where this operation was not conducted — Kosovo, for example — the conflict was not politically resolved.

Since the signing of the Oslo Agreements, despite 11 years of nonstop terror, Israel has persisted in its wrong-headed policy proclaimed by the late Itzhak Rabin: "We shall fight terror as if there were no peace negotiations and we shall conduct negotiations as if there were no terror."

The consequences of this policy have horrifying statistics: over 1,400 Israelis — women and children, young and old, military and civilian — were murdered, and tens of thousands wounded, with many crippled for the rest of their lives.

Clearly, without eradicating terror any attempt at political settlement is doomed.

Let me remind you that the political settlement and the revival of economy of European countries after WWII became possible only after the complete victory over Nazi Germany and its complete unconditional capitulation. As long as Hitler was alive, he submitted to no agreements and broke all treaties — just like Arafat, for whom all the agreements signed with Israel and the states are pieces of paper.

Political settlement and the revival of economy of Afghanistan became possible only after the United States removed the Taliban from power. Similarly, in Chechnya no steps toward settlement were possible without decisive military measures and removing Basayev and Maskhadov from the regional stage.

To date, not one Israeli government has taken a strategic decision for full and complete eradication of terror. All their actions were of limited tactical nature — revenge for terrorist acts.

A military operation makes no sense in the absence of a final political objective set by the government. In order to eradicate terror, the government must conduct a large-scale military operation with a specific objective: Palestinian representatives must sign an act of unconditional capitulation.

Terrorists will capitulate to Israel if the terror infrastructure is destroyed: training camps, terrorist bases, explosive labs, weapons factories. The militants must be completely disarmed, terrorist organizations must be dismantled, and their leaders brought to justice.

Palestinian Representatives Must Sign an Act of Complete Unconditional Capitulation

The results of the military operation on the territory under the Palestinian Authority will become irreversible only when Israel achieves full and unconditional capitulation of Arafat's terrorist regime.

For a variety of reasons, this was not done in 1982, and the conflict was allowed to smolder for 18 years.

Only after the Palestinians sign an act of capitulation can we open negotiations about a political settlement.

A Palestinian Partner in Constructive Negotiations

Creating a basis for political settlement requires two sides capable of conducting a normal dialogue.

Both sides must be interested in a settlement and work toward a signed agreement that would stop the bloodshed. Israel needs a partner for actual constructive dialogue, rather than endless empty talk. Such a partner exists on the Palestinian side. But the story of Abu Mazen and Dahlan appointments clearly suggests that as long as Arafat holds sway in Palestinian Authority, he will be able to neutralize any partner acceptable to Israel.

Therefore, banishing Arafat or having him join Hamas' leaders Sheik Yassin and Rantissi in the ground is a *sine qua non* for starting the political negotiations.

Improving Economic Situation on the Palestinian Side

Both negotiating parties must derive practical benefits from the cessation of the conflict. Palestinians must learn in no uncertain terms that signing an agreement with Israel will bring them first and foremost economical benefits and an improved quality of life.

Arafat realizes that, too, which is why he makes every effort to worsen the economical situation in Palestinian areas. The living standards of Palestinians fell radically since Arafat came back from Tunis in 1993.

At the same time, European and international aid to the Palestinian autonomy runs into billions of dollars. Yet not one resident of a refugee camp has experienced the slightest improvement in his situation, since most of this aid was stolen and transferred to the personal bank accounts of Arafat and his coterie.

It seems that the Palestinian Authority has developed a firm strategy toward their people, deliberately driving it to despair and hopeless misery. Those who have nothing to lose grab at *shaheed* belts as if those were life-savers.

It is no incident that many terrorist attacks were aimed at Erez industrial zone, where thousands of Palestinians are employed, earning a living for themselves and their families. Other attacks are aimed at Karni checkpoint, an important economic artery for Palestinians, since this is where most humanitarian shipments pass through to the Gaza Strip.

By striking these targets, Arafat and his underlings strike at their own people. PA leaders do not need gainfully employed subjects capable of providing for their families. They need their subjects to be hungry and desperate, ripe for turning into live bombs.

Consequently, improving the economical situation in Palestinian territories and creating conditions for economic growth must become a priority and a national concern for Israel.

Neighboring Arab Countries Must Participate in Israel-Palestinian Negotiations

Israel must ensure that the agreement with Palestinians is regional in nature; neighboring Arab countries must be involved in the settlement process.

This is necessary for the following reasons:

1. Once involved in the process, Arab countries will assume certain responsibilities for the implementation of the agreements.

2. The threat of fundamentalism in whatever Palestinian structure emerges will not be aimed at Israel alone, but at Egypt and Jordan as well.

This means that both Egypt and Jordan must have a vital interest in contributing to the development of an Israeli-Palestinian agreement on political settlement.

The Palestinian problem should not be resolved at the expense of Israel alone. Egypt and Jordan must make a contribution and assume certain obligations in resolving the conflict.

The Egyptian leadership, especially, must realize acutely that everything that happens in the "Palestinian street" directly affects Egyptian public mood. Moreover, Palestinian actions may directly endanger the authority of the Egyptian president.

Therefore we must make sure that Egypt assumes part of the solution of economic problems in the Palestinian territories adjoining the Sinai Peninsula.

Egypt must provide Palestinians with employment opportunities at oil and gas fields in Sinai and tourist resorts on the Red Sea shores, from Taba to Sharm-al-Sheikh. Egypt must also assume responsibility for security in the Palestinian territories adjoining the Sinai Peninsula.

Should Egyptian leadership refuse to assume the above-mentioned obligations, Israel must request that influential Jewish organizations in the States (AIPAC and others) lobby for suspending financial and military aid to Egypt.

Since Israel playing the "American card" is a nightmare for President Mubarak and the entire Egyptian leadership, consequences of Egypt's refusal must be clearly outlined.

The royal dynasty of Jordan is also perfectly aware that a country where Palestinian Arabs make up 70 percent of the population is particularly vulnerable to Islamic extremism, which can at any time result in the situation similar to Black September. Therefore, Jordan also has a vital interest in the settlement of the conflict; it must provide active support to Israeli effort and assume partial responsibility for the adjoining Palestinian territories in Judea and Samaria.

Territorial Contiguity of the Palestinian Entity Cannot be a Precondition

From the very start, we must decisively reject the idea of the contiguity of the Palestinian entity, i.e., building a special transport artery, or a so-called "safe corridor" between Judea and Samaria on the one hand,

and the Gaza Strip on the other. In practice, this territorial contiguity will result in the trans-Palestinian highway splitting Israel from north to south and make it easy for thousands of armed terrorists to reach any area of the country. The "safe corridor" will inevitably turn into a constant security risk for Israel.

The world history has only one precedent of such a "corridor." The Treaty of Versailles, signed after WWI, provided Poland with the so-called Danzig Corridor to the Baltic Sea at Prussia's expense. The corridor was a source of constant friction and reciprocal claims between Poland and Germany, and eventually became a key reason for German invasion of Poland, and thus WWII.

Besides, we should keep in mind that the territories of Gaza, Judea, and Samaria have never been linked either geographically or historically. Moreover, between 1948 and 1967 they made parts of different countries: Egypt (Gaza) and Jordan (Judea and Samaria).

In my opinion, the eventual configuration of the political settlement should take the form of natural geographic cantons, with their subsequent inclusion in confederations with Egypt and Jordan.

Palestinians Must Relinquish Their Claims to Return Inside Israel

We should bear in mind that after 1948 Arabs were leaving Israel of their own volition, despite the appeals from the leaders of the Jewish state created in accordance with the U.N. mandate. Conversely, after Israel declared its independence in 1948, hundreds of thousands of Jews were banished from Arab countries.

Currently, about 3.7 million so-called Palestinian refugees are scattered all over the world. About 2 million of them live more or less comfortably in Europe, Canada, or Saudi Arabia, and will never come back here. There are 1,600,000 impoverished embittered Palestinians living in refugee camps in Syria, Lebanon, Iraq, Jordan, and Tunis, and it is they who are interested in returning.

From the start, Israel must unequivocally state its position on the refugees' return:

1. The return will be possible only to the territory of the Palestinian entity to be created in the settlement process. There will be no return to the territory of the state of Israel.

2. Refugees will be allowed to return to the territory of the Palestinian entity only if they are guaranteed a subsistence minimum. Otherwise, hungry impoverished crowds, resettled on

the Palestinian territory in the vicinity of Israel, will turn the entire Gush-Dan area, from Hadera to Kfar Saba, into living hell. At best, they will turn to theft, robbery, and raids on border areas; at worst, they will join the ranks of terrorist gangs and turn the peace agreements to nothing.

Exchange of Territories and Populations: Jews Go One Way, Palestinians Go the Other Way

We should not hope that removing Jewish settlements will change the nature of relations between Jews and Arabs in the state of Israel.

I consider the issue of liquidating Jewish settlements impermissible and radically erroneous. Israel has repeatedly dismantled settlements in the past without achieving any kind of political agreement. The settlements are not the obstacle.

I will remind you that most settlements were built *after* 1975. The settler movement Gush Emunim was started in 1974.

An obvious question is, wasn't there terror before 1974? Before the Six-Day War? Before the liberation of Judea, Samaria, and Gaza? There were no *fedayeen* raids in the '50s and '60s? There was no point-blank execution of the passengers of a bus in Ma'ale Akravim in 1953? There was no terror before the state of Israel was established in 1948?

We did not forget the story of Tel Hai settlement; the murder of Iosif Trumpeldor; the pogroms in Hebron; the explosion in the Palestine post offices.

Therefore, it is absolutely clear that the roots of the conflict do not lie in the settlements, or controlled territories, or even the creation of the state of Israel, but in the constant confrontation of Jewish and Arab populations residing in the same territory.

In order to reach a political settlement, we must remove the points of contact between Jewish and Arab populations — to separate the two physically. This can be done only by re-dividing the territory between River Jordan and the Mediterranean, with Jews and Arabs being on different sides of the border.

It should be noted that the separation of two peoples must necessarily include the Arabs residing inside the 1967 borders, many of whom identify with Palestinians. They even call themselves Israeli Palestinians. This ambiguity must be removed. Israeli Arabs must make up their minds once and forever to which country they owe loyalty.

Once and again, I wish to focus on the impossible situation with Israeli Arabs who call Israel's Independence Day the Catastrophe Day and maintain openly anti-Israeli positions. In recent years, most Israeli Arabs have been actively involved in terrorism, directly or indirectly fighting Israel in the ranks of Palestinian terrorist organizations. Arabs who hold Israel citizenship, including Knesset members and local authorities, openly support terrorists. Examples are numerous: support of Marwan Bargouti, indicted by Israeli court for killing the Jews; support of Hizbollah, of Sheik Yassin, and others. Clearly, this group will never identify with Israel.

Unlike American or Russian Jews, who, despite spiritual closeness to their brothers in Israel, owe their first loyalty to their state, most Israeli Arabs are unlikely to ever feel they are Israeli citizens.

Naturally, the Arab majority currently forming in Negev and Galilee will more and more insist on autonomy, and then inevitably will demand full independence from the Jewish state.

Experience shows that physical separation — demarcation — of two groups is the only effective solution. We are not talking about deportation or a transfer, whether voluntary or forced, but about re-dividing the territory between River Jordan and the Mediterranean, with Jews and Arabs being on different sides of the border. It is this measure that promoted peace and stability in Cyprus, where after a prolonged confrontation Greeks and Turks were resettled in two different areas.

Another example is the story of the Sudeten Germans, who after WWII were resettled from Czechoslovakia to Germany.

In the recent decades, the population exchange involved tens of millions of people — Turks who left Bulgaria, Russians who left former Soviet republics, Armenians and Azerbaijanis, Volga Germans, and many others. In many of these cases, the exchange took unlegislated spontaneous forms.

In this case, demarcation will be implemented in accordance with the Political Settlement Agreement; that is, it will be agreed on by both sides and backed by the world community, out of realization that only this plan — as opposed to the "New Middle East" projects — is the only tangible means of stopping the conflict and removing its causes.

In order to implement the demarcation and population exchange program, Israel must lay down a proper legal foundation. A number of laws regulating this process must be adopted, in particular the citizenship law, according to which every person upon reaching the age of 16 and receiving an internal identification paper will have to take an oath of loyalty to the state of Israel, Declaration of Independence, Israeli flag and anthem, as well as assume an obligation to be drafted, whether for military or alternative service — a procedure similar to the one used to obtain U.S. citizenship.

Arabs who live within 1967 territories and carry Israeli citizenship will have to take an oath, sign a declaration of loyalty, and sign up for military or alternative service. Israeli Arabs who refuse to take the oath or sign up will be legally deported to the Palestinian territory. The same measure will be taken concerning Arabs who signed the declaration but violated their oath.

In order to reach true demarcation and avoid contact between Israel and Palestinian populations, infiltration of Palestinians to Israel has to be excluded altogether or at best reduced to a minimum. Therefore, no employment for Arabs should be created in Israel; rather, such employment should be created on the territory of Palestinian entity or in the Sinai.

Following the signing of the political settlement agreement, every effort should be taken, with the help of the world community, to develop economy in the Palestinian entity: industry, agriculture, and transportation.

Jerusalem is the Single and Indivisible Capital of the State of Israel

At this stage it doesn't make sense to draw maps for future territorial and demographic changes. As we mentioned above, these will be elaborated in the course of the negotiations with Palestinian representatives following their signing of Act of Capitulation.

Yet there is one clause in the political settlement agreement that should be committed to paper right now. Jerusalem shall forever remain united and the indivisible capital of the state of Israel under full Israel sovereignty.

Conclusion

I am not saying that an agreement is impossible with Palestinian Arabs — only a voluntary one. As long as Arabs retain at least a spark of hope of getting rid of us, they will not sell this hope for any sweet words or the most nutritious sandwiches, exactly because they're not just a bunch of vagrants, but a people. However backward, they are a people.

A live people makes concessions on huge dramatic issues only when there is no hope left — when not a loophole is left in the iron wall. Only then can radical groups with their "Never Surrender" slogans lose their charm, and the moderates can take over. Only then will the moderates come to us with offers of mutual concessions; only then will they negotiate in good faith practical issues like guarantees against displacement or equal rights or national uniqueness. And I do believe and hope that then we will be able to provide them with the guarantees that will put them at peace, and the two peoples will be living in peace and decency side by side. But the only path to such an agreement lies through an Iron Wall, i.e., creating in eretz Israel such a Jewish power that will not be shaken by any Arab influence or effort. In other words, the only way for us to reach an agreement in the future lies through an absolute rejection of any attempts to have an agreement in the present.

These words were written by Ze'ev Zhabotinsky in 1923 in an article called "The Iron Wall." They ring true now as much as they did then.

An agreement of political settlement with Arabs can be achieved only from the position of force. It is true not only, and not so much, because force provides one with a better bargaining position, but mostly because this is the only position that provides the other side with a motivation to seek a settlement. An agreement achieved from the position of weakness provides the other side with a motivation to violate it and thus gain new advantages.

Israel strives for normal relations with all our neighbors, including Palestinians, or at least for security without having to hear daily reports of terrorist bombings. Any plans to settle the conflict based on one-sided concessions continue to give the other side the hope that one day they will be able to get rid of us, and so only serve to take us further from our objectives.

At the time of the first Summit, **BENNY ELON** served as the minister of tourism for the state of Israel. Since his election to the Knesset in 1996, Benny Elon has served on a number of committees, including Constitution, Law and Justice; Ethics; House; Foreign Affairs & Defense (observer); and Internal Affairs and Environment. He is the chairman of the Moledet faction that is part of the Ha'Ichud Ha'Leumi party in the present government.

The Right Road to Peace

by Benny Elon

Preface

"And you shall dispossess the inhabitants of the land . . . and dwell in it. For I have given you the land to possess it" (Num. 33:52–53).

The statement "The land of Israel belongs to the people of Israel" that forms the foundation for the return to Zion, unfortunately seems to many people to be irrelevant when dealing with the Israeli-Arab conflict. The various peace plans that have been proposed for decades, and which have taken a heavy toll of lives from the Israelis, are all based on an attempt to ignore this fundamental statement, and consequently always fail.

This disregard is a case of burying one's head in the sand.

The Jewish people's return to its land is the major geo-political factor in the region. This is in fact a miraculous event: A nation that was absent from its land for hundreds of years is now returning to it, by being uprooted from the countries in which it has been dispersed, and this very same process is driving out Arab residents from here. Only those who know how to read the Bible can understand the phenomenon and are capable of proposing a realistic political solution. Peace will only be achieved in our region after acceptance of the return to Zion, acceptance that must begin in Israeli society and spread to all the nations involved.

Those who wish for life at the present time must examine ways to achieve real and lasting peace, must identify the roots of the conflict that is spilling our blood, and must seek a solution with honesty and creativity. Those who make such an effort and study the questions at issue and the forces acting in the region, discover that the sole real chance to achieve peace lies with a plan based on Israeli sovereignty extending over the entire width of our little Western eretz Israel, from the Jordan to the Mediterranean. This is the plan presented here.

The Israeli-Arab conflict focuses on two points. The first, deep, issue is that of the land: To whom does this land belong? Does the land of Israel belong to the Jewish people, or, God forbid, is it merely another Arab estate? The second issue is the question of the Arab refugees: What should be done with the refugees who fled from the bounds of Israel during the 1948 War of Independence, and have retained their status as refugees until the present?

These two questions may be answered in only one of two ways. The first is that the land is an Arab one. This approach also implies the answer to the question of the refugees, in the form of the "right of Arab refugees to return to their former homes." Such an answer turns the entire Zionist movement into an illegitimate colonial one, and leads directly to the destruction of Israel as a Jewish state, and to the reversal of the process of the ingathering of the exiles.

The second answer, based on the recognition and the certainty that the land belongs to the Jewish people, leads inevitably to striving to achieve the rapid and generous rehabilitation of Arab refugees in Arab countries. This is the sole solution. Any partition of the land and any delay in the rehabilitation of the refugees means adoption of the PLO strategy of perpetuating the conflict, a strategy aimed at implementing the first approach: the destruction of the state of Israel and the return of the refugees to their former homes in Haifa, Jaffa, and Ashdod.

* * *

Only those who are familiar with and accept the biblical verses "The strength of His deeds He said to His people, to give them the inheritance of nations," "To you and to your seed I shall give this land, for ever," and

"Do not fear them" [Josh. 1:1–9], are capable of leading the state of Israel in standing up for its own interests, and advancing a peace plan based on Israeli sovereignty and on solving the problem of the Arab refugees created in the War of Independence.

However, those who possess belief must propose a real alternative, and not rely solely on biblical verses. A political plan that addresses all the issues involved in the conflict in the Middle East and is based on accepted principles of international law is essential in order to advance the vision of the return to Zion in the world of political action. Such a plan is presented in the following pages.

Introduction

"The Palestinian Problem," or the refugee problem, feeds the Israeli-Arab conflict for two generations, and is used to strengthen the Arab claim in the debate on who this land belongs to. It is not by chance that the "right of return" and the rehabilitation of the refugees were kept as open issues in all of the accords signed with the Palestinians: It is part of their strategic plan to avoid the termination of the conflict whatsoever.

All the plans which are based on the partition of Western Palestine to two entities, "Palestine" and Israel, are disastrous from an Israeli point of view. They do not offer a solution to the Palestinian problem (because they propose to the Palestinians no more than a tiny and densely populated quasi-state, which is totally dependant on Israeli economy), and they include a practical declaration that this land does not belong to the people of Israel. These two characteristics of these plans ensure that they strengthen the Arab war toward the destruction of Israel as the Jewish state.

* * *

From every aspect – geographic, economic, and demographic — it is clear that it will be impossible to resolve the problem within the small, overcrowded area between the Jordan River and the Mediterranean Sea.

Only with application of a *regional solution* that includes the entire territory of British Mandatory Palestine (land of Israel) can the peace process be delivered from its impasse. A regional solution based on *geopolitical and economic logic* can provide the Middle East with long-term peace, prosperity, and stability.

The American and British victory in Iraq has spurred an American commitment to instill *democratic values* in the Middle East and establish a new political map. This is a historic opportunity to enable the Arab nations to be part of the solution to the Palestinian problem and garner *international support and funding.*

The Elon Peace Plan addresses the fundamental issues related to the conflict and offers a comprehensive solution for Israel, Palestinian Arabs, and surrounding countries.

Expanding the solution to include both sides of the Jordan River creates a new reality in which:

- Israelis and Palestinian Arabs exist alongside one another in two genuine, sovereign states that seek stability and peace.

- A well-defined natural border would be established, far from population centers.

Both states would have strategic depth and ample land reserves. Dealing directly with final-status issues, the Elon Peace Plan offers:

- Removal of the threat to Israel's existence as a Jewish state

- Realization of the covenant regarding the ownership of the land of Israel

- The granting of national expression and full rights for all Palestinian Arabs

- Building an opportunity for removing the demographic threat of Israeli Arabs

- Full and comprehensive rehabilitation of Palestinian refugees

- An immediate permanent-status settlement to end the conflict

KEY PRINCIPLES OF THE ELON PEACE PLAN	
Dissolution of the Palestinian Authority	Immediate dissolution of the Palestinian Authority, a non-viable entity with no future, whose existence precludes the termination of the conflict.
Eradication of terror infrastructure	Israel will uproot the Palestinian terror infrastructure. All arms will be collected, incitement will be stopped, and all the refugee camps, which serve as incubators for terror, will be dismantled. Terrorists and their direct supporters will be deported.

Recognition and development of Jordan as the Palestinian state	Israel, the United States, and the international community will recognize the Kingdom of Jordan as the only legitimate representative of the Palestinians. Jordan will once again recognize itself as the Palestinian nation-state. In the context of a regional economic development program, Israel, the United States, and the international community will put forth a concerted effort for the long-term development Jordan, to rehabilitate its economy and enable it to absorb a limited number of refugees within its borders.
Israeli sovereignty over Judea, Samaria, and Gaza	Israeli sovereignty will be asserted over Judea, Samaria, and Gaza (the West Bank). The Arab residents of these areas will become citizens of the Palestinian state of Jordan. The status of these citizens, their connection to the two states, and the manner of the administration of their communal lives will be decided in an agreement between the governments of Israel and Jordan (Palestine). The Palestinian-Jordanian citizenship will be offered subsequently to the Arab citizens of Israel.
Rehabilitation of refugees and completion of population exchange	Israel, the United States, and the international community will allocate resources for the completion of the exchange of populations that began in 1948, as well as the full rehabilitation of the refugees and their absorption and naturalization in various countries.
Peace and normalization	After implementation of the above stages, Israel and Jordan-Palestine will declare the conflict terminated. Both sides will work to normalize peaceful relations between all parties in the region.

CLARIFICATIONS OF KEY PRINCIPLES

The Dissolution of the Palestinian Authority and the War on Terror

1. Immediate dissolution of the Palestinian Authority, a non-viable entity with no future whose existence precludes the termination of the conflict.

2. Israel will uproot the Palestinian terror infrastructure. All arms will be collected, incitement will be stopped, and all the refugee camps, which serve as incubators for terror, will be dismantled.

3. Terrorists and their direct collaborators will be deported.

The Palestinian Authority — An obstacle to Peace

After the eradication of the Taliban and the regime of Saddam Hussein, it follows logically that another of the world's most dangerous regimes, the Palestinian Authority (PA), be immediately dissolved.

- The PA has funded and dispatched homicide terrorists to carry out terror attacks in Israel.

- Senior PA officials have plundered large sums from funds contributed by donor nations.

- The PA is indoctrinating its children toward hatred and violence.

- The PA plays a leading role in the international terror network.

- PA strategy is to pay lip service in the Western media to "peace," while delivering the opposite message for domestic consumption.

The absence of responsible leadership in Judea, Samaria, and Gaza encourages criminal activity, Islamic extremism, and long-term damage to the infrastructure and ecology of the region. Israeli control over Judea, Samaria, and Gaza will be a stabilizing influence.

The establishment of a Palestinian state in Judea, Samaria, and Gaza would:

- Foster, continue, and intensify terror

- Perpetuate day-to-day friction between Jews and Arabs

- Represent a constant demographic danger to the very existence of Israel as a Jewish state

Such a state, dissected, demilitarized, its economy totally dependent on Israel, would evolve into a protectorate whose main function would be to supply cheap labor to the state of Israel. It would be unable to provide its citizens with national pride, civic freedoms, or economic hope, and offers no solution to the refugee problem.

The Cessation of Terror — Using Military Means

The Camp David talks between Ehud Barak and Yassir Arafat in the summer of 2000 brought in their wake an unprecedented wave of terror. With the encouragement and funding of the Palestinian Authority, many hundreds of Israelis have been killed and thousands injured in terror attacks. Proportionately, Israel has sustained losses equivalent to ten times the number of Americans killed in the 9/11 tragedy.

Israel's generous territorial offers and support of the Palestinian Authority did not stop the terror. Furthermore, equipping it with arms has caused terror to mushroom to intolerable proportions.

Israel's intense and relentless military activity against the terrorist strongholds in the Palestinian Authority led to a dramatic drop in the number of attacks.

Today, more than ever, the world understands that the only way to fight terror is by firm and unequivocal action. Israel has the means to dismantle the Palestinian Authority and its security apparatus quickly and efficiently.

Refugee Camps — Hotbeds of Terror

The refugee camps lying alongside the Arab cities in Judea, Samaria, and Gaza must be dismantled. Dominated by poverty, despair, and virulent hatred, the refugee camps breed terror. They produce the motivation for terror and enable terror squads to be formed, providing them with a safe haven. The population of the camps is at the mercy of terrorists and provides cover for their activities.

The continued existence of these camps more than 50 years after they were established is a humanitarian disgrace as well as a threat to the security and peace of the Middle East.

The dismantling of the camps, combined with the establishment of a mechanism to rehabilitate the refugees, will strike a mortal blow to the terror infrastructure.

Recognition and Development of Jordan as the Palestinian State

Israel, the United States, and the international community will recognize the Kingdom of Jordan as the only legitimate representative of the Palestinians. Jordan will once again recognize itself as the Palestinian nation-state.

In the context of a regional economic development program, Israel, the United States, and the international community will put forth a concerted effort for the long-term development of Jordan, to rehabilitate its economy and enable it to absorb a limited number of Palestinian refugees within its borders.

The Hashemite Kingdom of Jordan Is in Fact a Palestinian State

Both sides of the Jordan River are considered the "land of Israel" in the Bible. The Jews have never conceded their claim for the land of Reuben, Gad, and Menasheh on the eastern side of the river. Nevertheless, the Israeli Jews recognize the fact that on these lands there is an Arab Palestinian state, since 1922 — the Hashemite Kingdom of Jordan.

At the end of WWI, the League of Nations convened in San Remo and gave Britain a mandate over Palestine — east and west together — so it could build there a "national home for the Jewish people." In contradiction with this mandate, Britain gave in 1922 all the eastern part of this territory to Abdullah, the Hashemite prince, and established there an Arab-Palestinian state, decades before the dreamed Jewish state was established.

In 1948, Jordan crossed the Jordan River to the west, and took control over what was called from then on "the West Bank" — Judea and Samaria, the mountainous heartland of western Palestine and of the ancient Jewish kingdoms. Jordan unilaterally annexed these areas and granted citizenship to all its Arab population, both residents and refugees. It enacted a number of major constitutional amendments expressing Palestinian-Jordanian unity.

For many years, the PLO competed with Jordan over who would represent the Palestinian Arabs. Only after Israel's weak response to the first "intifada" in 1987 and the subsequent strengthening of the PLO, which resulted in Israel viewing the PLO as the representative of the Palestinian Arabs, did Jordan withdraw from its connection with the "West Bank."

The new reality in the Middle East provides a historic opportunity to rectify that error and once again establish Jordan as the Palestinian nation-state — the exclusive representative of the Palestinian Arabs.

From Refugees to Citizens Once Again

On July 31, 1988, Jordan revoked the Jordanian citizenship of all the Arabs living in Judea, Samaria, and Gaza. As a Palestinian state, Jordan-Palestine will return this citizenship.

Even if they choose to continue to live in Israel, these citizens will enjoy national and political rights in the Palestinian state, whose capital is Amman.

> NOTE: *In February 2003, 22 Palestinian unions in Judea, Samaria, and Gaza appealed secretly to King Abdallah for his economic intervention in these areas — despite their knowledge of Arafat's strong objection to such machinations. This act testifies to the fact that the current mood would support the renewed link with Jordan and the dissolution of the Palestinian Authority.*

No to a Second Palestinian State

A Palestinian state in Judea, Samaria, and Gaza would in fact mean the establishment of a second Palestinian state. This would not be a solution of "two states for two nations," but rather "three states for two nations" — one for the Jews and two for the Palestinians.

A second Palestinian state in Judea, Samaria, and Gaza would pose a threat to both Israel and Jordan. It would serve as a springboard to turn all of the land of Israel — from the Iraqi desert to the Mediterranean Sea — into a single Palestinian Arab state.

What Would Jordan Gain from Becoming Part of the Regional Settlement?

The current Jordanian regime is friendly to Israel for the most part. Its stability, however, is currently in danger because of its delicate pro-Western geopolitical status.

The lack of clarity concerning the status of its Palestinian majority and the danger posed to it by the establishment of an additional Palestinian state would foment unrest among the Palestinian population of Jordan against the government.

The dissolution of the Palestinian Authority and the subjugation of the PLO establishment would elicit a sigh of relief in Amman and pave the way for the underscoring of the Palestinian character of Jordan, whose absolute majority — including the queen and numerous senior government officials — is Palestinian.

A comprehensive development program for Jordan, accompanied by moderate reforms to bolster its Palestinian character, is likely to be welcomed in Amman and would move the kingdom forward to a more hopeful future. Jordan's principal problems are economic. It could be significantly strengthened by Israel and the United States in the context of a regional "Marshall Plan" integrated with the rebuilding of Iraq.

A comprehensive, internationally funded development plan for Jordan, most of whose territory is undeveloped, would facilitate the absorption and naturalization of the Arabs of Judea, Samaria, and Gaza.

Israel has a profound interest in the development of Jordan as a Palestinian state. The transfer to Jordan of significant portions of American military aid to the Middle East could significantly transform Jordan's economy. The normalization of relations and cessation of hostilities would significantly reduce the need for major U.S. foreign defense aid, part of which could also be re-allocated to boost Jordan's economy.

Israeli Sovereignty Over Judea, Samaria, and Gaza

Israeli sovereignty will be asserted over Judea, Samaria, and Gaza (the West Bank). The Arab residents of these areas will become citizens of the Palestinian state in Jordan.

The status of these citizens, their connection to the two states, and the manner of administration of their communal lives, will be decided in an agreement between the governments of Israel and Jordan (Palestine).

The Palestinian-Jordanian citizenship will be offered subsequently to the Arab citizens of Israel.

Assertion of Sovereignty — Restoration of Stability

The areas of Judea, Samaria, and Gaza, including the eastern part of Jerusalem, were part of the British mandate territory that was intended for the establishment of the Jewish homeland. Since the end of the British mandate, these areas have not received any recognized legal status. They were annexed by Jordan after the War of Independence, but were never recognized as part of Jordan in international law.

During the Six Day War in 1967, Israel liberated these territories and returned them to the Jewish people. Eastern Jerusalem was officially annexed to the state of Israel in 1981.

The status of the remainder of these areas remained unclear. Israel evaded determining the future of these areas. This encouraged Palestinian aspirations for establishing an additional Palestinian state in these areas, which, through their topographical advantage, directly threatens the densely populated Israeli coastal plain and Jerusalem basin.

The areas of Judea, Samaria, and Gaza are the only places in the Western world where Jews cannot move without fear, where extensive Arab criminal activity is openly carried out, and where there is widespread abuse of environmental issues. Assertion of Israeli sovereignty on these areas will end this grave situation.

As part of the plan to end the conflict and create a new and stable map in the Middle East, the border between Palestine and Israel must be drawn at the Jordan River, and all the areas west of the Jordan must be formally annexed to the state of Israel.

Judea and Samaria — The Cradle of Jewish Civilization

Judea and Samaria represent the historical "spinal cord" of the land of Israel. The central mountain range, whose heart is Jerusalem, reminds us of who we are.

It was here that Abraham walked with his son, Isaac, and here Jacob set up his tents. It was here that our forefathers, under Joshua, conquered this land by divine decree from the Canaanite nations.

In the hills of Judea and Samaria we find dozens of holy sites and a myriad of others with historic importance, many of which have not yet been researched.

The handing over of Beit El, Shiloh, Bethlehem, and Hebron to foreign (hostile) hands would signify the severance of the Jewish people from its roots and lead ultimately to the loss of recognition of their right to the land.

The biblical and eternal capital of Israel, Jerusalem, is surrounded on three sides by Judea and Samaria. Whoever is concerned for the future of Jerusalem — and is aware of its centrality in the prophetic vision of the return to Zion — cannot allow it to become once again a border settlement in the heart of hostile Arab land.

In the hills of Judea and Samaria and the Gaza coastal plain we have witnessed the development of Jewish villages and towns that manifest national strength and exceptional individual and communal quality. Unsettling these places would be a devastating moral blow to Israel that is liable to damage the very fabric of society and create a severe civil crisis.

The Status of the Palestinian Arabs

In the framework of the eradication of terror, the terrorist heads and inciters will be deported from Judea, Samaria, and Gaza. The dismantling of the refugee camps, part of the rehabilitation process, will reduce the Arab population in these areas and lessen the poverty and density in the Palestinian Arab towns.

The Arab population that will continue to reside within the new areas of the state of Israel will benefit from the civil rights conferred by Israel, but its citizenship will be Palestinian, and its political rights will be actualized in Amman.

The actual administration governing the Arab sector will derive its authority from the Israeli sovereign, but will enjoy limited autonomy in a form to be determined in negotiations between Israel and the Hashemite Kingdom of Palestine.

This distinction between residency and citizenship is also valuable for the Arabs living in Israel today. Those residents that would prefer not to declare loyalty to the Jewish state could realize their political rights in Amman's parliament. This way the Jewish character of the state of Israel will be strengthened, without uprooting anyone.

In order to keep its Jewish character in the future, the Israeli government will adopt a systematic policy of encouraging emigration of Arabs from all of the land of Israel, and will help every one who wants to find their future in other countries.

Dialogue Between States — A Positive Dynamic

The negotiations with the Hashemite Kingdom regarding the precise status of the residents of Judea, Samaria, and Gaza will differ in its essence from those conducted until today between Israel and the Palestinian Authority. When the two parties to discussions are sovereign nations, both of whom are interested in stability and peace, it is possible to reach a real solution.

It is even possible to postpone some of the harder decisions for the future, with the confidence that a positive dynamic of cooperation and mutual interests will develop over the years. As is well known, agreements between democratic nations last for many years. Israel is a true democracy, while the Hashemite Kingdom is a constitutional monarchy undergoing a process of democratization. It has one of the most progressive regimes in the Arab world, with a clearly pro-Western orientation.

The Rehabilitation of the Refugees and Completion of Population Exchange

Israel, the United States, and the international community will allocate resources for the completion of the exchange of populations that began in 1948 and the full rehabilitation of the refugees and their absorption and naturalization in various countries.

After implementation of the above stages, Israel and Jordan-Palestine will declare the conflict terminated. Both sides will work to normalize peaceful relations between all parties in the region.

The Refugee Problem Must be Resolved

The refugee problem in the Middle East has burgeoned into dangerous proportions, in sharp contrast with all other refugee populations from the 1940s who were resettled and rehabilitated decades ago.

From a few hundred thousand Arab refugees in 1948, Palestinian refugees now number in the millions, including second and third generations. Their refugee status is not only the product of education and propaganda, but also the result of many years of neglect and lack of desire on the part of the Arab world to rehabilitate them.

The resolution of the refugee problem must be a primary element of any final status arrangement. For many years the Arab world has done its best not to rehabilitate the refugees in order to undermine Israel's right to exist.

An important ingredient in the resolution of the refugee issue is predicated on international insistence on the need to rehabilitate the refugees and the reallocation of American foreign defense aid to the absorption of refugees.

It's Time to Complete the Population Exchange Begun in 1948

The relocation and rehabilitation of the Palestinian refugees in Arab lands will complete the population exchange process begun in the 1940s. The state of Israel absorbed millions of Jewish refugees from all over the world and, within a few years, these refugees became citizens of the state with full rights. Almost one million of these refugees fled from Arab lands leaving behind property and wealth for which they were never compensated.

At the same time, the 1948 War of Independence created hundreds of thousands of Arab refugees who fled to Arab lands. While the Jews displaced from Arab lands were rehabilitated and naturalized in Israel, the Arab countries refused to do the same for Arab refugees.

The resettlement of these refugees and their descendants will complete a historic circle of population exchange. This will result in the emergence of countries where the majority of their population shares a common nationality and culture.

Refugees from the War of Independence, 1948

600–700 thousand Arabs from Israel

860 thousand Jews from Arab countries

The End of the Process

Various peace processes initiated between Israel and the Palestinian Arabs until now have all failed to bring about the end of the conflict. The principal reason for this is that the PLO, the Palestinian Authority, and its leaders remain intransigent and have no interest in terminating the conflict. This is indicative of the fact that the PA is not a genuine peace partner and, in fact, is a hindrance to peace.

In contrast, however, the Elon Peace Plan can bring about the end of the conflict, because:

- The parties to the final-status settlement are sovereign states that have a vested interest in peace and stability.

- The basic issues will be unequivocally dealt with, leaving no prospect for the future destruction of the state of Israel.

- Weapons will be confiscated, weapons factories destroyed, and the refugee camps dismantled.

- The refugee issue will be resolved as all refugees will be granted citizenship and the potential for economic rehabilitation.

The Elon Plan proposes a *simple*, sustainable solution that achieves *historic justice* and advances the *vision of the prophets*. It addresses the *human tragedies* of all sides and does not harm Israeli *deterrence*.

Underlying Principles of the Elon Peace Plan

No other proposal addresses final-status issues. The Elon plan offers a way to translate the achievements of the war in Iraq into a new "Marshall Plan" for the Middle East, a plan that is based, on the one hand, on Israel, the only stable democracy in the region, and, on the other, on Jordan which has a quasi-democratic government, thus removing the Palestinian terrorist regime from the picture. This plan is a way to take part in the realization of the prophecy and the covenant between the Lord and His people, and between His people and His land. The Elon Peace Plan manifests:

Biblical Validity

God gave this land (Canaan, later called Palestine) to the Israeli people — the descendants of Abraham, Isaac, and Jacob. The historical continuity of God's people, Israel, with God's covenant has been unbroken since patriarchal times and was reaffirmed in the Torah and Neviim (prophetic books of history), commonly called in the Christian world "the Old Testament" (Covenant).

People of the Book (Jews and Christians), who recognize the ultimate authority of God's Word for all of history, understand that what God declared stands as covenant truth through the ages and cannot be altered by human will or force. This plan is the only practical plan based on the Bible.

Simplicity

Two states for two nations on either side of the Jordan River. This solution offers a natural and logical border, separation of hostile populations, and an end to the human tragedy that has continued since the War of Independence.

Sustainability

This plan grants the Palestinian Arabs citizenship in a real state that has the ability to sustain itself economically and politically, with clear and final borders. This state would not find itself in constant conflict with Israel, and its future would not be predicated on the destruction of Israel as a Jewish state.

Morality

This plan prioritizes the treatment of human issues over empty symbols. "Peace" proposals that are based on continued conflict perpetuate poverty, violence, and ignorance. The Elon Peace Plan brings about a solution to the Palestinians' suffering without capitulating to terror and violence.

Deterrence

An Israeli withdrawal of any kind would severely harm Israel's national strength while reinforcing the motivation for terror. The Elon Peace Plan preserves Israel's deterrent capabilities, making it possible for the first time to delineate secure and recognized borders.

Justice

The secure existence of Israel corrects a historic injustice. The essence of Zionism is to establish a state for the Jewish people, a safe haven for millions of Jewish refugees from all over the world including from the Arab countries.

The Arab world must be involved in a resolution of the Arab refugee issue, using its vast territorial expanses and abundant natural resources.

This is not only justice in its most elementary sense — that of human decency — but also draws on deep biblical sources, which view the Jewish people as a nation with a unique destiny and place in history. This plan is founded on the fundamental historic and biblical truth that the land of Israel belongs to the Jewish people.

However, it realizes only part of this principle because it accepts the existence of a Palestinian state east of the Jordan River, part of the biblical land of Israel.

The realization of the Zionist dream — the return of the Jewish people to its land from all corners of the earth — is a historic event of global significance.

Only when Israel's Arab neighbors accept its right to exist within secure boundaries as a fundamental reality will regional peace and prosperity be achieved.

RAND FISHBEIN, Ph.D, is president of Fishbein Associates, Inc., a public policy consulting firm based in Potomac, Maryland. He is a former professional staff member of both the U.S. Senate Defense Appropriations and Foreign Operations Appropriations subcommittees, where he was responsible for the budgeting and oversight of $35 billion in annual defense expenditure and the drafting of the annual U.S. foreign aid bill, respectively. Dr. Fishbein conceived of and developed numerous programs to strengthen the U.S.-Israel security relationship. He was one of only two foreign policy/intelligence analysts on the Senate Iran-Contra investigating committee and was a principal author of its final report. He serves on the boards of both the Jewish Institute for National Security Affairs (JINSA) and the Center for Security Policy (CSP).

Is the Elon Plan Viable? An Assessment

by Rand Fishbein

The events of September 11, 2001, and the overthrow of Iraq's Ba'athist regime have dramatically altered the Middle East political landscape.

They have led many in the foreign policy community to question a number of the fundamental assumptions that have guided U.S. and Israeli polices in the region for well over half a century. Some of these include the beliefs:

- that all but a small portion of the Arab and Muslim worlds are committed to peaceful coexistence with the West and, by extension, Israel

- that despotic regimes will eventually moderate their behavior and place the good of their people over their own self-aggrandizement

- that the borders which have crisscrossed the region since the end of World War I are holy and immutable

Yet these are the very assumptions that have Balkanized minority communities throughout the Middle East, forged nation-states out of peoples incapable of reconciling their ethnic and religious differences, and fueled the animosity and despair of generations.

This is the legacy handed to us by the region's imperial forbearers and the corrupt regimes that have followed in their wake — regimes sustained on little more than greed, political intrigue, malevolence, and patronage — regimes for whom terrorism is a way of life and democracy is but a contagion.

With September 11, though, we entered a new era, one which allows us to challenge the mantras of the past and examine new approaches to Middle East political organization that are grounded in the realities of the region. And nowhere is this reevaluation more appropriate, or more vital, than in the case of the Israeli-Palestinian conflict.

Profound change is now afoot in Iraq and Afghanistan.

Syria, Iran, and Saudi Arabia each stand on the precipice of social and political upheaval. A regime change for each looms large on the horizon.

Only the Palestine dilemma defies corrective action — that is, until now.

With the collapse of the Oslo process and the Bush administration's Roadmap for peace in a state of suspended animation, now is the time for Israel and the United States to press for a focused redrawing of the demographic map of greater Palestine.

For nearly a century, the current map has forced Jews and Arabs into both competition and conflict over the same piece of land and brought bloodshed and sorrow to countless tens of thousands of innocent people on both sides.

If nothing is done — and if the false hopes of the Oslo dreamers continue to be pursued — then both peoples will have missed yet another historic opportunity to redress some of the wrongs of the past and create a more stable, secure, and prosperous environment in the future.

The first step in this process must be to discard or retool the ill-fated Roadmap so that it provides for the eventual separation of Israel from the emerging Palestinian state. In the final analysis, only the Jordan River can serve as the border between the two.

It is my view that the plan put forward by Minister Binyamin Elon comes the closest to fulfilling the vision outlined by President Bush in his landmark June 24 speech of last year.

As a former professional staff member of the U.S. Senate Appropriations Committee, it is my opinion that the Elon plan embodies many of the essential ingredients necessary for both Palestinians and Israelis to chart their own destinies, free of most social, political, or economic entanglements. Its elegance lies in its simplicity and the obvious fact that rivers, mountains, and oceans have for millennia served as mankind's best borders.

A patchwork of isolated villages — or settlements — spread like islands across the West Bank is not a formula that will ever bring peace. It is an approach that is doomed to pit Arab against Jew in perpetuity — one that is provocative, economically unproductive, and ultimately indefensible.

A gerrymandered Palestinian state is no more viable in the West Bank than would be an attempt to link all of the Indian reservations in the United States into a single sovereign entity.

In this respect, the Elon plan is a return to historical reality — a reversal of the colonial fragmentation of historic Palestine. Now is the time to untie the knot that began with the Sykes-Picot Agreement of 1916 and the Cairo Conference of 1921 and has continued to this day.

The Elon plan is grounded in two fundamental, irrefutable realities:

- First, that the historic paths of Israelis and Palestinians are diverging. Co-existence, together, on the same plot of land, is impossible. Israel's continued administration of a growing and increasingly radicalized population is unworkable and unsustainable.

- Second, that the demography of the region is working against Israel. The Palestinian birth rate is now an average of 6.2 children per woman while the comparable Israeli Jewish birthrate is only 2.3.

By 2020, the Palestinians will be a majority and, as a consequence, victory will then be theirs by default — without bombs, without guns, and without U.N. resolutions!

Terrorism, and the absence of a clear political solution that will bring the violence to an end, has transformed Israel into a Middle Eastern *shtetl* [a *shtetl* is a small Jewish village in pre-Holocaust Europe] — recreating in the heart of the Jewish homeland many of the same conditions that Jews sought to escape from in Europe.

It was the decision of the British and the French to divide the land of Palestine following WWI that brought chaos to the region. Since then,

we all have been paying the price for this imperial folly. Two political entities were then created from one contiguous piece of land — the Palestine
Mandate and the Kingdom of Trans-Jordan.

In the ensuing decades, this historical and geographical anomaly has
permitted the myth to arise that the Palestinians are a stateless people
when nothing could be further from the truth.

My friends, Jordan is, and always has been, PALESTINE! In fact, it
constitutes the majority of historic Palestine.

With upward of 65 percent of Jordan's current population considering itself Palestinian, the country is as much Palestinian as Canada is
Canadian, France is French, and Britain is British.

An answer, albeit a partial answer to the current malaise, might exist
right before our eyes.

Is the Elon plan viable? The answer is, most assuredly, YES.

A Palestinian state already exists east of the Jordan River in all but
name. A two state solution will reach its full realization only when Palestinians now residing west of the river come under the full administrative
control of Jordan. If, as Mr. Arafat would have us believe, the Palestinians
are truly one nation, then why not let them come together in a region of
this ancient land where today they are a majority?

In the wake of so much suffering on both sides of the Arab-Israeli divide, this is the only approach that, in my view, has any real chance of gaining traction in a land littered with unrealistic expectations and false hopes.

What we all should have learned from Oslo is that political reconciliation cannot be achieved outside of history.

What the Elon plan offers is what the Palestinians do not now have,
and that is self-determination. And it provides a way to attain this objective that is both compassionate and humane.

At a time when the Palestinians have demonstrated little compassion
and humanity toward their Israeli neighbors, this fact alone should make
the Elon plan worthy of serious consideration.

What the Palestinians will not gain through the Elon plan is what
some in their community desire above all else — the destruction of Israel.
If Tel Aviv, Haifa, and Jerusalem remain the destinations coveted by the
Palestinian leadership, then there is no plan, or peace "processing," that
will ever resolve this conflict.

My friends, the suffering of both peoples need not persist forever. Yet,
in order to move forward we must discard the failed paradigms of the past
— recognizing, as we always must, that the devil is in the details.

The fundamental questions are these: What must be done to win the
support of the U.S. administration and the American public for the core

principals of the Elon plan? And how can this be accomplished while there is still time?

You will have noticed that I have not included the international community in my formulation. Not only do I believe this is an impossible task, but, more importantly, I don't believe that a global consensus is necessary to advance Mr. Elon's vision. The United States, Israel, Jordan, and the Palestinians can themselves engineer the needed change.

So, what must now be done?

First, Israel must take the lead by making it clear that it will no longer accept the status quo.

Israel holds leverage over jobs, water, electricity, travel, and commerce in the West Bank. Instability there causes instability in Jordan. Israel and the United States need to make it clear to the king that if he is not part of the solution then, to paraphrase President Bush, he is part of the problem. Israel's support for the Hashemites over the last four decades has been a principal reason why the Kingdom has survived. It is well known, for instance, that intelligence sharing between Israel and Jordan saved the late King Hussein from assassination on a number of occasions and helped to ensure the stability of his country during the Palestinian uprising in September 1970, an event remembered by most Hashemites as "Black September."

However, Israel's continued support for the monarchy should not be unconditional. It should hinge on the degree to which the new king, Abdullah, cooperates in transforming Jordan into a home for the Palestinians. Jordan must restore Jordanian citizenship to the Palestinian population of the West Bank and immediately open its doors to a voluntary Palestinian repatriation program.

The Elon plan does not envisage, nor could the United States ever support, any forced resettlement of Palestinians. More importantly this is not the Jewish way.

Not so for the Palestinian Moslems who, over the last decade, have engineered the mass exodus of Christians from their homes in towns like Bethlehem and Beit Jalla. This is a fact largely ignored by the international community, but instructive nonetheless.

Second, Jordan must NOT be given the choice of opting out. Every incentive must be given to the Kingdom to go forward — money, technical assistance, and political support.

The consequences of not supporting this plan must be spelled out clearly and directly to King Abdullah.

Third, bringing the United States on board will require a sweeping educational effort both inside and outside of Washington.

The essential points to remember are these:

- Oslo failed, in large part, because it did not recognize the fundamental incompatibility of Palestinians and Israelis to live commingled and co-dependent within the confines of the Jordan River and the sea. History has imposed a burden on both peoples that neither can escape. Making Jordan the custodian for the Palestinians is a vast improvement on the Oslo paradigm.

- The U.S. public is tired of the incessant warfare between Israel and the Palestinians. A solution to the problem of Palestinian statelessness is essential as we enter the 21st century. As Mr. Elon has aptly noted, nearly 850,000 Jews from Arab lands were absorbed into Israel between 1948 and the present day. Surely the same is possible for the Palestinians — refugees and non-refugees — seeking to build a new life in Jordan/Palestine.

- It is also a fact that with U.S. military commitments expanding around the world, particularly in the Middle East, a solution to the Palestinian problem now is imperative. The conflict is draining on the U.S. national will. Its escalating cost and constant political engagement is a distraction from other equally pressing policy concerns such as the emerging threats posed by North Korea, China, and Iran, and the proliferation of weapons of mass destruction. It seems to me these are reasons enough for the United States to reassess its strategy in dealing with the question of Palestinian statehood.

- Next, the implementation of the Elon plan could be one of the beneficial outcomes of the Iraq war. Cooperation between Jordan and Iraq in the reconstruction effort could provide the jobs and needed capital to sustain a Palestinian economic renaissance in Jordan.

For the Elon program ultimately to succeed, the U.S. government and public must embrace the vision, not because it is good for Israel, but because it is good for the United States.

Israel, though, needs to take the lead in making this a matter of national policy. Members of Congress will not get out ahead of the Israeli government.

In the end, only the United States has the capacity to persuade Jordan that it must assume responsibility for the Palestinians.

There are some specific actions that if unilaterally taken by the United States and Israel could advance the objectives of the Elon plan. These include the following:

- First, continue efforts at reform and institution-building within the Palestinian community.

- Second, remove the CIA from the role of peace monitor and PA trainer. This is a clear conflict of interest that has only undermined the chances for peace.

- Third, the United States should immediately recognize Jerusalem as the Israeli capital as provided for in U.S. law. Free access to all of the world's religions would be guaranteed.

- Fourth, Israel should assume sovereign control over all of Judea and Samaria while recognizing Jordan as the de facto Palestinian state.

- Fifth, carefully monitored financial incentives should be offered to Jordan for infrastructure development. These would include incentives for water, electricity, schools, and industry. They also would support the establishment of world bank lending programs and the creation of an international donor stabilization fund.

- Sixth, the United States and Israel must end talks with the P.A., disavow its legitimacy as it has Yassir Arafat, and immediately begin a dialogue with Jordan. U.S. talks with the Palestinians should only take place with individuals who have not directly or indirectly been implicated in murder or other terrorist acts. The United States should work for a new Palestinian leadership with no ties to any Palestinian terrorist organization or affiliate.

- Seventh, the Palestinian refugee camps should be phased out and UNWRAA administration ended. The U.N. should consider reallocating UNWRAA funds to Jordan to support Palestinian welfare needs.

- Eighth, the United States and Israel should reaffirm support for Hashemite sovereignty. If Jordan rejects the plan, Israel and the United States should withdraw their support, aid, and protection for the Kingdom.

- Ninth, the United States and Israel should pursue a policy which isolates Syria and supports efforts at regime change. The Syrian Accountability Act, now pending in Congress, which imposes economic sanctions on Syria for its role in aiding and abetting terrorism, is a good place to start.

Again, I repeat: The United States and Israel must not wait for the international community to buy into the idea that Jordan is Palestine. Rather, Jordan should be handed a fait accompli.

Conclusion

All efforts at Middle East peace have failed over the last 50 years. Why? Because they all have assumed that Palestinian coexistence with Israel is possible given time, money, and good will.

Today, all of these things are in very short supply. The radicalization of all elements of the Palestinian population argues for only one thing — placing as much distance as possible between Israelis and Palestinians.

Let's be clear. Israeli settlements are not the problem, Arab ideology is! It is an ideology that eschews any solution to the Israeli-Palestinian dispute that does not provide for the eventual destruction of Israel. A decade of Oslo concessions proved this point beyond any shadow of a doubt.

The "Jordan is Palestine" option is the last best option, the most humane option left today.

Time is not on Israel's side. Time is not on the side of the United States. Delay in implementing this new approach will only weaken Israel and in the process bring about untold suffering on both sides of the Israeli and Palestinian divide. Delay will only set back the extraordinary gains already made by the United States and its coalition allies in its fight against global terrorism. More importantly, perhaps, our hesitation at this critical hour will stymie our efforts to reshape the political contours of the Middle East along more democratic and peaceful lines.

MANDELL GANCHROW, a retired associate clinical professor of surgery, served with distinction as a decorated combat surgeon in Vietnam. As an American Israel Public Affairs Committee (AIPAC) leader, and as founder and president since 1982 of the Hudson Valley Political Action Committee — one of America's largest Pro-Israel PACs, he has been in the forefront of the Pro-Israel communities' efforts in Congress to project a strong U.S.-Israel relationship.

In 1994, he retired from surgery to serve for six years as the full-time-voluntary president of the Orthodox Union — America's largest Orthodox synagogue group. Today, he serves as executive vice president of the Religious Zionists of America, as well as serving on various boards and foundations.

Summary of the Ideas Raised at the First Jerusalem Summit

by Mandell Ganchrow

1. Terrorism must be defeated in a proactive manner using all means available, including and especially, military victory.

2. No negotiations should take place until terror has been defeated.

3. Radical Islamic fundamentalism (Islamists) seeks not to capture our hearts or our territories but to destroy the civilized world and its culture.

4. Israel as a target of Islamic fundamentalism is secondary to the primary target — the United States.

5. The concept of Israeli occupation of Judea and Samaria represents a dangerous and libelous attempt by our enemies to portray Jews and Israel as morally corrupt. History, theologically

and demographically, proves this to be a lie that is repeated even by friends. It should be a main objective of ours to present the truth.

6. The U.N. is morally bankrupt and cannot function as the instrument of justice. Alternatives must be examined.

7. Peace can be accomplished only by facing the truth.

8. Jerusalem is the eternal indivisible capital of Israel and the center of spiritual opportunity to unite the world.

9. The right of return of so-called Arab refugees is non-negotiable and would represent the demise of Israel.

10. Demographically, historically, and legally, Jordan is an already existing Palestinian state. To create a second Palestinian state in Judea, Samaria, and Gaza means to establish a new terror base on the shores of Mediterranean, which will destabilize the entire Middle East.

11. There can never be peace until anti-Jewish/Israel incitement ceases — including children in schools.

12. The PA is a failed institution and incapable of bringing peace.

13. The Palestinian people have to be liberated: not from the so-called "Israeli occupation" but from a tyrannical corrupt regime of PA that brings death and misery both to Jews and Arabs.

14. It is time for a serious discussion and evaluation in Washington and Israel of the realistic, efficient, and humane alternatives to the failed approaches of Oslo and the Roadmap.

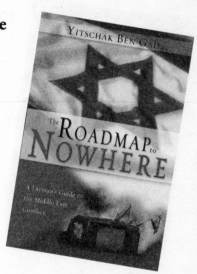

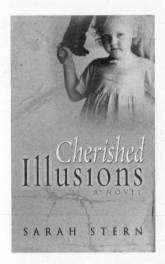

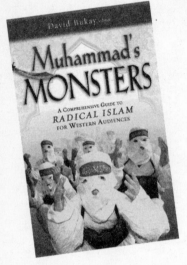

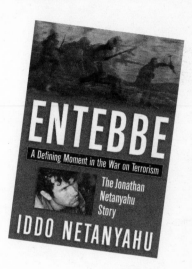